"As the church journeys through the murky terrain of post-Christendom we are looking for clarity, conviction and insight. Schoon provides a close reading of the contours and distinctiveness of the Missional Church Movement. He encourages a missional approach to worship that is a praxis-oriented discipleship rooted in place. This well researched project will invite you to examine your assumptions of church."

—DALLAS FRIESEN, Director of Church Life and Leadership, Canadian Baptists of Ontario and Quebec

"Robust Trinitarian worship and contagious Christian witness belong together, shaping congregations which abide deeply in Christ and which welcome many who are being engrafted into Christ, the vine. What a gift to see this symphonic vision shared so compellingly through Chris Schoon's careful analysis."

—JOHN D. WITVLIET, Calvin Institute of Christian Worship, Calvin College and Calvin Theological Seminary

"What does a disciple-making, missional, worshipping community look like and what are the themes that will support such a project? In this astute book, Chris Schoon bridges, dialogues with and provides generous critiques that bring key insights and even contrarian perspectives together. The academic and the practitioner will find abundant material here to deepen research and practices that will benefit both. Schoon provides a curated analysis that answers big questions and helps us understand the challenges of being a community of faith in this age."

—JUL MEDENBLIK, President of Calvin Theological Seminary

"Chris Schoon here brings together his pastor's heart and his scholar's head to create a unique contribution to the missional conversation. He shows the organic theological connections between mission, worship, discipleship, and evangelism. What does it mean for worship to be missional in character? And how does mission-oriented worship help shape disciples who care about evangelism? I for one find myself convinced that such a blend is much needed, life-giving—and possible."

—**John P. Bowen**, Professor of Evangelism,
Wycliffe College, University of Toronto

"Schoon presents a helpful corrective by showing how worship, discipleship, and evangelism are not independent activities but function like points on a Hoberman sphere; all are interconnected and what happens at one point impacts all the others. In order for that inter-relatedness to work he lays out a robust Trinitarian theology of worship that illuminates worship's true meaning and purpose. This book brings together conversations from various disciplines providing the church with the means to articulate some of what we are seeing happening around us and what we hope for in the future."

—**Joyce Borger**, editor of Reformed Worship, Director of
Worship Ministries of the Christian Reformed Church

Cultivating an Evangelistic Character

Cultivating an Evangelistic Character

Integrating Worship and Discipleship in the
Missional Church Movement

Christopher James Schoon

WIPF & STOCK · Eugene, Oregon

CULTIVATING AN EVANGELISTIC CHARACTER
Integrating Worship and Discipleship in the Missional Church Movement

Copyright © 2018 Christopher James Schoon. All rights reserved. Except for brief quotations in critical publications or reviews, no part of this book may be reproduced in any manner without prior written permission from the publisher. Write: Permissions, Wipf and Stock Publishers, 199 W. 8th Ave., Suite 3, Eugene, OR 97401.

Wipf & Stock
An Imprint of Wipf and Stock Publishers
199 W. 8th Ave., Suite 3
Eugene, OR 97401

www.wipfandstock.com

PAPERBACK ISBN: 978-1-5326-4430-6
HARDCOVER ISBN: 978-1-5326-4431-3
EBOOK ISBN: 978-1-5326-4432-0

Manufactured in the U.S.A.

All Scripture quotations, unless otherwise indicated, are taken from the Holy Bible, New International Version®, copyright © 1973, 1978, 1984, 2011 by Biblica, Inc.™ Used by permission of Zondervan. All rights reserved worldwide. www.zondervan.com.

To Hennie:
my faithful partner, beloved wife, and closest friend—
the one I laugh with, live for, dream with, love;

and

To our children: Josh, Nate, Tim, and Karis—
who continue to open my heart to possibilities I had not imagined.

Contents

Acknowledgments | ix
Abbreviations | xi

Chapter 1. Introduction | 1
    Thesis Statement and Other Introductory Matters | 1
    Methodology | 14
    Delineating the Missional Church Movement | 17
    Procedure and Outline | 39

Chapter 2. Literature Review | 42
    Previous Enquiries | 44
    Identifying Gaps in the Conversation | 80

Chapter 3. Missional Ecclesiology | 85
    What Makes the Church *the Church*? | 86
    Reaction against Christendom Ecclesiology | 90
    Toward Character Marks: Outlining a Missional
        Ecclesiology | 98

Chapter 4. A Missional Approach to Worship | 111
    The Transformative Presence of the Holy Spirit | 112
    Smith's Reflections on the Formative Capacity of Christian
        Worship | 118
    Proposing a Missional Approach to Worship | 122
    Missional Worship Needs a Praxis-Oriented Discipleship | 140

Chapter 5. Integrating a Missional Approach to Worship with a Praxis-Oriented Discipleship | 142
    Integrating Worship with Discipleship: Remembering and Anticipating | 143
    Three Contours of a Praxis-Oriented Discipleship | 157
    Hospitality and Compassion | 164

Chapter 6. Communally Embodying the Gospel of Jesus Christ
Jesus Christ's Evangelistic Character | 168
    Two Missional Perspectives on Evangelism | 174
    Affirmations from Conversations in Post-Christendom Evangelism | 181
    Communally Embodied Expressions of the Gospel of Jesus Christ | 190
    Implications and Potential Contours for Further Conversation | 192

Bibliography | 197
Index | 211

Acknowledgments

With deep gratitude, I recognize that this project, as with the whole of life, is not truly my own. Those influencing my engagement with these ideas far outnumber the references included in the footnotes. As this project enters a more public stage, I see the crowd of witnesses surrounding me and recognize their voices reverberating through these pages.

To briefly name a few for whom I am particularly grateful:

Thank you to the three congregations that have graciously welcomed me into their communities as a seminarian, outreach minister, and lead pastor: Madison Square CRC, Plymouth Heights CRC, and First Hamilton CRC. You have reminded me again and again that it all comes back to God's lavish grace in Jesus Christ.

Thank you to the academic communities with whom I have journeyed. For the faculty and staff of Calvin Theological Seminary, among whom I learned to value the life of the mind as a gift meant to be given away in service within God's kingdom. For Wycliffe College and Toronto School of Theology, especially John Bowen, David Reed, and Bill Kervin, who advised, encouraged, taught, and befriended me, as they walked with me through each stage of my doctoral program. For Redeemer University College, where I have been able to dip my toes into the teaching side of the academic world.

Thank you to my friends and family who challenged, sacrificed, encouraged, rebuked, endured, tolerated, comforted, humored, indulged, and loved me in a thousand other ways. Among them, I want to particularly recognize the Demik family for their generosity with housing for us when we moved to Ontario; the guys weekend crew—Brad, Tom, Kris, and Jason, along with my brothers-in-law, Brandon and Ryan—who welcome me home each year and remind me of who I am; and the Heeremas, whose steadfast friendship embodies God's goodness—even when camping.

Thank you as well to our families. To our siblings—Gerrit and Kathy, Tess and John, Rol and Sheryl, Tam and Ry, Amy and Jeremy, and Megan and Brandon—who have endured my theological rabbit trails, long-winded responses to the simplest of questions, and persistent academic distractions, and yet somehow have still found it in your hearts to love me. To my in-laws, Hank and Rolina, who have remained steadfast in their support and prayers, and whose love has been a constant encouragement to us. To my mom, Ruth Schoon, who has been my cheerleader, listening to my crazy ideas and challenging me to seek God's face. She continues to inspire me with her consistent devotional life and her pervasive compassion for the least of these. To my dad, Steve Schoon (2011), whose generous hospitality taught me so much about the love of God, whose love for words cultivated my imagination, and whose love of telling others about Jesus continues to encourage me. I only wish he could be here to celebrate this part of the journey with us.

Josh, Nate, Tim, and Karis: Thank you for your incredible patience. You remind me daily that life is way more than books and ideas. You amaze me with your insights. You encourage me with your curiosity. You inspire me as you discover how to follow God with everything God has entrusted to you. I am absolutely delighted to be your dad.

Hennie, you have freely given more than I ever could have asked. You believed in this dream before I did and you have not wavered in your steadfast love and encouragement along the way. Thank you. Thank you. Thank you. I could not have begun and would not have finished this project without you.

Abbreviations

ASM	American Society of Missiology
CRCNA	Christian Reformed Church in North America
GOCN	The Gospel and Our Culture Network
MCM	missional church movement

1

Introduction

Thesis Statement and Other Introductory Matters

Thesis Statement and Primary Research Question

THIS BOOK CONTENDS THAT the missional church movement (MCM) can more fully cultivate an evangelistic character among God's people by integrating a missional approach to worship with a praxis-oriented discipleship. Bringing worship and discipleship together in this way serves to form God's people as communally embodied expressions of the gospel of Jesus Christ. While ultimately directed toward the formation of these communities, the project's primary focus rests on the capacity of a missional approach to worship to participate in cultivating an evangelistic character among God's people. Admittedly, such a project could encompass wide-ranging conversations in multiple disciplines, including liturgical theology and Christian ethics. However, this particular endeavor seeks to advance the MCM's conversation regarding the development of an evangelistic character among God's people, particularly in relationship to the movement's theology and practice of communal worship.

The impetus for this research emerges from the question: Within the MCM, how might a missional approach to worship contribute to cultivating an evangelistic character among God's people? This question itself developed from interaction with several MCM sources, but owes particular acknowledgment to Newbigin's chapter "The Congregation as the Hermeneutic of the Gospel" in *The Gospel in a Pluralist Society*.[1] There, Newbigin suggests that "the only possible hermeneutic of the gospel is a congregation

---

1. Newbigin, *Gospel in a Pluralist Society*, 222–33.

which believes it."[2] This declaration summarizes his broader argument surrounding Jesus' formation of a new community. He writes:

> Jesus, as I said earlier, did not write a book but formed a community. This community has at its heart the remembering and rehearsing of his words and deeds, and the sacraments given by him through which it is enabled both to engraft new members into its life and to renew this life again and again through sharing in his risen life through body broken and the lifeblood poured out. It exists in him and for him. He is the center of its life. Its character is given to it, when it is true to its nature, not by the characters of its members but by his character. Insofar as it is true to its calling, it becomes the place where men and women and children find that the gospel gives them the framework of understanding, the 'lenses' through which they are able to understand and cope with the world.[3]

This missional vision—in which Jesus' character is cultivated among God's people through worship and leads into their communal embodiment of that character in the world—lies at the heart of this project. Stated directly, this project's primary research topic is the capacity of communal worship within the MCM to participate in cultivating an evangelistic character among God's people.

Importance of and Objectives for the Proposed Research

The importance of and objectives for pursuing this research are threefold. First, the project derives its primary importance from its capacity to address a lacuna within MCM literature related to how the movement's desired evangelistic character can be formed. While rooted in *missio dei* theology,[4] MCM literature has only recently attended to practices that encourage the formation of a missional identity capable of sustaining ongoing personal and communal engagement within God's mission.[5] Notably, these practices

---

2. Ibid., 232.

3. Ibid., 227.

4. The *missio dei* concept serves as the foundational theological conviction of the MCM. For contemporary roots of this concept, see Newbigin, *Gospel in a Pluralist Society*, 66–79, 89–102, 222–33; and Bosch, *Transforming* Mission, 389–93. For a broader discussion, see Laing, "Missio Dei," 89–99; and Richebacher, "Missio Dei," 588–605.

5. For example: Minitrea, *Shaped by God's Heart*; Helland and Hjalmarson, *Missional* Spirituality; and Woodward, *Creating a Missional Culture*.

bend toward organic, praxis-oriented discipleship approaches.[6] Treatments considering the potential role of worship in forming God's people remain rather scant.[7] Guder, among others, has recognized this deficiency, urging MCM advocates "to address the questions of worship, of sacramental practice, and of church discipline," in order "to equip us for our 'sent-outness,' for our apostolate as the church dispersed."[8] Entering into this conversational field, this project contends that the desired evangelistic character of God's people can be formed more fully when worship and discipleship work together, rather than in isolation from each other. To this end, the primary purpose of this project is to address the worship-related gap in MCM conversations about the formation of a missional identity among God's people.

Secondly, in order to fulfill the primary objective stated above, this project needs to engage—and to a large extent propose—contours for a missional approach to worship. Thus far, much of the MCM commentary surrounding worship has been limited to passing remarks about the centrality of worship for the church,[9] to reflections on particular liturgical practices,[10] or to a deconstruction of Christendom emphases on institutional approaches to worship.[11] The few substantive reflections on missional worship express a great degree of diversity surrounding the shape and importance of communal worship gatherings for God's people.[12] The research that follows enters this second lacuna by proposing a missional approach to worship, both in terms of identifying significant theological themes and with regard to locating potential attendant practices.

---

6. See in particular Breen and Cockram, *Building a Discipling Culture*. Additionally, see Huckins, *Thin Places*; Hirsch and Hirsch, *Untamed*; and Maddix and Akkerman, *Missional Discipleship*.

7. Concern regarding a shortage of resources related to worship and the formation of God's people predates and extends beyond the MCM. See Davies, *Worship and Mission*, 9.

8. Guder, "Worthy Living," 424–32.

9. Van Gelder indicates that "worship serves a centering function in the life of the church" yet offers no direction regarding what this worship might look like from a missional perspective (*Essence of the Church*, 151–52).

10. For example, Tizon, *Missional Preaching*; Lange, "Communal Prayer and the Missional Church," 9–21; and Guder, "Theological Significance of the Lord's Day," 105–17.

11. Frost's chapter "Exiles at the Altar," 275–300, provides a clear and extended example of this deconstructive approach.

12. Compare the high view of institutional worship throughout Schattauer's *Inside Out* with the rejection of Christendom worship patterns in Frost, "Exiles at the Altar," 275–300.

Finally, this research brings the MCM into dialogue with related conversations from three other settings: liturgical theology, Christian ethics, and post-Christendom evangelism[13]—each of which has the capacity to address aspects of the above identified lacunae. By engaging in deliberate dialogue with specific elements of these other settings, this project seeks to expand the MCM's cross-disciplinary familiarity with more developed conversations regarding the intertwining natures of Christian worship, discipleship, and mission.

Thus, this project has three objectives. The primary objective is to demonstrate the potential for integrating a missional approach to worship with a praxis-oriented discipleship. The second objective is to articulate a missional approach to worship, including attention to theological contours and potential attendant practices. The final objective is to facilitate cross-disciplinary engagement for the MCM with related conversations in three other disciplines: liturgical theology, Christian ethics, and post-Christendom evangelism.

Potential Implications

Through these three objectives, this project has the capacity to impact both academic studies in practical theology and tangible practices within the MCM. These potential implications are offered at the outset in order to provide a more complete view of the conversational context within which this research occurs.

With regard to academic impact, at least three implications can emerge from the research. Foremost, this project provides an opportunity to recognize the MCM as a valuable subject area for academic consideration within pastoral departments. For most of its short history, the MCM has been primarily situated either in biblical hermeneutics or in contemporary ecclesiology.[14] While enriching both of those arenas, the MCM foundation rests on Newbigin's critique of the church's engagement within Western culture, giving attention to how the communal life of God's people embodies the gospel.[15] In other words, the MCM is originally a practical theology con-

---

13. In one sense, this project invites participants from liturgical theology, Christian ethics, and post-Christendom evangelism to lend their wisdom to the MCM conversation regarding the role of worship in cultivating an evangelistic character among God's people.

14. Hunsberger, "Proposals for a Missional Hermeneutic," 309–21. Also note the ecclesiological focus in early missional contributions: Guder, *Missional Church*; Frost and Hirsch, *Shaping of Things to Come*; and Brownson et al., *StormFront*.

15. See Roxburgh, "Practices of a Missional People," who critiques how missional conversations have become ecclesiocentric and lost sight of Newbigin's broader vision for the church's engagement in Western culture.

versation. However, academic research related to the MCM in relationship to ethics, catechesis, liturgics, or evangelism is only recently receiving attention.[16] By attending to the conversation regarding a missional approach to worship, this project advances the MCM as a viable research subject within practical theology.

Second, this project proposes an integrative approach to three practical theology conversations—liturgical theology, Christian ethics, and post-Christendom evangelism—that frequently unfold in isolation from each other. While a variety of robust conversations have occurred related to worship and Christian ethics,[17] few efforts have articulated an ethically appropriate approach to evangelism or mission.[18] Similarly, while liturgical theology has a long history of demonstrating the outward focus and justice implications of worship,[19] these efforts have not yet produced a substantive engagement with conversations in post-Christendom evangelism. By engaging all three of these conversations together, this research offers a footprint for a more integrative dialogue between currently isolated conversations within practical theology.

Thirdly, while acknowledging Christianity's historical entanglements with colonialism and proselytism,[20] this project roots conversations regarding missiology and evangelism within a community's capacity to faithfully embody God's character. This rooting replaces the previous approach to evangelism, which was built around techniques designed to solicit individual decision-oriented conversions from people who previously self-identified

---

16. Guder called for a broadly engaged missional theology in his 2008 ASM presidential address ("Missio Dei," 63–74). Notably, however, he does not engage aspects of practical theology, such as preaching, worship, and pastoral care. One might consider recent program developments at Calvin Theological Seminary, Wycliffe College (University of Toronto), and Tyndale Seminary (Toronto) as examples of academic institutions seeking to integrate missional theology within their academic programs.

17. See Hauerwas and Wells, eds., *Blackwell Companion to Christian Ethics*, which will be considered more directly in chapter 5; and Wells, *God's Companions*, which served as a complementary volume to the first edition of *The Blackwell Companion to Christian Ethics*.

18. Thiessen, *Ethics of Evangelism*, serves as an extended treatment of this concern.

19. For example, Saliers, *Worship as Theology*, 25–38; Cavanaugh, *Theopolitical Imagination*, 112–22; and Koester, *Liturgy and Justice*.

20. Tineou offers an initial suggestion for the church to operate from its weakness and with dependency on Christ's grace rather than on perceived strengths related to membership, cultural sophistication, or economic capacity ("Dare to Make New Mistakes," 19–29). Despite sustained critique and warning against paternalism and colonialism in mission, entanglements with neocolonial practices persist. See Kim, "Mission to the 'Graveyard of Empires'?," 3–23.

outside of Christianity.[21] Though several substantive contributions have been offered recently,[22] this project argues for a shift in academic dialogue regarding evangelism, so that the emphasis rests on a community's capacity to faithfully embody Jesus' character in their relationships with each other instead of on an individual's capacity to solicit momentary conversions.[23] This repositioning has the capacity to guard against the weeds of colonialism and proselytism that have seemingly choked off the potential for meaningful dialogue regarding a positive place for evangelism within the academy.

Additionally, this proposed research has several implications for strengthening practices within the MCM. First, this research encourages practitioners to consider how their communal worship practices participate in cultivating the movement's desired evangelistic character among the people of God. A few attempts, such as Webber's *Ancient-Future Worship*[24] and Schmit's *Sent and Gathered*,[25] encourage this practical application of missional theology. In dialogue with these and other such resources, this project invites worship leaders to recognize the potential for cultivating an evangelistic character among God's people through their worship practices.

Secondly, by pointing toward an integration of liturgical rhythms, a praxis-oriented discipleship, and evangelism, this project encourages MCM leaders to collaborate across ministry areas. Far too often, those in ministry leadership experience a silo approach by which focus areas of worship, discipleship, and evangelism have little interaction, or can even become competitive and territorial toward one another.[26] This project encourages practitioners to look for ways in which worship practices can extend beyond the communal gathering into tangible discipleship opportunities; and, in turn, for ways in which a praxis-oriented discipleship can nurture and fuel communal worship gatherings. As such, the trajectory of this research points toward the development of resources that specifically expand the capacity for practitioners to facilitate an integrated approach to ministry.[27]

---

21. Language regarding a community's faithful witness leans decidedly toward Anabaptist perspectives on evangelism. See Stone, *Evangelism after Christendom*, who considers evangelistic implications of Yoder's ecclesiology.

22. Van Gelder, "Future of the Discipline of Missiology," 39–46; and Bowen, "Towards Scholarly Evangelists and Evangelistic Scholars," 113–25.

23. See Adeney, *Graceful Evangelism*; and Hybels, *Just Walk Across the Room*. Additionally, Cahill, *One Thing You Can't Do in Heaven*, reaffirms a decision-for-Christ methodology with the purpose of "winning souls."

24. Webber, *Ancient-Future Worship*.

25. Schmit, *Sent and Gathered*.

26. Hauerwas, "Worship, Evangelism, Ethics," 205–18.

27. For example, my webinar, "Missional Worship for Missional Living."

Finally, this research encourages practitioners to focus their resources primarily on the character formation of their respective communities rather than on equipping particularly gifted and interested individuals in evangelism techniques.[28] The intention here is not to dismiss the unique gift of evangelism in a few people, nor to undermine the benefit of training in personal evangelism and apologetics. Rather, the implication is that God's people would be well served by a greater emphasis on their common calling to embody an evangelistic character in their life together. Thus, this project suggests that practitioners would better serve their whole congregation by equipping their respective communities to more faithfully embody Jesus' character.

Hermeneutical Location

This project is written within a particular, if not peculiar, hermeneutical landscape.[29] Admittedly, I rest comfortably within the juxtaposition of a Reformed emphasis on transformational engagement and Hauerwas's advocacy for what is typically an Anabaptist emphasis on alternative community. The approach engaged in this project proceeds on the trajectory indicated by Goheen, who suggests that a new model of mission may be found in creatively integrating "the insights of contrasting traditions," such as "the scriptural emphases of the Anabaptist and Reformed ecclesiologies while avoiding their corresponding weaknesses."[30] While differences between these traditions occasionally emerge,[31] this project operates with the premise that the respective strengths of both traditions are complementary.

Beyond integrating aspects of Reformed and Anabaptist traditions, I also resonate with a missional hermeneutic marked by deep appreciation

---

28. This project is not the first to suggest this shift. See, Abraham, *Logic of Evangelism*; Bowen, "Scholarly Evangelists and Evangelistic Scholars," 117; and Bowen, *Evangelism for "Normal" People*.

29. Though beyond my capacity to explore directly in this project, I am aware that my engagement here is impacted (likely beyond my cognizance) by my privileged location as a middle-class, married, heterosexual, Caucasian male, raised in the Midwest United States and now living in Southern Ontario, who experienced the stability of a two-parent home, received a private Christian education, and has completed several graduate degrees.

30. Goheen, "Missional Church," 488. Also, Keller, "Being Salt & Light in Culture," http://www.youtube.com/watch?v=i1Q6Zun2v-8.

31. Smith's and Fitch's exchange around "Knitting While Detroit Burns?" provides a clear example of how these differences can emerge. In particular, Fitch, "'Knitting While Detroit Burns?,' The Reformed 'Both/And' vs. the Anabaptist 'First/Then,'" which responds to Smith, "Knitting While Detroit Burns?"

for Christopher Wright's efforts,[32] value Hauerwas's narrative approach to the life of God's people,[33] and draw upon my pastoral experience within the Christian Reformed Church in North America (CRCNA).[34]

The missional hermeneutic shaping this project resonates closely with Christopher Wright's work in *The Mission of God*. While recognizing the interpretative complexities attendant with multiethnic, pluralistic readings of the biblical text,[35] Wright details a hermeneutic rooted in God's self-revelation and shaped by the missional contexts in which the Bible was written. As Wright states, "the whole canon of Scripture is a missional phenomenon in the sense that it witnesses to the self-giving movement of this God toward his creation and us."[36] Moreover, many of the biblical texts "emerged out of events or struggles or crises or conflicts" with which God's people struggled to understand their identity in response to "God's revelations and redemptive action in the world."[37] Thus, scripture is simultaneously an expression of and a response to God's mission.

Relying on O'Donovan, Wright describes biblical authority as permission-giving freedom that authorizes God's people to live faithfully in relationship to the reality of God at work in the world. As Goheen and Bartholomew argue, such a missional hermeneutic interprets scripture in a way that always calls its readers to respond personally, communally, and contextually in congruence with the biblical narrative.[38] Scripture, then, depicts

---

32. Wright provides an intricate account of how a missional hermeneutic developed (*Mission of God*, 48–69), which follows earlier works by Newbigin, *Gospel in a Pluralist Society*, 89–102; Brownson, "Speaking the Truth in Love," 479–504; and Bauckham, *Bible and Mission*.

33. Hauerwas, "Story-Formed Community," 171–98.

34. Over the past decade, I have served two congregations within the Christian Reformed Church of North America (crcna.org); the first seven years as an outreach minister in Grand Rapids, Michigan, and more recently as a lead pastor in Hamilton, Ontario.

35. Wright, *Mission of God*, 33–47, particularly 38–41 for the impact of global readings and 45–46 on plurality without relativism. Also Brownson, "Speaking the Truth in Love," 479–504, who argues for an irreducibly multicultural understanding of God's presence; and Bauckham, *Bible and Mission*, 49–54 for the scandal of Jesus as the access point to God's universal plan of salvation, and 90–94 on how the biblical metanarrative "is hospitable to considerable diversity and to tensions, challenges and even seeming contradictions of its own claims."

36. Wright, *Mission of God*, 48.

37. Ibid., 49.

38. Bartholomew and Goheen contend: "[i]f our lives are to be shaped by the story of Scripture, we need to understand two things well: the biblical story is a compelling unity on which we may depend, and each of us has a place within that story" (*Drama of Scripture*, 12–13, 196–206). They attribute the basic metaphor of the Bible as drama to N. T. Wright, *New Testament and the People of God*, 139–42.

the story of God's mission in order to create a people who will faithfully conform to the realities the kingdom of God is making.[39] In this context, mission, according to Wright, involves humanity without being "primarily a matter of our activity or our initiative." Rather, mission is "the committed participation of God's people in the purpose of God for the redemption of the whole creation. The mission is God's."[40]

Within this hermeneutic, I contend that sin is primarily a refusal to participate in God's mission and not simply a transgression of divine law or honor.[41] Salvation, rooted in God's work in Jesus Christ and the Spirit, restores relationships between humanity and God, among all people, and with the whole of creation, so that each person is able to participate faithfully as both a recipient of and collaborator within God's mission. Furthermore, this hermeneutic is eschatological. This posture constantly reinterprets the past while engaging the present in light of an anticipated future, within which all of God's creation will mutually contribute to each other's flourishing in God's presence.[42]

This hermeneutic also values Hauerwas's narrative approach to the life of God's people. Through analyzing *Watership Down*, Hauerwas contends that stories form both the people who tell them and the people who hear them, providing a narrative identity for a community of God's people.[43] This narrative identity resonates with Smith's reflections on cultural liturgies[44] and with Green's call for a robust theological imagination in *Imagining God*.[45]

39. Bartholomew and Goheen, *Drama of Scripture*, 51–54.

40. Wright, *Mission of God*, 61–67.

41. See my essay "Confessions of a Former Skeptic," where I write: "Surprisingly, the fall and the consequences that follow do not remove our creational vocation, its attendant commands, or the organizing structure of the family. Genesis 3 begins with Adam and Eve in the centre of the Garden. They have not been fruitful and they have not gone forth. The first sin is not one of commission, but of omission: humanity has personally, communally, and institutionally failed to embrace their vocation of ruling over creation through the intergenerational sending forth directives that God gave them."

42. See Plantinga, "Epilogue," in *Engaging God's World*, 137–44, where he calls for a faithful anticipatory demonstration of the fullness of life in God's coming kingdom. Also, Bartholomew and Goheen, *Drama of Scripture*, 206.

43. Hauerwas remarks: "To be sure, we have often been unfaithful to [Jesus'] story, but that is no reason for us to think it is an unrealistic demand. Rather, it means we must challenge ourselves to be the kind of community where such a story can be told and manifested by a people formed in accordance with it—for if you believe that Jesus is the messiah of Israel, then 'everything else follows, doesn't it?'" ("Story-Formed Community," 198).

44. Particularly in Smith, *Desiring the Kingdom*, who relies on the paradigmatic work of Taylor, *Modern Social Imaginaries*.

45. Green, *Imagining God*.

Such a narrative approach encourages dynamic considerations of ethical living through constant engagement with ever-changing cultural contexts and an ever-expanding understanding of the Bible's grand narrative. Within this approach, ethical decisions emerge from engaging questions about how to be faithful to the story of God's self-revelation within the particular contours of the reader's current cultural circumstances. Therefore, a missional hermeneutic recognizes that there is never a cultureless gospel[46] and that the good news of Jesus Christ offers an important metanarrative that is always particularized, so that it can only be told and retold, embedded and re-embedded, within specific, dynamic cultural contexts.[47]

My hermeneutical location is also shaped by my role as a Christian Reformed church pastor.[48] This particular expression of my vocation carries with it two implications relevant to this project: (1) the academic agenda pursued here is influenced by day-to-day practices of shepherding a community of God's people; and (2) I breathe the air of a Calvinist Reformed theology[49] filtered primarily through Dutch Reformed theologians during the late 1800s to the mid-1900s.[50] The high value placed upon gathered

---

46. I am indebted to John Bowen, who over the past six years has prompted me on this point, initially in response to Donovan, *Christianity Rediscovered*. Also, Bosch: "There never was a 'pure' message, supracultural and suprahistorical. It was impossible to penetrate to a residue of Christian faith that was not already, in a sense, interpretation" (*Transforming Mission*, 422).

47. See my essay "Ruminating around a Backyard Fire," 7–10, where I write: "without being intertwined within any given culture, the gospel is nothing more than speculation about a distant deity, irreducibly irrelevant to us and our birth-through-life-to-death living. No matter how noble the desire to avoid passing along distortions and deformities from an evangelist's own culture, if the gospel is to be good news for anyone, the evangelist must proclaim a gospel that has been, is, and will be inculturated again and again among an ever increasing variety of peoples, customs, and places. The gospel is nothing if it cannot grow new life in each and every culture through which and into which it is proclaimed."

48. I belong to the Christian Reformed Church in North America. See crcna.org for further details on the history, beliefs, ministries, and stories shaping my context.

49. I identify more closely with the neo-Calvinist movement as opposed to the neo-Puritan movement. For further discussion on this distinction, see Oppenhiemer, "Evangelicals Find Themselves in the Midst"; Robinson, "So What's Wrong with Neo-Calvinism?"; and Pennings, "Can We Hope for a Neocalvinist-Neopuritan Dialogue?" Thanks to Robert Joustra for recommending Pennings's article.

50. The CRCNA is heavily influenced by Dutch Reformed theologians. Though far too extensive for a comprehensive list here, they include Abraham Kuyper, Herman Dooyeweerd, Herman Bavinck, and Louis Berkhof. Likewise, more recent theologians and philosophers, such as Cornelius Plantinga, Nicholas Wolterstorff, Lewis Smedes, Brian Walsh, Al Wolters, and James K. A. Smith, have also contributed to the continued development of this Reformed heritage and the CRCNA environment in which I am rooted.

worship, especially on preaching and on the sacraments of baptism and Communion,[51] has certainly influenced my consideration of how liturgical practices contribute to the ways God's people engage their communities.

My understanding of what it means to be Reformed has been assisted by a description of how three strands—doctrinal, pietistic, and transformationalist—simultaneously complement and also are frequently pitted against each other in various Reformed communities.[52] The doctrinal emphasis stresses the importance of understanding the beliefs of the Christian faith, particularly the centrality of God's grace, the nature of covenant, and the role of common grace. On the other hand, the pietistic strand attends to how God's people experience God's presence in Jesus Christ, through both the Holy Spirit and the fellowship of the church community. The central focus of the transformationalist strand rests on how Christians engage the world in response to the lordship of Jesus Christ. While affirming the need for all three strands, I tend to align most naturally with the transformationalist strand.

This broader Reformed environment celebrates the centrality of communal worship, the importance of lifelong discipleship, and the tangible, transformational engagement of God's people in all areas of life as they anticipate the advent of the new heaven and new earth.[53] More specifically, the CRCNA context influencing this paper is shaped by emphases on God's sovereignty, covenantal relationships, and a keen awareness of an already-not-yet eschatological understanding of God's kingdom.[54]

Presuppositions and Limitations

Finally, two key presuppositions influence the theological trajectory of this project. First, this project takes for granted that evangelism ought to occur

---

51. See Calvin, *Institutes of the Christian Religion*, 4.1.9, where the preaching of the word and the administration of the sacraments are held up as the criteria for being a church. For a consideration and critique of Calvin's theology on this point, see Moore-Keish, *Do This in Remembrance of Me*, 15–32. See also the Belgic Confession, Articles 29, 33–35; and CRCNA, *Our World Belongs to God*, 37–38, in which the priority on preaching and the sacraments is clearly seen. Both of these documents play a significant role in the confessional life of the CRCNA.

52. What follows is drawn largely from the CRCNA document *What It Means to Be Reformed*.

53. These emphases are clearly seen in *Our World Belongs to God*, particularly paragraphs 34–54.

54. See Wolters, *Creation Regained*. In particular, Wolters's reflections on structure and direction (72–95) demonstrate how Reformed theology can apply to particular opportunities for personal and societal reform.

and that evangelism can be engaged in an ethically appropriate manner.[55] The assumption is quite simply that evangelism not only happens, it ought to happen. As such, the argument here is not related to whether evangelism has a place in today's pluralistic environment. However, consistent with pursuing an embodied gospel, this project will contend for an expanded vision of what evangelism entails. To that end, the question considered here is in regard to nurturing the evangelistic character of the MCM, not with regard to evaluating (or even with establishing criteria for evaluating) evangelism methods, their efficacy, or their ethical implications.

Second, this paper weights the *lex orandi–lex credendi* dialogue[56] on the side of primary theology emerging in the context of communal worship, with a distinctive bent toward praxis. In other words, this book presupposes that the communal worship experience both gives and receives distinctive shape from how the people of God engage with each other and the world around them. While positioning this perspective toward *lex orandi*, the approach here recognizes the reciprocal nature of the original construction, in agreement with Kilmartin's summary:

> On the one hand, the law of prayer implies a comprehensive, and, in some measure a pre-reflective, perception of the life of faith. On the other hand, the law of belief must be introduced because the question of the value of a particular liturgical tradition requires the employment of theoretical discourse. One must reckon with the limits of the liturgy as lived practice of the faith. History has taught us that forms of liturgical prayer and ritual activity, however orthodox, often had to be dropped or changed to avoid heretical misunderstanding.[57]

Furthermore, this project perceives that the original formula of *lex orandi–lex credendi* is functionally tridirectional, not bidirectional. Stated more directly, this project operates on the idea that prayer and belief dialogue continually with praxis. Irwin makes a similar point when he concludes: "At various times in the Church's life *lex orandi* and *lex credendi* (implying always a *lex vivendi*) have been emphasized, reshaped, and reformulated

---

55. See Thiessen, *Ethics of Evangelism*, for an extended consideration of ethical contours involved with evangelism. Flett provides helpful critiques of Theissen's work with regard to complexities that need fuller consideration in a postcolonial, pluralistic, and post-9/11 context ("Ethics of Evangelism," 97). Also, Kerr, "Christian Understandings of Proselytism," 8–12.

56. Moore-Keish provides a succinct historical overview of the *lex orandi–lex credendi* discussion (*Do This in Remembrance of Me*, 61–85). For a more nuanced historical summary and contemporary analysis, see Irwin, "Lex Orandi, Lex Credendi," 57–69.

57. Kilmartin, "Theology as Theology of the Liturgy," 107–8.

to suit particular needs and challenges."[58] As such, the life of God's people in the particularities of their respective heres and nows participates in the *prima theologia* traditionally formulated in the ebb and flow of prayer and belief. Neither prayer nor belief is engaged in a contextless vacuum. People (personally and communally) bring their histories and their specific circumstances with them into their worship, expressing their theology with linguistic concepts from their respective cultural contexts. In other words, this thesis operates on the presupposition that the prayers and theology of God's people are in constant dialogue with the life of God's people.

However, this presupposition neither indicates how a liturgical gathering forms God's people nor naïvely asserts that such formation occurs automatically in any person or community that engages in liturgical practices. Assigning causal effect to the communal worship gatherings of God's people would implicate them too neatly within the mechanistic and industrial production modalities of modernity, an association this project would readily eschew. Quite simply, *lex orandi* does not guarantee orthodoxy or orthopraxis. As Romano Guardini argues, "The liturgy has no purpose, or, at least it cannot be considered from the standpoint of purpose. It is not a means which is adapted to attain a certain end—it is an end in itself."[59] Instead, this presupposition recognizes that the phenomenon of God's people gathered in worship provides a context within which theological understanding emerges and to which it returns.[60]

With regard to limitations, this project is not offering a defense for the MCM as a whole. Though responding to critiques of the MCM would be a worthwhile endeavor, critiques beyond the arena of worship and the formation of an evangelistic character are simply too far afield for the focused pursuit of this project. This book seeks to further understanding about the MCM, not to defend or challenge its existence. Thus, critiques about the MCM's hermeneutical approach;[61] its lack of racial, gender, and economic

---

58. Irwin, "Lex Orandi, Lex Credendi," 69.

59. Guardini, "Playfulness of the Liturgy," 41.

60. As will be noted in the conclusion of the project, the MCM stands to benefit greatly from dialogue with other disciplines, like ritual studies and phenomenology, particularly in relationship to this presupposition.

61. Jethani objects to an oppressive element of the hermeneutic, contending that "[a]n individual is either *on* the mission, the *object* of the mission, an *obstacle* to the mission, and *aid* to the mission, or a fat Christian who *should* be on the mission" (*With*, 84; emphasis original).

diversity;[62] its prioritization of missiology over ecclesiology;[63] and other perspectives not directly related to the role of worship in forming an evangelistic character will not be addressed by this project.

While readily evident in a wide spectrum of denominations, the MCM is still quite limited to Protestant traditions, and even then mostly to those within England, United States, Canada, Australia, New Zeeland, and South Africa. At this time, there is minimal representation in the literature of MCM practitioners or academics aligned with Roman Catholic[64] or Orthodox expressions of the Christian church. As such, this project focuses its energy on Protestant resources, avoiding those in Roman Catholic or Orthodox liturgical traditions or analysis.[65]

Methodology

Primary Literature

The primary literature for this project engages a subset of academic and popular MCM contributions that address the capacity for worship to participate in the formation of an evangelistic character among God's people. Rather than exhausting MCM resources on this topic, the selected contributions provide representative views on the role of worship in forming the evangelistic character of God's people. The lead sources are Schattauer's *Inside Out*, Kreider and Kreider's *Worship and Mission after Christendom*, Webber's *Ancient-Future Worship*, and Schmit's *Sent and Gathered*, along

---

62. While affirming the intent and need for the MCM, Smith, "Expanding the Missional Church Conversation," and Canty, "A Black Missional Critique of the Missional Movement," both contend that the MCM continues to ignore contributions from African-American practitioners. Furthermore, the MCM's lack of attention to women practitioners and academics is quite stark.

63. DeYoung and Gilbert, *What Is the Mission of the Church?*, challenge four aspects of the MCM: 1. that mission is the core of the church's identity; 2. an overemphasis on social justice and kingdom building; 3. confusion regarding the corporate and individual responsibilities; and 4. emphasizing world transformation to the detriment of disciple-making.

64. For a notable exception, see Bevans and Schroeder, *Constants in Context*, 286–304, who provide an extensive consideration of the *missio dei* theology from a Trinitarian perspective that would be an asset to current conversations within the MCM.

65. Pope Francis's *Evangelii Gaudium* expresses much about the sent nature of the church in response to God's missionary character and has the potential to contribute significantly to the further development of the MCM. However, the MCM as understood in this project is not rooted in or currently conversant with the missional trajectory expressed within the Roman Catholic Church since Vatican II and *Ad Gentes* and continued most recently by Pope Francis.

with chapters on worship from Fitch's *The Great Giveaway*, Frost's *Exiles*, and Tizon's *Missional Preaching*.[66] Additionally, the primary literature includes five articles and essays that have contributed to this topic: Dawn's "Worship to Form a Missional Community" and "Reaching Out without Dumbing Down," Goheen's "Nourishing Our Missional Identity: Worship and the Mission of God's People," Chilcote's "The Integral Nature of Worship and Evangelism," and Guder's "Theological Significance of the Lord's Day for the Formation of the Missional Church."[67]

Methods for Interpreting Primary Literature

The methodology for this proposed research consists of five aspects. The first aspect locates the primary sources in relationship to other MCM sources and with regard to understandings of ecclesiology, worship, and evangelism. As a comparative step, the research contrasts elements of a missional ecclesiology with those of a Reformed ecclesiology, particularly attending to the "marks of the church." This comparison recognizes that the MCM's ecclesiological marks differ from Reformed understandings of the *notae ecclesia*, which are primarily anchored within the liturgical acts of preaching and of the sacraments. This comparative orientation also acknowledges that early academic proponents of missional hermeneutics and ecclesiology appear to have had a disproportionate rooting within Reformed traditions as opposed to the practitioners currently contributing to the popular dialogue, where a fairly strong Anabaptist orientation is evident.[68]

A second dimension of the methodology is to summarize the relevant literature, so as to reveal the presence of two lacunae surrounding the role

---

66. Schattauer, *Inside Out*; Kreider and Kreider, *Worship and Mission after Christendom*; Webber, *Ancient-Future Worship*; Schmit, *Sent and Gathered*; Fitch, "Production of Experience," 95–125; Frost, "Exiles at the Altar," 275–300; Tizon, *Missional Preaching*, 24–34.

67. Dawn, "Worship to Form a Missional Community," 139–52; Dawn, "Reaching Out without Dumbing Down," 270–82; Goheen, "Nourishing Our Missional Identity," 32–53; Chilcote, "Integral Nature of Worship and Evangelism," 246–63; Guder, "Theological Significance of the Lord's Day," 105–17.

68. See Holsclaw, "More than Splitting the Difference," who contrasts an Anabaptist perspective with unspecified neo-Reformed persons. By way of observation—but not as documented analysis—Newbigin, Guder, VanGelder, Goheen, Hunsberger, all early proponents of the MCM, are rooted within Reformed traditions; whereas many contemporary practitioners, including Fitch, Holsclaw, Briscoe, and Cavey, engage from within an Anabaptist tradition. While beyond the scope of this particular research, the relationship between Reformed and Anabaptist orientations within the MCM would be a beneficial study.

of worship in cultivating an evangelistic character among God's people and the seemingly haphazard way that missional worship has frequently been discussed within the literature. This step is beneficial because it exposes how the paucity of resources related to missional worship is incongruent with the MCM's comments about the central importance of worship in cultivating a missional identity.[69]

Thirdly, these sources are supplemented with other available works related to this thesis, whether in print, blogs, video, or other media. Attending to other types of material as relevant secondary sources recognizes that conversations about the MCM's approaches to worship, discipleship, and evangelism are not strictly or even primarily academic at this point in time. Much of the MCM's conversation takes place through blogs, social media, and other non-traditional academic venues and media.

The fourth aspect in this interpretive process is to engage conversations within liturgical theology, Christian ethics, and post-Christendom evangelism that can assist in delineating potential opportunities and challenges accompanying the perspectives advanced within the primary literature. Additionally, this cross-disciplinary engagement has the capacity to illuminate beneficial entry points into the lacunae surrounding missional worship and evangelistic character formation.

Finally, the last aspect of this five-part methodology is to propose an approach to missional worship that, when integrated with a praxis-oriented discipleship, has the capacity to more fully cultivate the evangelistic character of God's people. This last methodological aspect also lends itself well to further, albeit still brief, reflections on potential implications regarding this research and to suggesting potential trajectories for furthering the conversations initiated and advanced through this thesis.

Framed by these aspects, the methodological approach facilitates internal dialogue and external contrast, deliberately engages secondary sources that include alternative perspectives, and orients the unfolding conversation in relationship to complementary conversations within related and often more developed disciplines. As such, pursuing the thesis with this methodological approach increases the likelihood that this research will generate dependable conclusions about the primary literature and will demonstrate the validity of the thesis statement.

---

69. Van Gelder indicates that "worship serves a centering function in the life of the church" yet offers no direction regarding what this worship might look like from a missional perspective (*Essence of the Church*, 151–52).

Delineating the Missional Church Movement

To assist in further clarifying the argument that follows, a few introductory descriptions related to the MCM are beneficial. These descriptions include an overview of core terminology utilized in this project, a summary of the history and trajectory of the MCM, and a brief acknowledgement of several other contemporary ecclesial movements that overlap with aspects of the MCM.

Core Terminology

The core terminology for this project is considered under five headings: *missional*, *missional church movement*, *worship and liturgy*, *praxis-oriented discipleship*, and *evangelism*. The synonymous terms of *missio dei* and *missio trinitatis* are treated together while explaining emphases within the *missional church movement*.

Missional

Admittedly, *missional* has accumulated a rather broad usage in its short history. The Missional Church Network acknowledges the frequent confusion around this term: "Some view missional as the latest church growth strategy, or a better way of doing church evangelism. Others see missional as a means to mobilize church members to do missions more effectively. While still others believe missional is simply the latest Christian fad that will soon pass when the next trendy topic comes along."[70] Hirsch observes that people appropriate *missional* "without the foggiest idea of what it actually means and the impact that it should have on our thinking and practices," leading to a situation where the meaning of *missional* "devolves to jargon."[71]

The devolution of *missional* toward jargon is due partly to basic definitions that communicate only the idea of "joining God in God's mission" or that serve as a simple replacement for pre-existing ecclesiological concepts like *missionary*, in which the status quo is maintained and to which a few particularly gifted individuals are called. These broad definitions leave enough room that people with dramatically different understandings of the relationship between the church and the world, and even with completely different religions,[72] can all utilize the term *missional* for their engage-

---

70. Missional Church Network, "What Is Missional?," http://missionalchurchnetwork.com/what-is-missional/.

71. Hirsch, series editor's preface in Frost, *Road to Missional*, 11–12.

72. Mikaelsson, "Missional Religion," 523–38.

ment with others.[73] On account of this diffusion, the term *missional* faces a constant danger of becoming meaningless.[74]

However, these variant uses of *missional* deviate from the central understanding of the term as advanced by early advocates of *missional* concepts. As Goheen notes, "The employment of the term 'missional' includes the superficial along with the profound, the culturally captive alongside the richly biblical."[75] Though overstating his case, MacIlvaine contends for a technical understanding: "The term 'missional,' on the other hand, has evolved to have a precise definition, rich in theological significance in four areas: theology proper, Christology, soteriology, and ecclesiology."[76]

The word *missional* began to appear in Christian missiological literature in the early 1980s,[77] particularly among those following Newbigin's cultural assessment of the Christian West as a contemporary mission field.[78] Newbigin's reclamation of Barth's *missio dei* construct served as the orienting theological basis for understanding the church as a people who are sent. For the early proponents, this *missional* ecclesiology is rooted in perceiving God as the God who sends. In *Missional Church*, Guder explained the ecclesiological implications: "With the term *missional* we emphasize the essential nature and vocation of the church as God's called and sent people."[79] The church's core identity is that they have been formed by God in order to be sent by God. Goheen contends further that "[a]t its best, 'missional' describes not a specific *activity* of the church but the very *essence and identity* of the church as it takes up its role in God's story in the context of its culture and participation in God's mission to the world."[80] Reflecting on how this identity is not simply a specific set of activities, Frost stresses that *missional* carries a life-encompassing response: The *missio dei* "is a lifelong calling to service, sacrifice, selflessness, and effort. It will be worked out in neighborhoods and people groups around the world, and fueled and led by the least likely saints."[81] In agreement with Frost, Tizon says *missional* "means *to join God's mission to transform the world, as the church strives in the Spirit to be*

---

73. Knight, "What Does Missional Mean?"

74. Raj, "Missional or Missionary," 101–3.

75. Goheen, *Light to the Nations*, 4.

76. MacIlvaine, "What Is the Missional Church Movement?," 90–92.

77. The term *missional* in its current understanding is generally attributed to Frances DuBose in DuBose, *God Who Sends*.

78. Hirch, "Defining Missional." Emphasis original.

79. Guder, *Missional Church*, 11.

80. Goheen, *Light to the Nations*, 4. Emphasis original.

81. Frost, *Road to Missional*, 21–22.

authentically relational, intellectually and theologically grounded, culturally and socio-economically diverse, and radically committed to both God and neighbor, especially the poor."[82] Within this project, *missional* will operate either as a shorthand way of speaking about the *missional church movement* or as an adjective conveying the missionary character of God, the church, or another aspect of the church's tangible participation in the *missio dei*.

Missional Church Movement

Recognizing the fluidity of the term *missional*, this paper relies more specifically on the term *missional church movement*. By considering the whole designation *missional church movement* (MCM) instead of only *missional*, an identifiable conversational field comes into focus.

Historically, the MCM is distinguished from several other contemporary ecclesiastical movements[83] by the primacy afforded to Newbigin's assessment of and vision for the church's engagement within Western culture as the hermeneutic of the gospel.[84] While GOCN and some initial gatherings took shape in the late 1980s and early 1990s, the movement's initial public contributions launched in 1996 with the publication of Hunsberger and Van Gelder's *The Church between Gospel and Culture* and Van Gelder's *Confidant Witness, Changing World*.[85] For the purposes of this project, the release of these two sources marks the beginning of the movement in the North American context.

More specifically, however, the MCM can be described through five common emphases: the centrality of the Trinitarian God's missionary character (*missio trinitatis*);[86] an understanding of the church as being sent as participants in God's mission;[87] the essential nature of an incarnational

---

82. Tizon, *Missional Preaching*, xxiii. Emphasis original. Tizon utilizes this language to reflect the various contributions offered by four missional-related movements as outlined in Sine, *New Conspirators*, 31–55.

83. Five contemporary movements are worth noting due to their similarity with the MCM: fresh expressions, new monasticism, integral mission, Christian community development, and emergent church. A brief consideration of each of these movements is included later in this chapter.

84. Newbigin, *Gospel in a Pluralist Society*, 227.

85. Hunsberger and Van Gelder, *Church between Gospel and Culture*; and Van Gelder, ed., *Confident Witness, Changing World*.

86. See Wright, *Mission of God*, 61–65; and Guder, *Continuing Conversion of the Church*, 19–21.

87. Guder, *Missional Church*, 77–141; and Van Gelder, *Essence of the Church*, 28–31.

mission dynamically expressed in locally contextualized ministry;[88] the assessment that the church's privileged position within Christendom has come to an end, resulting in an opportunity for the church to embody a servant identity;[89] and a commitment to a holistic gospel aimed at the reconciliation, restoration, and flourishing of all things in Jesus Christ.[90] While various academics and practitioners will offer differing suggestions regarding the number and importance of these emphases,[91] all five are discernible to some extent across the diverse expressions within the MCM.[92] To understand these emphases, and thus the shape of the MCM as considered within this project, attention is given here to an expanded description of each emphasis.

Trinitarian God's missionary character

The first emphasis is on *the centrality of the Trinitarian God's missionary character* (otherwise referred to as *missio trinitatis*),[93] which reflects the continuing development of the *missio dei* theological construct. In the context of the MCM, the *missio dei* construct has served as the central organizing concept, providing theological coherence amid diverse ecclesiastical expressions. Bosch provides a rudimentary yet, nonetheless, beneficial description of the primary premise within *missio dei*: "mission is not primarily an activity of

---

88. Roxburgh and Boren, *Introducing the Missional Church*, 77–90.

89. Frost and Hirsch, *Shaping of Things to Come*, 8–9, 14–15.

90. Frost, *Road to Missional*, 101–20; Keller, *Generous Justice*, 78–147.

91. The youthfulness of this movement is evidenced in the diversity of opinions surrounding what qualifies as indicators of the MCM. For example, the Missional Church Network offers three descriptors on its website; Minetrea, *Shaped By God's Heart*, describes nine priorities; Keller, *Center Church*, part 6, ch. 19, suggests four commonalities.

92. A closer examination of these emphases would also reveal nuanced postures among academics and practitioners as to why these emphases are important. For example, Keller's assessment in *Center Church*, part 6, ch. 19, under the heading "Missional Church Movement Today," where Keller suggests that for some the missional church is about evangelism, for others it is about being incarnational, while others focus on contextual ministry, and still others on a reciprocal and communal dimension of being missional.

93. I first encountered this term through blog posts by Mike Breen, particularly "Why the Missional Conversation Must Change." His usage of *missio trinitatis* emerges out of concern for the way that *missio dei* is frequently interpreted through the lens of Western individualism. Others consider *missio trinitatis* as a reflection of the historical origins of *missio dei* and as a corrective to the (mis)appropriation of *missio dei* to religious contexts beyond Christianity. See Kirk, *What Is Mission?*, 27; and Richebacher, "Missio Dei," 597–99. More substantively, Flett, "Missio Dei," 5–18.

the church, but an attribute of God. God is a missionary God."[94] Perhaps the most significant implications of this concept are (1) that it "has helped to relinquish mission from the ownership of the Western churches and to make it truly a worldwide phenomenon"[95] and (2) that the local church is no longer merely a sending institution but is primarily a sent people.[96]

Two primary objections have been raised in response to this concept. First, the question has frequently been posed as to whom or to what *dei* refers. The idea that *dei* could refer to gods in multiple religions is seen in the recent expanded application of the term *missional* to include Islam and Buddhism.[97] Samartha advances perhaps the most coherent argument for this broadened interpretation, contending:

> Without conversion there would have been no Buddhism or Jainism, and later on, Sikhism in India, and no Christianity emerging out of Judaism in the first century. Without mission there would have been no Buddhists in Tibet, Thailand, China, Japan and Sri Lanka, or Muslims in Indonesia and the Philippines. Before the sea route to India was discovered by Vasco de Gama in 1498, in central Asia for nearly a thousand years Hindu, Buddhist, Muslim, Christian and Jewish traders came together for commerce, in the course of which there was enormous interchange of religious and cultural ideas and experience leading to mutual enrichment. The results are to be seen in art, poetry, drama, sculpture and architecture, no less than in dress, food habits and cooking styles.[98]

Samartha later summarizes the argument, contending that "[i]n a religiously plural world, Christians, together with their neighbours of other faiths, are called upon to participate in God's continuing mission in the world."[99]

While these objections still surface upon occasion,[100] this multifaith approach runs counter to the historical roots of the *missio dei* concept and the operating paradigm within the MCM. As Richebacher notes, Barth's original usage of *missio dei* emerged from his understanding of the *opera*

---

94. Bosch, *Transforming Mission*, 390.

95. Pachuau, "Missio Dei," 234.

96. Laing, "Missio Dei," 92.

97. Tizon, *Missional Preaching*, xxiii. Tizon utilizes this language to reflect the various contributions offered by four missional-related movements as outlined in Sine, *New Conspirators*, 31–55.

98. Samartha, "Mission in a Religiously Plural World," 320–21.

99. Ibid., 322.

100. See Pachuau, "Missiology in a Pluralistic World," 539–55; MacIlvaine, "What Is the Missional Church Movement?," 97–98.

trinitatis. This emphasis is also observable in Hoekendijk and others at the Willingen Conference in 1952, who rooted their understanding of the *missio dei* in the activity of the Trinity.[101]

In conformity with the historical roots of the *missio dei* concept and in response to the multifaith expansion of *missional*, several contributors within the Christian community have suggested that *missio dei* ought to be clarified to more precisely indicate the Trinitarian God—Father, Son, and Holy Spirit—as revealed through Christian scripture.[102] In agreement with these concerns for clarity, the language of *missio trinitatis* will serve as the principle linguistic formulation of the *missio dei* concept within this project. However, where occurring in source material, *missio dei* will still be utilized within quoted material. Likewise, derivative phrases, such as *God's mission*, will be used interchangeably with *missio trinitatis* on account of their predominant usage within current MCM literature, where the Trinitarian understanding is frequently assumed.

Sent as participants in God's mission

A second distinguishing emphasis of the MCM is the ecclesiology that perceives the church *to be sent as participants in God's mission*.[103] Kirk bluntly states:

> Mission is so much at the heart of the Church's life that, rather than think of it as one aspect of its existence, it is better to think of it as defining its essence. The Church is by nature missionary to that extent that, if it ceases to be missionary, it has not just failed in one of its tasks, it has ceased being Church."[104]

Rooted in the *missio trinitatis*, this perspective on the missionary nature of the church is often described as a corrective in the relationship between

---

101. Richebacher, "Missio Dei," 590–92.

102. See n. 93.

103. Moltmann, *Church in the Power of the Spirit*, 10. Variants of Moltmann's declaration, "What we have to learn from them is not that church 'has' a mission, but the very reverse: that the mission of Christ creates its own church. Mission does not come from the church; it is from mission and in the light of mission that the church has to be understood," are loosely quoted within MCM literature, frequently without reference to Moltmann. Additionally, see Brunner, *Word and the World*, 108, where he writes: "Mission work does not arise from any arrogance in the Christian Church; mission is its cause and its life. The Church exists by mission, just as a fire exists by burning. Where there is no mission, there is no Church; and where there is neither Church nor mission, there is no faith."

104. Kirk, *What Is Mission?*, 30.

ecclesiology and missiology.[105] Whereas, during Christendom, mission was viewed as a task of the church, the MCM understands the church exists as a working out of God's mission. The ordering of this relationship is frequently described as moving from theology to missiology to ecclesiology, instead of theology to ecclesiology to missiology.[106]

In its clearest expressions, this missional ecclesiology emerges from a missional hermeneutic that perceives all of scripture as a revelation of God's mission. Tienou expresses this perspective well:

> Regardless of differences concerning the definition of mission, I hope it is agreed that the entire canon is about God's mission. The Scriptures unfold God's redemptive purposes for a humanity in rebellion against him. As God graciously reveals himself (in speech and acts) to a sinful and rebellious humanity, his purpose is to acquire a people who would know him, obey him and represent him in the world. Thus, God's redeemed people are the result of God's own mission. God also entrusts his mission to his people: in this, they (corporately and individually) become the agent of God's mission in the world.[107]

The MCM frequently describes this sending pattern in three progressive movements: God the Father sends the Son; God the Father and the Son send the Spirit; God the Father, Son, and Spirit send the church.[108] More poetically, *Our World Belongs to God*, a communal and contemporary testimony of faith developed within the CRCNA, expresses the sent nature of the church this way:

> Joining the mission of God,
> *the church is sent*
> with the gospel of the kingdom
> to call everyone to know and follow Christ
> and to proclaim to all
> the assurance that in the name of Jesus

---

105. Guder writes, "This trinitarian point of entry into our theology of the church necessarily shifts all the accents in our ecclesiology . . . In particular, we have begun to see that the church of Jesus Christ is not the purpose or goal of the gospel, but rather its instrument and witness" (*Missional Church*, 5).

106. See the following video clips from MCM leaders who identify this change: Cam Roxburgh, http://www.youtube.com/watch?v=pi4iKr7ExpU; Alan Hirsch, http://www.youtube.com/watch?v=dEnBLFQWgPI; Ed Stetzer, http://www.youtube.com/watch?v=YT_T88crkog.

107. Tienou, "Dare to Make New Mistakes," 25.

108. Wright, *Mission of God's People*, 210–21.

there is forgiveness of sin
and new life for all who repent and believe.
The Spirit calls all members
to embrace God's mission
in their neighborhoods
and in the world:
to feed the hungry,
bring water to the thirsty,
welcome the stranger,
clothe the naked,
care for the sick,
and free the prisoner.
We repent of leaving this work to a few,
for this mission is central to our being.[109]

As reflected in the CRCNA's statement, the church's central nature is that of a people who are sent by God to participate in God's mission within the world. In this way, the sentness of God's people is not dependent on geographical or circumstantial location. As Hammond and Cronshaw explain, "Sentness is not about taking a plane trip or joining a short-term mission. In fact, when we really understand being sent, we may not go anywhere," adding later: "If your imagination is grabbed by being a sent people, you will see all your life as mission."[110]

Dynamically expressed, locally contextualized incarnational mission

A third emphasis of the MCM is *the essential nature of incarnational mission dynamically expressed in locally contextualized ministry*. While missional identity is not dependent on a particular type of location, a church's immediate location provides the context within which that missional identity is engaged, deepened, and finds its fullest expression. Roxburgh contends for a dual focus with regard to the local context: "First, the focus must be on the ordinary lives of the people of a local congregation through which the Spirit is shaping a new future. Second, the focus must be on the local contexts as

---

109. Excerpted from Christian Reformed Church in North America, *Our World Belongs to God*. Reprinted with permission. Emphasis added.

110. Hammond and Cronshaw, *Sentness*, 54.

the venues for discerning and engaging that future."[111] Within this localized focus, the MCM has been on the front side of a renewal of parish language and practices, providing a communal corrective to what is perceived to be an overly individualistic understanding of the gospel and mission within much of the North American church context. As *The New Parish* authors comment, "Proximity in the parish allows you to participate in God's reconciling and renewing vision in ways you can't do as an individual."[112]

Three dimensions of this emphasis draw repeated attention in the movement: an imitation of Jesus' incarnation, the dynamic nature or constant change in a ministry setting, and the localized context within which mission is engaged. With regard to the incarnation, a deep reliance emerges around the manner in which God engaged humanity through Jesus Christ—by becoming fully human. God's salvation was not accomplished at a distance, but through intimate relationship with and among those Jesus was sent to save. As Frost and Hirsch explain, "It is from inside the human condition and experience that God fulfills his own requirements for the salvation of the human race."[113] Even then, Jesus Christ's humanity is made known in his specific familial, social, religious, and broader cultural location.[114]

This prioritization on the incarnation of Jesus Christ shifts attention within the MCM from a prescribed and universal set of Christian behaviors toward asking questions about how to be a "faithful presence" of God in a particular place. Goheen relates this presence to the identity of the church as an eschatological, Spirit-filled people. "Mission is the presence of God's people in the midst of the world and the powerful presence of God's Spirit in the midst of this people for the sake of the world."[115] According to Frost, the faithful presence of God embodied in Jesus Christ "demands that we neither retreat into a holier-than-thou Christian ghetto nor give ourselves over to the values of secular culture." Within such an understanding of the incarnation, the church is "called, like Christ, to be godly, but we are expected to live it out fully in the midst of others."[116] As Goheen emphasizes, "The power and love of God's presence in the Spirit works in and through the church to draw the nations. Each characteristic of God's people is fulfilled in Christ

---

111. Roxburgh, *Missional*, 167–68.
112. Sparks, Soerens, and Friesen, *New Parish*, 23.
113. Frost and Hirsch, *Shaping of Things to Come*, 35–41.
114. Sparks, Soerens, and Friesen, *New Parish*, 26–27.
115. Goheen, *Light to the Nations*, 197.
116. Frost, *Exiles*, 15.

and yet—and this is an essential point—*the missional implications of each characteristic remain with the church today.*"[117]

An emphasis on being an incarnational presence of God also recognizes the constant cultural change that demands a dynamic approach to expressing the gospel. Much attention has been given within the MCM to the rate of change and the sheer volume of change faced by the church over the last century.[118] The response to such rapid cultural change is to call for equally adaptable approaches to ministry. In pursuing faithfulness, no program is sacrosanct. Instead, ministries focus on consistently asking questions about what it might look like to more faithfully express God's presence here and now than has been done so far.[119] Frost and Hirsch contend that "the missional church is always outward looking, always changing (as culture continues to change), and always faithful to the Word of God. In many places it is so radical it barely resembles church as we know it. In other cases it might appear conventional but is in fact incarnating itself into its community in surprising and exciting ways."[120] *The New Parish* authors continue this shift toward creative contextual imagination when they urge their readers to "[a]llow the incarnation of God in Jesus Christ to form your imagination for faithful presence."[121]

In seeking to dynamically express God's presence, the MCM draws attention to the congregation's immersion in the local context. Van Gelder argues that the church "has the inherent capacity to fit into every culture, to be relevant within the organizational and institutional dimensions of any context," not because it is so generic, but because "the church through the Spirit is inherently translatable into every specific, cultural context."[122] In the practice of contextualizing, the MCM places significant weight on listening to those in the neighborhood around the church and on working for the good of the community.[123] This practice has encouraged MCM

---

117. Goheen, *Light to the Nations*, 196. Emphasis original.

118. Van Gelder highlights a few of the global shifts that shape the need for dynamic expressions of ministry ("Future of the Discipline of Missiology," 40–42). Fennell provides an extended consideration of the church's responses to rapid change in more localized contexts ("Canada's Ever-Changing Contexts," 21–34).

119. Guder, *Missional Church*, 14.

120. Frost and Hirsch, *Shaping of Things to Come*, 7.

121. Sparks, Soerens, and Friesen, *New Parish*, 46.

122. Van Gelder, *Essence of the Church*, 119. For an extended treatment of this concept, see Sanneh, *Translating the Message*.

123. Roxburgh provides an introductory explanation of what attention to local context could look like (*Missional*, 166–92). For a more robust consideration, see Gornik, *To Live in Peace*.

practitioners to recognize that "the Spirit works through the relationships of the neighborhood to teach us what love and faithfulness look like in that particular context."[124]

Servant Identity

The MCM is also recognizable through a fourth emphasis, which asserts that *the church's privileged position within Christendom has come to an end, resulting in an opportunity for the church to embody a servant identity*. Though certainly not the only movement to proclaim the end of Christendom, the MCM developed in a context where the culture no longer embraced the Christian narrative as authoritative and thus viewed the church's influence with skepticism.[125] In their analysis, Frost and Hirsch argue that Christendom has been declining for 250 years already. While broader society is considered post-Christendom, "Christendom, as a paradigm of understanding, as a metanarrative, still exercises an overwhelming influence on our existing theological, missiological, and ecclesiological understandings in church circles."[126] They later assert that "[t]he missional church is the hope of the post-Christendom era," in contrast to other Protestant church movements that continue to "operate out of the fallacious assumption that the church belongs firmly in the town square, that is, at the heart of Western culture."[127]

The response to this shift in relationship to Western society has been a call for the church to recover its servant identity. Such a response depends on recognizing that "the church must not be equated with the reign of God,"[128] but that "the church represents the reign of God by its deeds as the servant to God's passion for the world's life."[129] This representation is rooted

---

124. Sparks, Soerens, and Friesen, *New Parish*, 31.

125. Goheen, *Light to the Nations*, 9–14. See also Penner et al., *Hemorrhaging Faith*, 11–19.

126. Frost and Hirsch critique the Christendom church as being attractional, dualistic, and hierarchical, all of which are portrayed as shortcomings within the Western church model as developed from Constantine through the late 1900s (*Shaping of Things to Come*, 8–9). Their proposed antidote to the Christendom model is to embrace a missional model that is incarnational (instead of attractional) in evangelistic direction, messianic (instead of dualistic) in its cultural engagement, and apostolic (instead of hierarchal) in its development and exercise of leadership (ibid., 30). While their approach has potential for a postmodern milieu, their assessment of Christendom would have benefited from a more thorough engagement with other academic sources examining the nature of the Western church and the development of Christendom.

127. Ibid., 16.

128. Hunsberger, "Missional Vocation," 98.

129. Ibid., 105.

in the incarnation of Jesus Christ and gives particular attention to the ways Jesus extended love to others during his earthly ministry. Heuertz and Pohl comment: "If we really believe that the good news at its heart is a story of God's love for us, then mission is being faithful in loving God back—being faithful to God, and to what, whom and how God loves."[130] Such attention to the nature of God's mission in Jesus Christ reveals a daunting challenge to missional living. Frost observes: "How distressing to us that Jesus could be the Messiah, the human incarnation of God, second person of the Trinity for thirty years and no one at home noticed!...Somehow Jesus could be fully God and blend into Galilean society—hardly the most pious or sophisticated culture—without creating a ripple."[131] From Jesus' subversive ministry, expressed as it was through seemingly scandalous interactions with tax collectors, immigrants, widows, and prostitutes, the MCM derives that God's people are to engage God's mission as servants among those on the margins of society.

The MCM depicts the recovery of this servant posture as a "sign, witness, and foretaste of where God was inviting all of creation in Jesus Christ," asserting that "local churches should live as a contrast society right in the middle of their neighborhoods."[132] This contrastive lifestyle leads into a deepened engagement within the local congregation's community through exercising communal practices, particularly radical hospitality, that seek the well-being of the whole community[133] and by assuming a cruciform approach to one's resources, including time and relationships.[134] Commenting on the servant nature of the MCM, Metzger adds that it "will be unrelenting in freely expressing love, offering mercy and extending grace—with no strings attached, and no demands of response associated with the activity."[135]

---

130. Heuertz and Pohl, *Friendship at the Margins*, 73.

131. Frost, *Exiles*, 15.

132. Roxburgh and Boren, *Introducing the Missional Church*, 70. The language of "sign, witness, and foretaste" differs from Newbigin's formulation of "sign, foretaste, and instrument," described in Newbigin, "What Is a Local Church Truly United," 115–28. A comparative study relating Newbigin's intent to Roxburgh and Boren's (and perhaps other contemporary) uses of these metaphors could serve as a topic for further research.

133. See Pohl, *Making Room*, and her subsequent book, *Living into Community*.

134. Frost, *Road to Missional*, 89–92.

135. Stiller and Metzger, *Going Missional*, 64.

Holistic Gospel

Finally, the fifth emphasis within the MCM is *an insistence upon a holistic gospel that encompasses the reconciliation, restoration, and flourishing of all things in Jesus Christ*. In many ways, this view of a holistic scope to the gospel is rooted both in Jesus' earthly ministry and in the anticipated fullness of the new heaven and new earth. Hunsberger explains:

> Jesus' healings, exorcisms, calming of storms, feeding of the multitudes, and raising the dead to life were all signs. These signs revealed that in Jesus' life under the authority of God the reign of God was at hand. The deeds themselves were simply doing what ought to be done under God's reign. They also point to what God intends to bring about at the world's consummation, when all that creation was envisioned and imagined to be is made finally true. The actions of Jesus show forth the horizon of the coming world of shalom—peace, justice, and joy in the Holy Spirit.[136]

This broad understanding of the reign of God rejects both a separation of and also competition between word and deed ministries. Newbigin insisted that the church's "central reality is neither word nor deed, but the total life of a community enabled by the Spirit to live in Christ, sharing his passion and the power of his resurrection." He continues: "action for justice and peace in the world is not something which is secondary, marginal to the central task of evangelism. It belongs to the heart of the matter."[137] The MCM seeks to integrate the whole life of God's people in the mission of cultivating the reconciling life of God in Jesus Christ throughout all cultural contexts and all of creation. Frost depicts this holistic vision well:

> The missional Christian community should be at the forefront of relational reconciliation, as it was in the early years of the post-apartheid South Africa. The missional Christian community should be committed to the creation of a more just society, as it was in the launch of the Micah Challenge and the Millennium Development Goals, aimed at holding the UN to its commitment to end extreme poverty. And the missional community should be creators and purveyors of true beauty, whether it be great art, great music, great architecture, or great shoes. I would also want to add that not only should missional Christians

---

136. Hunsberger, "Missional Vocation," 105.
137. Newbigin, *Gospel in a Pluralist Society*, 137.

appreciate the beauty of nature, but they should actively participate in its protection.[138]

With such a view, the MCM conversation has been marked by dialogue around diverse topics, including creation care[139] and interfaith dialogue,[140] while frequently drawing from other conversations surrounding new monasticism and Christian community development.

Worship and Liturgy

This project also utilizes two closely related terms, *worship* and *liturgy*, fairly frequently. *Worship* refers to the participatory gathering of God's people by the Spirit wherein they are encountered by God's presence, formed by the story of God's covenantal faithfulness in Jesus Christ, and respond by the Spirit with renewed gratitude and commitment to participate in God's mission of making all things new. While agreeing that worship is life encompassing,[141] a narrower connotation of worship as a communal gathering of God's people will be utilized throughout this project. *Liturgy*, on the other hand, refers both to the structure of a worship gathering and to the particular movements within that structure. Within this project, *liturgy* does not refer to a specific liturgical tradition or prescribed ordering of a worship gathering.[142] An additional term, *liturgical rhythms*, will be introduced through this project in order to describe traits or emphases within the *liturgy* that spill beyond *worship* gatherings.

Praxis-Oriented Discipleship

The term *praxis-oriented discipleship* is intended to describe a shift in catechetical approaches that moves the central emphasis of discipleship from the transfer of information toward the formation of character. This shift has led to a resurgence in apprenticeship models of discipleship and to greater attention to ethical living in contrast to recitation of biblical texts and intellectual assent to creeds or confessions. Breen indicates that the two central areas of attention with regard to discipleship are character and competency.

---

138. Frost, *Road to Missional*, 115.

139. Kostamo and Kostamo, "Creation Care as Christian Mission," 167–79.

140. Berghoef, *Pub Theology*.

141. Van Gelder, *Essence of the Church*, 151; Hirsch, *Forgotten Ways*, 41; and Kreider and Kreider, *Worship and Mission after Christendom*, 29–31.

142. In other words, not a specific denominational tradition or liturgical form.

These lead the church to ask questions about its leaders like: "Are their lives characterized by grace? Peace? Love? Transformation? Patience? Humility?" And "Can they disciple people well who can then disciple others?"[143] Huckins further embeds this apprenticeship model by calling attention to six postures or practices that shape missional communities, arguing that "[t]here must be a dynamic interdependence that allows the Spirit to shape and fuel both individuals and communities as they seek to faithfully participate in the missio Dei."[144] Such a shift in discipleship coheres with similar transitions in educational theory and practice, where individuated education and project-based approaches have shifted attention to character formation and application competencies rather than to a restricted understanding of education as primarily (or simply) information dissemination and acquisition.[145]

Evangelism and Evangelistic

Within North America, *evangelism* has developed a negative reputation on account of exemplified practices that can appear intrusive (if not abusive), deceptive, or ingenuous by those being evangelized. Relying on a story from Margaret Atwood, Bowen describes how evangelism can be perceived in the same category as a flasher who exposes himself to an unwitting passerby on the street because of the abrupt way in which an evangelist suddenly exposes their spirituality.[146] Still others experience evangelism as being about the goals of the evangelist to secure a certain number of decisions for Christ. In these scenarios, the person being evangelized can feel objectified, as if the evangelist is not interested in them as a person, but only in leading them to pray the "sinner's prayer" or make some other verbal acknowledgment that they have accepted Jesus Christ as Lord and Savior.

In addition to questioning the social and ethical appropriateness of these scenarios, this project has two other concerns with evangelism when understood and encouraged in this manner. The first concern is the heavy focus on training individuals in specific evangelism techniques. In such an approach, the gospel is reduced to propositions to which a person is called to give intellectual assent as the primary part of a responsive decision to accept Jesus Christ. This kind of approach is frequently separated from the body of

---

143. Mike Breen, "Why the Missional Movement Will Fail, Part 2."

144. Huckins, *Thin Places*, 23.

145. For example, Roessingh and Chambers, "Project-Based Learning and Pedagogy," 60–71.

146. Bowen, *Evangelism for Normal People*, 18–26.

Christ, the community of God's people. These decision-focused techniques reinforce the perspective wherein people consider themselves spiritual but not religious, which reflects, at minimum, a heightened individualism and a disembodied understanding of the gospel.[147]

The second concern is that the practice of evangelism is frequently disconnected from discipleship and inclusion in the community of God's people. This project takes issue with evangelism approaches that make a clear distinction between evangelism and discipleship because the church is not called to make converts but disciples. To this end, the project relies on a centered-set approach to evangelism and discipleship that asks what direction a person is moving in relationship to Jesus Christ as a part of God's people. This theme will be considered more closely in chapter 6.

Moreover, this project draws attention to ways in which a community of God's people become evangelistic in their life together. The focus is on the character of their communal life, not on the mastery of particular verbal or pictorial summaries of the gospel. This attention is not intended to minimize the benefit and necessity of providing clear summaries of the gospel, of inviting others to make a decision to follow Jesus Christ, or of encouraging particularly gifted persons to initiate conversations calling others to faith in Jesus Christ. Rather, the attention on the people of God becoming evangelistic rests on a conviction that the whole life of God's people provides the context within which the gospel makes sense. Therefore, this project's consideration of evangelism focuses on how the community of God's people embodies the character of Jesus Christ in their relationships with one another and their neighbors, thereby becoming evangelistic. Thus, the call to evangelize is about God's people becoming evangelistic as they learn to faithfully embody the good news of Jesus Christ together.

Historical Roots and Trajectory

The historical roots of the MCM reach back to the 1930s and Karl Hartenstein's summary response to Barth's musings on the Trinitarian basis of Christian mission.[148] However, the *missio dei* concept, which animates the movement, emerged more popularly in dialogue surrounding the 1952 International

---

147. Kinnaman and Lyons, *UnChristian*.

148. Bevans and Schroeder trace the connection back to a paper that Barth presented at the Brandenberg Mission Conference in 1932, which influenced Hartenstein's coining of the phrase *missio dei* in 1934 (*Constants in Context*, 290).

Missionary Council held in Willingen.[149] While intended as a means of emphasizing both the Trinitarian basis of mission and the church's participation in that mission, the *missio dei* concept evolved rapidly to identify the church as a hindrance to God's mission and an emphasis on the work of the Holy Spirit apart from the church.[150] The concept languished within World Council of Churches conversations through the 1970s, when Lesslie Newbigin began to reclaim *missio dei* for its Trinitarian roots and its potential for the re-evangelization of Western culture in what was rapidly becoming a pluralistic and decidedly post-Christendom society. While Newbigin's influence is certainly the most significant, the influence of others, including DuBose's *God Who Sends*, Bosch's *Transforming Mission*, and Van Engen's *God's Missionary People*, is also evident in the early formation of the MCM.

Growing from these roots, the first clearly identifiable formation of the MCM in North America is evident in the launch of GOCN during the 1990s.[151] Under the influence of Darrell Guder, Craig Van Gelder, and George Hunsberger (among others), GOCN encouraged dialogue and published several significant texts related to missional approaches to ecclesiology and hermeneutics.[152] Nearly at the same time, Frost and Hirsch published *The Shaping of Things to Come*, which identified several elements of what became key emphases of the MCM, such as a priority on incarnational ministry, a recognition of the end of Christendom, and an ensuing necessity for discovering a new way of being church.

Shortly after these initial contributions, the MCM conversation broadened its scope through publications and networks related to leadership, neighborhood engagement, and discipleship in particular. Hirsch and Frost focused on developing a theological framework for missional leadership, emphasizing a fivefold office from Ephesians 4 (apostle, prophet, evangelist, pastor, and teacher).[153] Roxburgh shifted attention toward neighborhood engagement

---

149. Van Gelder comments on the significance of Willingen "reconceptualizing mission as *missio Dei*—the mission of the triune God in the world. It represented a fundamental shift from a Christology-based understanding of mission as being a church's responsibility to a trinitarian-based understanding of God's mission in the world as having a church" ("Future of the Discipline of Missiology," 50).

150. Bosch highlights distortions of the original intent of the *missio dei* designation, concluding that among some advocates "the church has become unnecessary for the *missio Dei*" (*Transforming Mission*, 390–92).

151. See Goheen, who notes distinctions in how North American and European applications of Newbigin's teaching ("'As the Father Has Sent Me,'" 434–40).

152. See http://gocn.org/network/about.

153. Hirsch, *Forgotten Ways*, is an early example of this approach to missional leadership. Woodward, *Creating a Missional Culture*, develops this fivefold approach in much greater detail.

and to leadership structures through Allelon, which later morphed into the Missional Network and collaboration with Van Gelder.[154] Breen has led the way in considering what missional discipleship might look like, particularly through his leadership within 3D Movements.[155]

A more comprehensive missional hermeneutic also developed during this time. Emerging from the early hermeneutical context of Brownson's article "Speaking the Truth in Love" and Bauckham's *Bible and Mission*, Christopher Wright articulated a thorough consideration of reading the scope of Christian scripture through the lens of *missio dei*, through his book *The Mission of God*. This metanarrative lens has also been attended to by others in the MCM, like Bartholomew and Goheen in their book, *The Drama of Scripture*, and has become essential in understanding both the *missio trinitatis* and the sent nature of the church.

Another sign of the ongoing development of the MCM has been the formation of several networks, such as Forge, the Missional Network, Missio Alliance, VERGE, Parish Collective, and 3D Movements. These networks have led to the creation of at least four annual conferences (VERGE, Sentralized, Inhabit, and Missio Alliance) and numerous smaller gatherings related to missional practices and theology. There have also been occasional academic conferences, like Calvin Seminary's "A Missional Reading of Scripture" in 2013, which continue to further academic considerations surrounding the MCM.[156]

Related Movements

While nearly impossible to exhaustively list the various adjective-rich descriptions of church that exist today, the MCM can be distinguished from five other conversations that have some parallel development with the MCM.[157] While sharing many similarities, these movements have developed with distinct emphases and characteristics. The five movements are:

---

154. See http://www.themissionalnetwork.com, through which *The Journal of Missional Practice* is now published.

155. See the 3DM website, http://3dmovements.com, for the various resources and blog commentary related to Breen's emphasis on missional discipleship.

156. November 20–21, 2013. Audio of the symposium is available at calvinseminary.edu/academics/continuing-education/missional-reading/.

157. For a different categorization of contemporary movements, see Richardson, who focuses more specifically on the American context, highlighting a multiethnic approach that distinguishes between community development and racial reconciliation and including a church multiplication movement ("Emerging Missional Movements," 131–36).

fresh expressions, Christian community development, integral mission, emergent church movement, and new monasticism.[158]

Fresh Expressions

Currently present in several countries, fresh expressions grew out of the Anglican context with a focus on facilitating opportunities for the church to grow in cultural settings in which it does not currently seem to have much traction. Sharing similar roots in Newbigin's teaching as the MCM has, fresh expressions has embraced a wide vision of experimentation in church planting and pioneer ministries, which also includes a closer embrace of new monasticism than the MCM.[159] Along these lines, the Anglican *Mission-Shaped Church* report observes that "no one strategy will be adequate to fulfill" the incarnational priorities of the Church of England. Though very rooted in their particular geographic communities, fresh expression practitioners have already realized that "[c]ommunities are now multilayered, comprising neighbourhoods, usually with permeable boundaries, and a wide variety of networks, ranging from the relatively local to the global. Increased mobility and electronic communications technology have changed the nature of community."[160] In this context of disconnect, Cray calls attention to how "Christians do not go to church. They are Church—sometimes gathered, sometimes scattered, but always interdependent."[161]

Christian Community Development

The Christian community development conversation has its roots in the work of Dr. John Perkins. Through his own experience of being called by God to return to Mississippi after achieving "the American dream" in California, Dr.

---

158. Compare this list with Sine, who describes missional related movements as: emergent, missional, mosaic, and monastic. Sine's emphasis on mosaic would encompass both Christian community development and integral mission, which, though having significant overlap, differ in their originating contexts, their particular emphases, and their cultural locations. Additionally, Sine's summary overlooks the unique perspective brought through fresh expression, particularly with regard to church expansion (*New Conspirators*, 31–55).

159. Cray, "On Not Knowing the End at the Beginning."

160. Church of England Mission and Public Affairs Council, *Mission-Shaped Church*, x. See the first chapter, "Changing Contexts," for a broad sweep accounting of the numerous changes that the Council observed impacting the Church of England in the British context.

161. Cray, "Why Is New Monasticism Important?," 2.

Perkins articulated a philosophy of ministry built around the three Rs—Relocation, Reconciliation, and Redistribution.[162] Perkins's vision for engaging communities marked by poverty has grown into an organized movement, the Christian Community Development Association, which is marked not only by the three Rs, but also five other values: leadership development, listening to the community, church-based, holistic, and empowerment.[163] Christian community development is similar to the MCM in its strong emphasis on the incarnation of Jesus Christ as a model for ministry and the insistence that the gospel is holistic. Old Testament images like the exodus from Egypt and Nehemiah rebuilding the walls of Jerusalem and prophetic passages like Jeremiah 29 (seek the peace of the city) and Isaiah 58 (restorer of streets with dwellings) play significant roles in shaping the ethos within Christian community development circles. To this point, the deliberate emphasis on economic and racial reconciliation within CCDA has been largely missing from MCM conversations. Conversely, though there are discernable adjustments being made, the emphasis on discipleship found in the MCM has often been a secondary or tertiary conversation within the CCDA context.

Integral Mission

Integral mission has emerged from within Central and South American contexts with a strong emphasis on holistic mission in an attempt to bridge what has frequently been viewed as a great divide between word- and deed-based ministries. As Bradbury comments, "in integral mission our proclamation has social consequences as we call people to love and repentance in all areas of life. And our social involvement has evangelistic consequences as we bear witness to the transforming grace of Jesus Christ."[164] Along with recognizing the radical impact of globalization, integral mission maintains a strong preference for attending to the poor and marginalized in ways that humanize them.[165] While advancing similar critiques as the MCM regarding the Christendom church's entanglements with political and corporate power structures, the historical roots of integral mission movement have a different genesis. Whereas the MCM finds its impetus within Newbigin, integral mission looks to Rene Padilla's work in evangelical conversations connected with the Lausanne Movement to shape its theological understanding

---

162. See Perkins, *Beyond Charity* and *With Justice for All*.

163. See http://www.ccda.org/about/ccd-philosophy for an overview of each of the eight values of the Christian Community Development Association.

164. Bradbury, "Micah Declaration on Integral Mission," 19.

165. Costello, "Integral Mission with the Poor," 110.

and vision.¹⁶⁶ From this orientation, integral mission places more emphasis on holistic and locally contextualized ministry and gives less attention to the sent nature of the church than the MCM does.¹⁶⁷

Emergent Church Movement

The emergent movement is probably the most readily confused with the MCM. The common recognition that Christendom has come to an end,¹⁶⁸ and the active self-identification within both movements by some advocates,¹⁶⁹ as well as the proliferation of the term *missional* within emergent conversations, has certainly contributed to the confusion. Roxburgh and Boren rightly conclude that, although there are similarities, the emergent and missional movements "are not necessarily the same thing."¹⁷⁰

In its short history, the emergent movement has resisted definition even more so than the MCM. In many ways emergent emphases are responding to the advent of postmodernity,¹⁷¹ by embracing an epistemological humility grounded in uncertainty¹⁷² and a hermeneutical prioritization on the reader's experience in their own context as the source of generative truth.¹⁷³ Fairly or not, the movement's attempts to de-emphasize historical

---

166. For a brief historical overview of integral mission, see Padilla's two chapters, "Integral Mission and its Historical Development" and "Integral Mission Today," in Chester, ed., *Justice, Mercy, and Humility*, 42–64.

167. See also Padilla's collection of essays, *Mission between the Times*, particularly his consideration of salvation in the essay, "What is the Gospel?" (83–101), which presents a more holistic understanding of the gospel than has been typically embraced within North American evangelicalism.

168. Roxburgh and Boren, *Introducing the Missional Church*, 53.

169. Dwight Friesen is one such person who contributes to both emergent and missional church conversations with some regularity. See http://dwightfriesen.com/.

170. Roxburgh and Boren, *Introducing the Missional Church*, 54.

171. Condor identifies the existing church according to its participation in modernity and the emerging church within postmodernity ("Existing Church/Emerging Church Matrix," 97–107). Also, Kimball, *Emerging Worship*.

172. Rollins, *Insurrection*.

173. As an example of how the reader's context takes priority within the emergent movement, see Scandrette, who writes: "You should not think that the 'real' emergence is happening elsewhere. You are invited to embrace your own celebrity—recognizing the importance of your own journey over simply being a fan of others'—and cultivate a local culture of faith-seeking. To address spectator tendencies, I give this unsolicited advice: no once can emerge for you. Make your own life. Host your own emergence. Stop reading so many books and blogs. Start your own conversations, and be a caring friend. The most important conversations happen between people who have the potential to live out their story together" ("Growing Pains," 25).

sources of authority are frequently interpreted as an inherent distrust for institutions and a blatant disregard for orthodox doctrinal statements.[174]

Over a similar developmental path, the emergent movement has been less concerned with understanding the *missio trinitatis* or the ecclesiology involved with seeing the church's identity as being sent, but has given more attention to the diversity of worship practices and affirming non-institutional expressions of church than has the MCM.[175] However, the primary difference between the two movements may well be the orienting point for their conversations: the MCM engages the intersection of gospel, church, and culture from the perspective of a missional hermeneutic largely operating from within an orthodox theological framework; whereas, the emergent movement enters the gospel-church-culture trialogue from the perspective of postmodern culture.

New Monasticism

With many striking similarities, the new monastic movement has developed significant overlap with each of the other movements identified above, including the MCM.[176] While there tends to be great appreciation within the MCM for new monastic practices, the two movements are not identical. In many ways, the new monastic movement has its central focus on participating in communal practices that affirm a locally contextualized approach to ministry, particularly among marginalized persons in urban contexts,[177] as a means of deepening faithful discipleship. Claiborne emphasizes that in new monasticism "[w]e are simply trying to remind the world of how good God is, in an age where one of the biggest obstacles to God has been Christians."[178] Seeking to combine orthopraxy, orthodoxy, and orthopathy

---

174. Wittmer, "Don't Stop Believing," 119–32.

175. Roberts asserts that "worship sits alongside mission as one of two core practices that constitute the church. Christians have a double calling: to be agents of God's transformation within the world through mission and to anticipate the consummation of the kingdom through worship" ("Rethinking Worship as an Emerging Christian Practice," 179–94). The MCM would disagree with the dualistic separation implied in such a statement.

176. Claiborne's description reveals how overlapping connections between Christian community development, emergent church movement, integral mission, and the MCM are readily evident in new monasticism ("Marks of New Monasticism," 19–36).

177. See Bessenecker, *New Friars*, for an intriguing glimpse at how new monasticism includes a recovery of the friar role, wherein a person or small team of people enter areas that have been hostile or resistant to the gospel for the sake of establishing the presence of God's people in places often deemed "God-forsaken."

178. Claiborne, "Marks of New Monasticism," 35.

into a holistic approach to life,[179] new monasticism places a high emphasis on becoming a community of disciples that does life together, so that salvation can be experienced among God's people in the extension of forgiveness and repentance.[180] By drawing from older monastic orders, new monasticism has placed significant emphasis on communal sharing of property and resources, on forming covenants around common practices (rules of life), and on prayer.[181] This emphasis on personal piety within the context of communal practices is perhaps the most significant difference between new monasticism and the MCM. Quite often, such piety and practice is only tangentially considered by MCM practitioners as one of the ways of establishing an incarnational presence within a local community.

Procedure and Outline

Project Development

As already evident, this project begins by presenting several introductory matters, including the thesis statement as well as a clear articulation of the hermeneutical location, the importance of the research, the methodology employed, and the trajectory for the remainder of the project. From here, the project proceeds with a substantive literature review in order to further locate the research in relationship to previous enquiries, while exposing the above identified lacunae. After briefly comparing a missional ecclesiology with a Reformed ecclesiology, this project will identify several contours of a missional theology of worship, highlighting the importance of liturgical rhythms that can extend beyond the worship gathering. Relying on these rhythms, a proposal for integrating this missional approach to worship with a praxis-oriented discipleship already present within the MCM is offered. This trajectory culminates by contending that such a combination of worship and discipleship cultivates an evangelistic character among God's people that could rightly be called a communally embodied gospel. The project then concludes by suggesting potential opportunities for ongoing

---

179. Mobsby and Berry, *New Monastic Handbook*, 51–65.

180. Wilson-Hartgrove connects this vision to the idea that "there is no salvation outside the church" when he writes: "if the Bible is a story about God's plan to save the world through a people, then my salvation and sanctification depend on finding my true home with God's people. Apart from the story of this people, I can't have a relationship with God. Without the church, there's no chance of becoming holy" (*New Monasticism*, 58).

181. Mobsby and Berry, *New Monastic Handbook*, 13–34.

dialogue regarding the relationship of worship, discipleship, and evangelism within the MCM.

Chapter Descriptions and Their Relationships to Each Other

Operating within the general trajectory identified through the introductory matters considered in this first chapter, the remaining chapters unfold according to the more specific contours identified in the following descriptions. The second chapter engages MCM conversations more directly, undertaking a review of relevant literature, focusing on three subsets of source material: those that consider the formation of an evangelistic character among God's people, those that describe or reference missional perspectives on worship, and those few sources that directly engage the capacity of a missional approach to worship to form an evangelistic character among God's people.

Addressing the question of "What makes the church *the church*?," the third chapter relates MCM understandings of the marks of the church to its Christology and ecclesiology. This chapter contends that the MCM understands the marks of the church in terms of practices that enable a community to more fully and faithfully embody God's character as expressed in Jesus Christ. Contrasting this perspective with the *notae ecclesia* confessed by churches associated with sixteenth- and seventeenth-century Reformation movements, this chapter shows how the MCM has oriented its theological priorities to move from Christology to missiology to ecclesiology.[182] This orientation toward embodying Jesus' character leads the MCM to emphasize communal practices that participate in the *missio trinitatis* over submission to creeds, confessions, or other institutional markers that often defined the church during Christendom.[183]

Operating within these ecclesiological contours, chapter 4 articulates a missional approach to worship, observing distinctive theological priorities and attendant practices that draw people as active participants into the narrative of God's mission. Engaging Smith's liturgical formation reflections, this chapter considers how an order of worship can participate in forming God's people within the character of Jesus Christ as active participants within the *missio trinitatis*. As this conversation unfolds, the MCM's

182. Hirsch, *Forgotten Ways*, 142–43.

183. Some advocates within the MCM criticize confessional and institutional as vestiges of the Christendom church. This perspective will be acknowledged and critiqued on a couple occasions in this project.

understanding of the Holy Spirit comes into focus as the central actor in forming the character of God's people.

Chapter 5 proposes an integration of a missional approach to worship with discipleship so as to increase the MCM's capacity to cultivate the character of Jesus Christ among the people of God. Continuing with themes from the previous chapter, this chapter demonstrates how the liturgical rhythms of remembering and anticipating can give shape to a praxis-oriented approach to discipleship. In the process of demonstrating the capacity for extending these liturgical rhythms into discipleship practices, this chapter considers how Hauerwas's and Wells's contributions can facilitate an integrative relationship between worship and discipleship within the MCM. Along with other personal and communal examples, practices of hospitality and compassion are considered here.

Drawing the project to a conclusion, the sixth and final chapter explores how the MCM's cultivation of Jesus Christ's character among God's people is essentially the formation of an evangelistic character that is communally embodied, particularly through practices of hospitality and compassion. Stone's *Evangelism after Christendom* and the contributions of a few others related to an embodied apologetics serve to anchor this chapter in broader discussions on evangelism in a post-Christendom context. The project then concludes by briefly identifying implications and outlining potential contours for furthering the conversations advanced within this project.

2

Literature Review

THIS CHAPTER SEEKS TO expose two worship related lacunae within MCM literature. The first literature gap centers on the role of worship in forming an evangelistic character among God's people. This gap in turn points toward the second lacuna, an absence of a clearly articulated missional approach to worship. In identifying these gaps, this literature review engages three subsets of missional church material: those that (1) address the formation of an evangelistic character among God's people, (2) offer perspectives on worship, and (3) consider the role of worship in forming an evangelistic character among God's people. Following the review, this chapter concludes with brief commentary on the two gaps, highlighting a few aspects of the MCM that may have contributed to their existence.

Three parameters shaped the selection of materials for this review. Firstly, the included literature is drawn exclusively from within the MCM. As outlined in chapter 1, the MCM is distinguishable by its roots within Newbigin's missiological critique of the church in Western society, his ecclesiological vision of the church as the hermeneutic of the gospel, and by five common emphases present within the MCM: *missio trinitatis*, the sent nature of the church, incarnational mission dynamically and locally contextualized, a recovery of a servant posture in a post-Christendom context, and a commitment to a holistic gospel seeking the reconciliation and renewal of all things in Jesus Christ.

Secondly, this review only considers MCM resources that address the formation of an evangelistic character or those concerned with communal worship. While perhaps obvious that not all MCM literature is concerned with worship, a temptation exists to assume that all MCM writings are focused on the formation of an evangelistic character among God's people.

However, simply glancing at published topics reveals a broader diversity among MCM literature than might be expected. Some sources advance new readings of scripture,[1] other contributions pursue denominationally located missional ecclesiologies,[2] and some attend to the sustainability of community engagement.[3] Therefore, rather than engaging the whole scope of MCM literature,[4] this review is particularly concerned with culling perspectives from those resources deliberately focused on cultivating an evangelistic character among God's people and those addressing worship.

Therefore, thirdly, sources rooted within the five related ecclesial movements[5] and those arising within liturgical theology and Christian ethics are excluded from consideration in this review. In particular, the exclusion of emergent church sources is important to recognize as the word *missional* frequently appears in their writings. Though using the word *missional*, the emergent movement embraces an uncertainty about God and a vision of the church's orientation to cultural engagement that differs from the MCM, resulting in an understanding of *missional* that is rooted primarily in cultural relevance rather than in faithfulness to the biblical narrative.[6] Additionally, sources in liturgical theology and Christian ethics that address relationships between worship, ethics, and mission are excluded from the review. While all these sources offer potential means for addressing gaps in the MCM literature, the MCM, as of yet, has not directly engaged these other conversations in a consistent manner.[7]

---

1. Gilbert, "Missional Relevance of Genesis 1–3," 49–64.

2. Marshall, "Missional Ecclesiology for the 21st Century," 5–21; and Rankin, "Perfect Church," 83–104.

3. Seibel, "Heart of God in the Heart of the City," 56–70.

4. From a pragmatic perspective, given the rapid proliferation of MCM-related material (whether through books, scholarly and popular articles, and myriad social media), a literature set composed of all sources associated with the MCM would be far too extensive for a single review.

5. As noted in the first chapter, the five related ecclesial movements are: fresh expression, Christian community development, emergent church, integral mission, and new monasticism.

6. Distinguishing between emergent and MCM resources is admittedly subjective. The central challenge revolves around these movements' overlapping use of the term *missional* while maintaining different operational descriptions of *missional*. Thus, conversational boundaries between the two movements are more fluid than the clear-cut distinctions a thesis project normally desires. Beyond the contrasts already noted in chapter 1, selecting which sources belong where has been mitigated by asking two questions: "Who are the primary conversation partners this source engages?" and "Do the referenced sources and practitioners primarily self-identify within the MCM?"

7. Several of these "outside" resources will be considered in later chapters as potential means of addressing the gaps identified through this literature review. Notably

With these qualifiers in place, this chapter proceeds in two parts. The first part engages material from previous enquiries under three headings: *cultivating an evangelistic character, perspectives on worship,* and *worship's role in cultivating an evangelistic character.* Drawing from this review, the second part highlights the presence of the two worship related lacunae, concluding with several suggestions as to how the shape of the MCM has been conducive for the development of these gaps.

Previous Enquiries

Cultivating an Evangelistic Character

At least five approaches to forming an evangelistic character among God's people are discernable within MCM literature: immersion in the story of God's mission, adjusting leadership approaches, promoting deliberate discipleship, attending to spiritual practices, and engaging with community. While offering a unique sight line into this conversation, each of these approaches remains dialogically dependent upon the other approaches to more fully describe the cultivation of an evangelistic character among God's people.[8] A close examination of the literature reveals that several sources blend two or more of these approaches and that some contributors have produced resources from one approach only to offer subsequent resources that follow a different approach.[9] Where occurring, these multiple approaches reflect the integrated and holistic nature of the missional church conversation rather than a conversion in the thinking of a particular author. This portion of the review is brief, highlighting one or two representative voices for each of the five approaches.

Immersion in the story of God's mission

The MCM's earliest approach to the formation of an evangelistic character is related to hermeneutics, specifically, those centered on the immersion of

---

excerpts from Smith, *Desiring the Kingdom*; Hauerwas and Wells eds., *Blackwell Companion to Christian Ethics*; and Wells, *God's Companions*, will impact chapters 4 and 5.

8. Hunsberger comments on the integral nature of the four emphases within missional hermeneutics applies to these approaches as well: "None of them is so independent of the others that it can stand alone. Each depends on and begs for the other accents" ("Proposals for Missional Hermeneutic," 318–19).

9. Compare, for example, Frost and Hirsch, *Shaping of Things to Come*, which focuses on structure and leadership, with Hirsch and Hirsch, *Untamed*, which focuses on discipleship.

God's people within the story of God's mission. Advocates of this approach describe how such an immersion requires ongoing rehearsal of the story, submission to the narrative's authority, and a lived response to the transformative nature of the story. Christopher Wright and Michael Goheen serve as the primary representatives of this approach.

Asserting that a missional identity is nourished by rehearsing the story of God's mission, Wright points to the Abrahamic roots of the church as "the vehicle of God's blessings to the nations," and then asks, "what else can the church be but missional? This is who we are and what we are here for."[10] Goheen adds that the North American church has become "oblivious to the rich resonances of the Old Testament sources in New Testament images of the church," and therefore to the church's "heritage as a missional people."[11] Collaborating with Bartholomew, he also suggests that such a loss is particularly tragic because "[t]he world of the Bible is *our* world, and its story of redemption is also *our* story."[12] Elsewhere, Goheen warns, "If we do not develop our self-understanding in terms of the role that we have been called to play in the biblical drama, we will find ourselves shaped by the idolatrous story of the dominant culture."[13] In such a light, Wright bemoans the persistent unfamiliarity with the biblical story, "even among Christians with great enthusiasm for world missions.[14]

Wright and Goheen also insist that God's people need to submit to the authority of the story.[15] To make this point, Wright argues that the great commands of scripture only make sense "within the context of their foundational indicatives, namely, all that the Bible affirms about God, creation, human life in its paradox of dignity and depravity, redemption in all its comprehensive glory, and the new creation in which God will dwell with his people."[16] Submission to the authority of the biblical narrative means accepting that how the Bible describes reality depicts the world in which God's people live. As such, Goheen argues that the truth of the biblical story

---

10. Wright, *Mission of God's People*, 73.
11. Goheen, *Light to the Nations*, 23–24.
12. Bartholomew and Goheen, *Drama of Scripture*, 196.
13. Goheen, *Light to the Nations*, 5.
14. Wright, *Mission of God's People*, 39.
15. Van Gelder remarks: "Being governed by the Word means that the church's life and ministry are to be defined by the biblical story. The church must live into this story, seeking to understand the full purposes of God. The church must also live out of this story, applying God's purposes to its life and ministry" (*Essence of the Church*, 144).
16. Wright, *Mission of God*, 51–61.

becomes a commitment that shapes the way God's people engage "every aspect of what God has created."[17]

Therefore, submitting to the authority of the biblical story calls for living that is congruent with the reality revealed through Christian scripture, not merely for obeying particular commands. Moreover, commitment to the story of God's mission creates tension with the expectations and norms of the surrounding culture.[18] As Goheen notes, the early church experienced this tension in such a way that "their alternative communal life was on the margins of mainstream society yet was attractive to many and publicly challenged the reigning idolatry of the empire."[19]

Such cultural engagement reveals the transformative nature of the biblical story, serving in part to cultivate an evangelistic character among God's people.[20] As Bartholomew and Goheen write, "If we recognize that we have been called to provide our world with a preview of God's coming kingdom, the hope of that kingdom's coming will shape all that we say and do in the here and now."[21] The transformative nature of the story leads to the recognition that "God's chosen people do not exist for themselves. Rather, they exist for the sake of God's glory and his mission, and for the sake of others toward whom God's mission is directed."[22] This project will return to this perspective when considering missional approaches to worship and discipleship.

Adjusting Leadership Approaches

Other missional advocates argue that cultivating an evangelistic character among God's people involves adjusting leadership approaches. While widely present in MCM literature,[23] this emphasis is seen clearly in Van

17. Goheen, *Light to the Nations*, 18.

18. Along these lines, Hendrick contends: "The beginning point for developing a missionary congregation will be that it understands itself to be living in a cultural situation that in many, if not most, ways is antithetical to the life, teachings, and gospel of Jesus" ("Congregations with Missions vs. Missionary Congregations," 304).

19. Goheen, *Light to the Nations*, 8.

20. See Bartholomew and Goheen, who describe this identity through three modes of continuing mission: "Being a Light to the World: Continuing the Mission of Israel"; "Introducing the Kingdom: Continuing the Mission of Jesus"; and "Bearing Faithful Witness: Continuing the Mission of the Early Church" (*Drama of Scripture*, 198–201).

21. Ibid., 206. Also, Hendrick, "Congregations with Missions vs. Missionary Congregations," 306.

22. Goheen, *Light to the Nations*, 26.

23. See Roxburgh and Boren, who contend that rather than setting the vision for the church, a missional "leader creates space and experiences for others to imagine what the Spirit is calling forth," therein emphasizing the priesthood of all believers through

Gelder's *The Ministry of the Missional Church* and Woodward's *Creating a Missional Culture*.

Van Gelder contends that "the exercise of *leadership* and the development of organizational *infrastructure*" function at the center of core missional practices.[24] He asserts that visionary leadership lies "at the heart of the life and ministry of a Spirit-led, missional congregation,"[25] requiring leaders "to engage in discernment and decision making"[26] in a way that participates in the Spirit's ministry, which "is always to lead the church into redemptive ministry that seeks to transform both human behavior and organizational life as the church participates in God's mission in the world."[27] For Van Gelder, then, the purpose of church leadership and the attention to infrastructure are intended to empower the local congregation to "be a community of God's people called, gathered, and sent to bear witness to the redemptive reign of God as they seek to participate in God's mission in the world."[28]

Within this framework, Van Gelder advocates for leadership and organizational structures that are "communally discerned," "theologically framed," and "theoretically informed," culminating in "strategic action."[29] However, Van Gelder does not specifically describe what leadership roles might be involved in such an approach, contending that "leadership and organization need to be understood as always being contextual and therefore always being provisional in character."[30] Van Gelder depicts an ideal congregation as being Spirit-led, aware of its geographical, cultural, and social location, and structured so that "a larger number of persons in both formal and informal roles" participate in shaping the congregation's ministry.[31] Though vague on specific roles, Van Gelder clearly locates the development of a congregation's missional identity—and therefore its evangelistic character—within a congregation's attention to their respective leadership and organizational structures.

---

the active participation of the congregation in discernment and decision-making (*Introducing the Missional Church*, 138–139). Also, Frost and Hirsch, *Shaping of Things to Come*, 165–200.

24. Van Gelder, *Ministry of the Missional Church*, 147. Also, Van Gelder, *Essence of the Church*, 155–84; and Van Gelder, *Missional Church and Leadership Formation*, 9–44.

25. Van Gelder, *Ministry of the Missional Church*, 148.

26. Ibid., 97.

27. Ibid., 54.

28. Ibid., 146.

29. Ibid., 104–14.

30. Ibid., 122.

31. Ibid., 140–48.

Woodward, on the other hand, articulates a specific approach to missional leadership, based on Ephesians 4:11, where Christ gives the church apostles, prophets, evangelists, pastors, and teachers to equip the rest of the church.[32] Often referred to as APEPT,[33] this fivefold leadership approach reacts against a professional, hierarchical clergy model, elevating the diverse gifts present throughout Christ's body.[34] Woodward indicates that the church needs "to shift from a hierarchical to a polycentric approach to leadership, where [leaders] live as cultural architects cultivating a fruitful missional ethos that fully activates the priesthood of all believers."[35]

Within this polycentric approach, the gathered community discerns and names the gifts present within the community. Woodward perceives leadership gifts this way:

- *Apostles*: create a holistic discipleship culture, focused on living into the missional nature of God's people, while also calling God's people to actively participate in the expansion of God's kingdom translocally.[36]
- *Prophets*: attend to God's heart, revealing God's social order and calling the people of God to adjust their own hearts so that they will stand with those who are oppressed.[37]
- *Evangelists*: tell God's story in a way that enables the people of God to proclaim the gospel and to participate as redemptive agents in the world, for the sake of the world.[38]

---

32. Woodward, *Creating a Missional Culture*, 58–59.

33. See Frost and Hirsch, *Shaping of Things to Come*, 165–81; and Hirsch, *Forgotten Ways*, 157–59, 169–72. Breen and Cockram take a different hermeneutical approach to Ephesians 4:7–16, focused on personal discipleship instead of church leadership. As such, they insist the Bible teaches "that each one of us has received a portion of grace in one of five roles" (*Building a Discipling Culture*, 136).

34. Woodward, *Creating a Missional Culture*, 113–14.

35. Ibid., 60.

36. Ibid., 123–30. APEPT is also at times referred to as APEST, where the S stands for *shepherd* instead of *pastor*. Also Hirsch, *Forgotten Ways*, 149–177, who depicts apostolic differently than Woodward, emphasizing that the apostolic is foundational to the other APEPT gifts and to the missional movement as a whole. Hirsch writes: "Quite frankly it is hard to conceive of metabolic, organic, missional movements existing let alone lasting, without apostolic influence in its varying forms. This is because apostolic ministry is entrusted with the mDNA [missional DNA] of Jesus' church" (177).

37. Woodward, *Creating a Missional Culture*, 131–40.

38. Ibid., 141–49.

- *Pastors*: heal souls, cultivating a spirituality that gives life to God's people and that leads to reconciliation, so that the congregation embodies God's love among each other.[39]
- *Teachers*: give light, empowering the congregation through immersion in scripture and by showing the congregation how to faithfully live within God's story.[40]

While not the first to express this fivefold ministry idea,[41] Woodward's *Creating a Missional Culture* thoroughly develops the concept,[42] maintaining an underlying premise that the five equippers empower the church to become more like Jesus Christ, "to be God's masterpiece, his living letter to the world, for the sake of the world."[43] For Woodward, then, adjusting the church's leadership approach creates a formative environment in which an evangelistic character can be cultivated.

Promoting Deliberate Discipleship

Other missional advocates turn toward discipleship in order to cultivate a missional character among God's people. Frequently anchored in an apprenticeship model, discipleship proponents promote common practices to form their missional identity in relationship with each other.[44] As Maddix and Ackerman summarize, "Missional discipleship represents the missionary nature of the triune God with the purpose of forming congregations to embody the gospel and to equip Christians to participate in the restorative

---

39. Ibid., 150–59. Hirsch has renamed *pastors* as *shepherds*. See http://theforgottenways.org/apest.

40. Woodward, *Creating a Missional Culture*, 160–67.

41. For a brief historical background on the fivefold ministry concept, see Frank Viola, "Rethinking the Five-Fold Ministry."

42. See Woodward's website, http://jrwoodward.net/equippers, where he provides an overview of the APEPT equippers model and links to one-page descriptions and video clips related to each.

43. Woodward, *Creating a Missional Culture*, 121.

44. Boren, *Missional Small Groups*, 63. Also, Hirsch's description of missional discipleship in a video clip from VERGE: "[missional discipleship] is not simply about Jesus in my heart kind of thing that we've got up to. That's included, but it's not just that. In my healing and your healing, my friends, in my redemption and your redemption is the redemption of the world. 'Cause God wants to use me and you and the churches we inhabit to channel his eternal purposes to redeem the world. That's missional discipleship" (Hirsch, "Missional Discipleship," http://vergenetwork.org/2013/08/12/what-is-missional-discipleship-alan-hirsch).

and redemptive mission of God in the world."[45] While the literature around missional discipleship is burgeoning, the basic contours of this approach are particularly evident in two sources: the Hirschs' *Untamed* and Mike Breen's *Building a Discipling Culture*.

Through their book *Untamed*, Alan and Debra Hirsch proceed with a core conviction "that everyone, young and old, male and female, spiritually mature and immature, rich and poor—everyone—gets to play a role in the unfolding drama of the church as Jesus designed it to be."[46] Admitting that this conviction has yet to be realized, they contend that Christian witness is challenged by the continuing impact of false ideas about God and a lack of experiencing God's love,[47] both of which they name as discipleship issues. They insist on attending to these challenges because "we are never going to be the movement Jesus wants unless we first get the issues of discipleship right."[48] From their perspective, recovering a "Shema Spirituality" (a deep, persistent engagement within Jesus' summary of the two greatest commandments, found in Mark 12:28–34) is the key to a renewed discipleship.[49]

As such, the Hirschs' vision of discipleship focuses on becoming aligned with the holiness of God through the work of the Holy Spirit. This discipleship approach shifts away from learning propositions about God toward an ongoing relationship with the Holy Spirit, who oversees "the change process by which we become holy." They insist that this holiness is "incredibly redemptive, highly missional," and not abstract.[50] Contending that the holiness they envision is rooted in Jesus Christ, they provocatively ask:

> What is it about the holiness of Jesus that caused 'sinners' to flock to him like a magnet and yet managed to seriously antagonize religious people? This question begs yet another, even more confronting question: Why does our more churchy form of holiness seem to get it the other way around—to comfort the religious and antagonize the sinners?[51]

Commenting further, they describe Jesus' holiness as "a redemptive, *missional*, world-embracing holiness that does not separate itself from the

---

45. Maddix and Akkerman, *Missional Discipleship*, 18.

46. Hirsch and Hirsch, *Untamed*, 136–37. This quote also reflects how immersion in the story of God's mission has permeated some of the other approaches.

47. Ibid., 55–81.

48. Ibid., 17.

49. Ibid. Much of the book explores impediments and potential means of freeing people to love God and their neighbors. See in particular: 27–28, 62–64, 188–90.

50. Ibid., 92.

51. Ibid., 45.

world, but rather liberates it."⁵² They assert that in Jesus Christ and through the Holy Spirit "God is extending his sanctity over ever-increasing portions of life until all is made holy. God is never a detached observer, but is deeply involved in the sanctification of the world. In fact he leads the charge!"⁵³ For Hirsch and Hirsch, then, the desired holiness of Jesus' disciples "is not gained by withdrawal from the world but by active, redemptive engagement in the world" with the Holy Spirit.⁵⁴

Breen takes a different approach to discipleship rooted in a conviction that "effective discipleship builds the church, not the other way around."⁵⁵ From Breen's perspective, this reversed approach exposes a problem wherein Western church leaders have been primarily "educated and trained to build, serve and lead the organization of the church. Most of us have actually never been trained to make disciples."⁵⁶ In this context, Breen contends that missional discipleship is absolutely essential: "We need to understand the church as the *effect* of discipleship and not the *cause*."⁵⁷ Carrying this assertion further, Breen adds: "If you know how to disciple people well, you will always get mission. Always."⁵⁸

Breen's remedy for this discipling deficiency has been to develop an apprenticeship model for discipleship. Senior pastors are coached to disciples others, who will disciple still others with the goal of creating a disciple-making culture within a congregation. Using "Huddles,"⁵⁹ the leader actively disciples Huddle members through a combination of organized group gatherings and informal interactions to model how disciples are to follow Jesus Christ. One of the primary tools in this method is the use of "life shapes"—simple drawings by which the Huddle learns a common language of discipleship.⁶⁰ Breen insists this approach is not another quick fix

52. Ibid., 46.
53. Ibid., 93.
54. Ibid., 93.
55. Breen and Cockram, *Building a Discipling Culture*, 12.
56. Ibid., 11. They assert even further that "[a]s we look around as Christendom is crumbling and the landscape of the church is forever changed, a stark revelation emerges: Most of us have been trained and educated for a world that no longer exists."
57. Ibid., 12.
58. Ibid., 13.
59. Ibid., 45. "A Huddle is the group of four to ten people you feel God has called you to specifically invest in, and you will meet with them regularly (at least every other week) to intentionally disciple them in a group setting. The best discipling relationships always have an intentional, 'organized' component to them, as well as a less formal, 'organic' component."
60. Breen identifies eight "life shapes"—images that help to explain different aspects of growing as a disciple—from desire to be a lifelong learner to prayer to personal

to discipleship "[b]ecause above all else, Huddles aren't a program; they are life-on-life discipleship. Transformation actually happens."[61]

While somewhat of a pragmatic model—how can one person disciple a whole congregation?—Breen's approach insists that only within a disciple-making culture will God's people develop an evangelistic character that is bent toward making new disciples. To this end, the desired discipleship growth is not larger Huddles, but that each Huddle member will start their own Huddle leading to a continual multiplication of Huddles through which more and more people become disciple-making disciples of Jesus Christ.[62]

The MCM's attention to Jesus' character reflected in the Hirschs' approach and the underlying praxis orientation present in both of these discipleship approaches will be expanded upon within chapter 5.

Attending to Spiritual Practices

More recently, MCM practitioners have pointed toward spiritual practices as the key to cultivating an evangelistic character among God's people. While closely aligned with discipleship approaches,[63] these contributors draw attention to the formative capacity of the spiritual practices themselves. Along these lines, Helland and Hjalmarson's *Missional Spirituality* along with Chester and Timmis's *Total Church* serve as primary examples. Contending that "missional spirituality is about enlarging the size of our hearts,"[64] Helland and Hjalmarson contend that "spiritual disciplines will *form* us, and doing the Father's work in community will *feed* us."[65] They contrast this approach with "temple spirituality," which they perceive to be dualistic, isolating God's people "from the nonreligious world outside." Instead, Helland

---

calling to mission engagement. See the brief depiction of each life shape in Breen and Cockram, *Building a Discipling Culture*, 60–61. Each life shape is then considered more fully in the eight chapters that follow, 63–197.

61. Ibid., 57.

62. Ibid., 204.

63. Maddix and Akkerman, *Missional Discipleship*, 21.

64. Helland and Hjalmarson, *Missional Spirituality*, 95. For a pointed critique of *Missional Spirituality*, see Hardy and Selvidge, "Review Essay," 109–21. Responding to the critique of temple spirituality, Hardy and Selvidge admonish: "The church, in its engagement with persons and communities whose spiritual lives are inexorably bound up with buildings, institutions, leaders, and rituals, needs to understand these as part of incarnational ministry, rather than as *ipso facto*, in opposition." Additionally, they provide other insightful critiques regarding Helland and Hjalmarson's failure to account for personality differences and for cultural location in proscribing practices associated with missional spirituality.

65. Helland and Hjalmarson, *Missional Spirituality*, 27. Emphasis original.

and Hjalmarson argue that God's people are called "to be at home with God (in spirituality) as they also serve his agenda in the world (in mission)."[66] Their approach is anchored in four theological foundations: the Trinity, the incarnation, the priesthood of all believers, and the Jesus Creed,[67] and developed through tangible inward and outward practices, so that God's people "are formed according to the culture of the Father's house."[68] These practices are highlighted through extended considerations of Jesus' two-pronged response to "what is the greatest commandment?" and carry a primary emphasis of preparing God's people for mission in the world.

For example, in considering how to love God with heart and soul, they encourage "a practice of *missio* reading and prayer," which is "a disciplined approach where the practice of *obedience* to Scripture is integrated with the practices of prayer, attentiveness to the Spirit, in the context of relationships, which will feed and facilitate mission located in the ordinary junctures of life."[69] They also emphasize a recovery of enchantment, whereby God's people learn to "view God's world as a sacramental place that reveals his tangible and yet hidden presence, his nearness and transcendence."[70] They conclude that the purpose of spirituality is to form the character of God's people in preparation for serving the world as Jesus's disciples:

> We must see our identity and function as disciples of Jesus who are missionaries in our communities and workplaces… This means that when we *gather* in worship services and small groups, our purpose is to worship God, connect with others, and be equipped in missional spirituality so that when we *scatter* we go as missionaries of Jesus.[71]

Chester and Timmis also reflect on the importance of spiritual disciplines for cultivating an evangelistic character among God's people. In a shorter section of *Total Church*, Chester and Timmis reframe spirituality around a threefold vision that merges reading God's word, prayer-filled response, and community engagement. They insist that "[b]iblical spirituality is not about contemplation; it is about reading and meditating on the word of God. It is not about detached silence; it is about passionate petition. It is

---

66. Ibid., 28.

67. Ibid., 53–74. Here they refer to Mark 12:28–34, openly borrowing Scot McKnight's language of *Jesus creed* from McKnight, *Jesus Creed*, and the language of *Shema spirituality* in Hirsch and Hirsch, *Untamed*.

68. Helland and Hjalmarson, *Missional Spirituality*, 92.

69. Ibid., 112. Emphasis original..

70. Ibid., 124.

71. Ibid., 197–198. Emphasis original..

not about solitude; it is about participation in community."[72] Challenging common notions of disciplines as means of achieving a mystical union with Christ, they argue that "[g]ospel spirituality is the exact opposite. Union with Christ is not the goal of spirituality, it is the foundation of spirituality. It is not attained through disciplines or stages; it is given through childlike faith."[73]

While not ignoring the need for personal prayer, Chester and Timmis emphasize accountability and reconciliation with others in relationship to God.[74] They hold a conviction that "[o]ur hearts are never far from sin, unbelief, hardening, and deception."[75] This viewpoint leads them to advocate for the communal nature of spiritual disciplines believing that "[t]he living, active word of God does its heart-softening work through gospel people reminding one another daily of gospel grace."[76] Spiritual practices, then, serve to form God's people for mission as God's people are embedded in a specific community of God's people. Thus, from their perspective, the gospel is experienced within the daily communal practice of spiritual disciplines. This idea of communal practices will inform part of the conversation about a praxis-oriented discipleship in chapter 5.

Engaging with Community

The final approach considered in this portion of the review focuses on engagement with community. This approach frequently attends to Jesus' incarnation because, as Fitch and Holsclaw remark, "It is the way God works to bring salvation, justice, and righteousness into the world."[77] Engaging within community serves to imitate Jesus' incarnation, and facilitates an ongoing encounter with God and neighbors, whereby an evangelistic character is cultivated among God's people. Huckins's *Thin Places* and *The New Parish* by Friesen, Soerens, and Sparks serve as examples of this emphasis on engagement with community.

Huckins offers *Thin Places* as a way of describing the missional postures shaping NieuCommunties in San Diego, California. They see themselves as "[a] community of apprentices" who are "a band of Jesus followers who seek to communally follow Jesus by living missionally every day."[78] The

---

72. Chester and Timmis, *Total Church*, 141.
73. Ibid., 143.
74. Ibid., 149–150.
75. Ibid., 150.
76. Ibid., 150.
77. Fitch and Holsclaw, *Prodigal Christianity*, 146.
78. Huckins, *Thin Places*, 138.

members covenant to grow together through a set of common practices, called postures.[79] In summarizing these postures, Huckins says the postures involve "becoming an alternative community within the neighborhood in such a way that neighbors participate in the rhythms of this new community.[80] In other words, practicing these postures forms the community of disciples while simultaneously creating a hospitable and invitational welcome for others in the broader neighborhood to become part of the community of disciples. In a way, then, there are always two communities in view for Huckins and NieuCommunities: the community of disciples and the community of neighborhood. This concept will inform the move from praxis-oriented discipleship to missional evangelism in chapter 6.

Within the community of disciples, each member has a coach, who asks "questions that lead to realizing what the Spirit is already putting on our hearts."[81] Through this form of embedded spiritual direction, community members embody a counternarrative to an "extractional" model of church. Huckins explains that model further:

> the traditional church is extractional in the sense that it extracts people from their local contexts to attend a church service and inadvertently teaches us that church is something we go to rather than who they are in the places they inhabit. Many of these people have been taught that attending a church service and serving in it is the central act of our Christian vocation."[82]

With this critique and the coaching model in mind, Huckins contends that the community's growth involves participation within the divine imagination, which frees God's people "to live into a new story that is marked by kingdom anticipation, advancement, and hope."[83] This new story is profoundly relational and reflects God's desire "to be in intimate relationship with humanity" in a way that embraces God's design for all of creation to function together "in a rhythm, of communal interdependence."[84] Huckins concludes that this relational, communal approach to being God's people seeks "to intentionally form others toward lives of Jesus apprenticeship

---

79. See Huckins, *Thin Places*, 28, for a brief description of the six postures: *listening, submerging, inviting, contending, imagining,* and *entrusting*. Huckins provides a more thorough exploration of each posture in the subsequent chapters.

80. Ibid., 6.

81. Ibid., 37. Huckins roots this practice within the Quaker tradition of clearness committees.

82. Ibid., 50.

83. Ibid., 115.

84. Ibid., 116.

with that expectation that they will be sent into something new."[85] Yet, rather than focusing on spiritual disciplines themselves, Huckins contends throughout that the act of being a community embedded within a specific, shared geographic neighborhood is the essential and transformative context for cultivating the community's evangelistic character.

The authors of *The New Parish* cover similar terrain while offering a slightly different angle into this conversation. Noting that "all of us are born dependent on others,"[86] they challenge the tendency to idolize an isolated individualism detached from location. Their proposed response to the cultural isolation is to practice being God's people *within* a specific geographic and relational neighborhood by collaborating *in* that place *with* the other people of that place.[87]

Sparks, Soerens, and Friesen argue that God's people are formed through rooted engagement within community, because "God is up to something in neighborhoods" and discovering what God is up to "could help the church learn to give itself away in love to the world around it.[88] The discovery process unfolds through a number of practices, including listening to how God's story, one's personal story, and the parish's story weave together.[89] Admitting that "most of your presence in the neighborhood is incredibly ordinary," they further contend "that doesn't mean it shouldn't be intentional."[90] As personal practices of engagement become consistent rhythms of being present within the parish, Sparks, Soerens, and Friesen encourage their readers to develop collaborative relationships with wider circles, including others in their congregation, other Christians and churches in the parish, people of other faith traditions, and even with created and built environments.[91]

Their goal is not to reject church as it has been, but to reintegrate the church's practice of being a community of God's people within its respective parish setting. Through engaging life in the parish, "each member of a local congregation" will learn to ask: "How can our participation in a particular gathering grow our capacity to be a living expression of the church together

---

85. Ibid., 138.

86. Sparks, Soerens, and Friesen, *New Parish*, 24.

87. Ibid., 35–48. The authors spend their second chapter reflecting on church history through a series of prepositions (*in, for, to, with*) that convey the church's relational posture toward the surrounding location. Their conclusion is that a combination of *with* and *in* is necessary for faithfully living as God's people today.

88. Ibid., 77.

89. Ibid., 119–127.

90. Ibid., 137.

91. Ibid., 138–48.

in everyday life?"⁹² As such, for *The New Parish* authors, the deliberate process of personal engagement within the church's geographic neighborhood, embraced throughout an entire congregation and across congregations, cultivates an evangelistic character among God's people in a particular here and now.

Perspectives on Worship

The second portion of this literature review attends to perspectives on worship. Two types of source material are considered here: those that offer passing remarks and those that provide extended engagements with worship as they articulate an overall vision for missional worship. The comments offering passing commentary are organized around two topics: the nature of missional worship, and missional implications of encountering God's presence in worship. For the extended engagements with worship, contributions by Webber, Schmit, and Frost will serve as primary examples.

Comments on Worship as a Way of Life

For the MCM, worship is seen as a way of life and not simply as a located event.⁹³ This vision tracks with *The New Parish* authors' cautionary critique that worship disconnected from lived practices leads to idolatry:

> for your church to invest its primary energies on worship events without a meaningful integration of mission, formation and community would be to move toward a form of idolatry. While your church would order its gathered life in the name of Christ who gave his life for others, you would not live into this mission yourselves. Church leadership would value attendance over communal life. And because liturgy was disconnected from life, the church would end up supporting cultural accommodation more than being formed as a tangible manifestation of an alternative story. This would be a grotesque distortion of the body of Christ with only the look of a worshipping community. If this were taken to an extreme, one would have to wonder what exactly was being worshiped.⁹⁴

---

92. Ibid., 84.
93. Chester and Timmis, *Total Church*, 18.
94. Sparks, Soerens, and Friesen, *New Parish*, 89–90.

Their pointed critique resonates with others in the MCM. For instance, the Hirschs assert that "[w]orship cannot, and must not, be limited to simply singing songs to God, although it should be included. Worship is nothing less than *offering our whole world back to God*."[95] Developing a similar theme, Hammond and Cronshaw contend that "God's call on our lives is more than attending a Sunday show and listening to someone chat. God's call is to serve God in the world. We need the gathering of church to empower us for that."[96]

These perspectives expose a rather pervasive indictment of Christendom worship practices that missional worship seeks to correct. Huckins rejects the "misguided" notion of inviting others to church so they can attend "a worship service on a Sunday morning or Wednesday night."[97] In similar fashion, Hammond and Cronshaw remark that "[a] shalom of spirituality discourages navel-gazing, private, individual spiritual practices limited to Sunday temple events. It does not extract people from their world, but encourages us to engage our 'worldly' responsibilities with attentiveness to God's purposes for the world."[98]

This attention to God's purposes prompts the Hirschs to contend that recovering a Shema spirituality will help Jesus' disciples to "rediscover the true nature of worship,"[99] wherein "worship is a matter of allegiance: whom or what shall deem worthy of glory, honor, and dominion? To whom shall we ascribe ultimate authority in our lives?"[100] This perspective resonates with Van Gelder as well, who contends that "intentionally living in a relational community in right relationship both with God and with another is equivalent to obeying the rigorous details of the Old Testament law. This spiritual worship characterizes all of life."[101] The NeiuCommunities covenant points to this life-encompassing view of worship when describing people as being "worshipers and lovers of God," implying that this identity involves, "cultivating an attitude of thankfulness, a lifestyle of prayer and worship, a deep and responsive engagement with Scripture, a reliance on the provision and guidance of the Holy Spirit, exploring and practicing a diversity of spiritual disciplines, discovering God's goodness and beauty in

---

95. Hirsch and Hirsch, *Untamed*, 76.
96. Hammond and Cronshaw, *Sentness*, 178.
97. Huckins, *Thin Places*, 71-72.
98. Hammond and Cronshaw, *Sentness*, 90.
99. Hirsch and Hirsch, *Untamed*, 28.
100. Ibid., 78.
101. Van Gelder, *Essence of the Church*, 151.

his created world, and the intentional participation in the gift of Sabbath."[102] Therefore, in opposition to worship that draws people out from the broader culture, these passing comments reveal a trend in MCM conversations to see worship as "world-engaging and transformative."[103]

The MCM, therefore, recognizes two aspects of worship, as Van Gelder explains:

> Specific worship takes place as the community gathers to praise God, give glory to God, and listen to God. Such worship serves as a centering function in the life of the church. The spiritual empowerment received in worship flows into other dimensions of ministry. In turn, the energy and fruit of the other ministry practices flow into the corporate worship. Congregations that cultivate the practice of joyful, devoted worship gain perspective and power for living all of life as worship.[104]

Such an external focus is not intended to be dismissive of worship gatherings. Rather, as Wright admonishes, "Those whose reason for existence on earth is to bring others to praise the living God . . . need to be doing so themselves or their whole mission is a hypocritical impossibility."[105] Huckins emphasizes further the desire to integrate specific and all-of-life worship.

> This is not to denigrate the importance of formal teaching times at church but rather to emphasize the need also to bring teaching out of the pulpit and embed it in life . . . The gospel word should be central to a formal meeting, but it also has to be the heart of all we do as the people of God and how we relate to the world.[106]

Taken together, these passing comments reveal a desire that local, particular worship gatherings would cultivate an environment within which God's people recognize that they are continually being sent as participants within God's world-engaging, transforming mission. Such worship gatherings are both invitational and anticipatory in practice. As Wright remarks,

> since glorifying God and enjoying him forever will be the joyful privilege of the redeemed humanity in the new creation for all eternity, to engage in such praise and prayer here and now is an act of anticipation, a signpost toward the future. And when we do it boldly and affirmatively, we invite others not only into the

---

102. Huckins, *Thin Places*, 154.
103. Ibid., 76.
104. Van Gelder, *Essence of the Church*, 151.
105. Wright, *Mission of God's People*, 247.
106. Chester and Timmis, *Total Church*, 117.

present experience of worship, but also into the future glory of a redeemed community.[107]

Comments on Worship as an Encounter with God's Presence

Other passing comments within MCM conversations focus more directly on the missional implications of encountering God's presence in worship. For instance, Bauckman asserts that because "God's presence is now among his people in the metaphorical Temple they themselves compose,"[108] so that the church engages God's mission as "the community that manifests God's presence in its midst by its life together and its relationship to others."[109] Likewise, the Hirschs remind their readers that "[i]f our encounter with God does not require something of us, we have to ask whether it really was God we encountered."[110] Similarly, Fitch and Holsclaw remark that the church needs to reclaim God's hospitality in the Table celebration "as an organizing tool for the kingdom in the neighborhood."[111] In agreement, Maddix succinctly states: "As Christians gather in worship around both the word and the table, God's healing mission begins,"[112] and then adds: "As the church encounters the renewing love of God in the communal worship of Scripture, prayers, offering, and the Eucharist, it is transformed to proclaim hope and forgiveness to be God's flesh and blood to the world."[113] For the MCM, the presence of God encountered in gathered worship leads God's people to live as an extension of God's presence in their relationships with each other and their neighbors outside of the worship gathering.

Sustained Reflections on Missional Worship

In addition to these passing comments, a few MCM contributors have offered more sustained perspectives on an overall vision for worship. While at times acknowledging the formative capacity of worship, these contributions are focused primarily on articulating a broad vision for missional worship. To highlight the diverse viewpoints being offered in this regard,

---

107. Wright, *Mission of God's People*, 247.
108. Bauckham, *Bible and Mission*, 76.
109. Ibid., 77.
110. Hirsch and Hirsch, *Untamed*, 77.
111. Fitch and Holsclaw, *Prodigal Christianity*, 112.
112. Maddix, "Missional Communities," 74.
113. Ibid., 75.

three contributions are considered here: Webber's *Ancient-Future Worship*, Schmit's *Sent and Gathered*, and Frost's "Exiles at the Altar," a chapter from his book *Exiles*.[114]

Webber's *Ancient-Future Worship* provides a wealth of insights about missional worship, particularly in framing how worship "remembers God's work in the past, anticipates God's rule over all creation, and actualizes both past and future in the present to transform persons, communities, and the world."[115] Writing to a broad audience of those engaged in worship planning, Webber's objective is to show "how worship does God's story" and how that story connects to the spirituality of the congregation.[116] While emphasizing an ongoing immersion within the whole biblical narrative, Webber contends "worship, which reveals Christ, forms" God's people according to the "pattern of living into the death and resurrection of Jesus."[117] Moreover, because God is the primary subject acting within worship, the participation of God's people "is not reduced to verbal response or to singing" but forms them by God's Spirit with Jesus "to die to sin and to live in the resurrection."[118]

Before explaining how this emphasis can unfold in worship, Webber observes how the historical development of worship lost sight of God's grand redemption of creation, exchanging it for more of an individualized salvation during the Reformation period.[119] With regret, Webber comments that "God's mighty deeds" have been further reduced in both traditional and contemporary songs to the point that "[t]here is very little awareness in evangelical music that God does more than save *me*."[120]

While acknowledging that the entire worship gathering has the capacity to form God's people through remembering and anticipating,[121] Webber gives particular attention to preaching and to celebrating the Eucharist. In preaching, God's story is remembered in the proclamation of Jesus Christ,

---

114. Webber, *Ancient-Future Worship*; Schmit, *Sent and Gathered*; Frost, "Exiles at the Altar."

115. Webber, *Ancient-Future Worship*, 43.

116. Ibid., 24.

117. Ibid., 93.

118. Ibid., 111.

119. Ibid., 77.

120. Ibid., 90. This remark by Webber may in fact say more about his preferences related to certain types of music. Though beyond the scope of this project, a field study comparing song content and styles of congregations with mission activities outside of worship would be helpful in shedding light on whether there is any basis to Webber's assertion here. I am indebted to David Reed for this insight.

121. Ibid., 110.

who is the central person "in the greatest drama of human history—*the drama of God who becomes one of us to rescue the world.*"[122] In the Lord's Supper, God's people see the full scope of God's story from creation through the new heavens and new earth[123] in such a way that they respond by manifesting "God's purposes for the world in the worship of our lips and lives."[124] For Webber, then, missional worship orients God's people through remembering and anticipating the movements of God's mission in Jesus Christ, leading to a way of life that makes the narrative of God's mission known.

Webber's work differs from this project in several ways. First, in reference to remembering and anticipating, Webber focuses specifically on preaching and the Lord's Supper, contributing only a few comments about the rest of the worship gathering.[125] By contrast, this project considers remembering and anticipating as rhythms present throughout the liturgy, and not primarily in association with preaching and the sacraments. Second, whereas Webber is concerned with recovering a narrative understanding of the liturgy, this project focuses on the liturgy's overall capacity to participate in cultivating an evangelistic character among God's people. Third, while Webber acknowledges that there are ethical implications for communal worship, he explains little about the relationship between worship, ethics, and evangelistic witness, choosing instead to focus on the experience of God's presence within the worship gathering.[126]

By contrast, Schmit portrays worship as an opportunity to reinforce the missional perspective that the church is sent. Applying MCM ecclesiology to worship, Schmit's *Sent and Gathered* considers how the sent identity of the church might impact the structure of worship. Addressing a broad, four-part *ordo* (sending, word, sacraments, gathering), Schmit presents a manual for missional churches that is accessible to worship planners across denominations and differing expressions of liturgical formalities. Working from Volf's contention that worship involves two rhythms of adoration and action,[127] Schmit develops his work on "an understanding that there is no such thing as an adjournment of worship. That which concludes the Sunday

122. Ibid., 121. Emphasis original.
123. Ibid., 141.
124. Ibid., 147.
125. Ibid., 177.
126. Webber remarks: "the truth of Christ remembered and envisioned in worship . . . forms me by the Spirit of God to live out the union I have with Jesus by calling me to die to sin and to live in the resurrection." However, Webber does not specify ways in which worship is "to live in the resurrection beyond the worship gathering" (*Ancient-Future Worship*, 111).
127. Volf, "Worship as Adoration and Action," 203–11.

service is not dismissal, but dispersal, in the sense of going forth, being driven or distributed: it is a sending."[128] In describing missional worship, he begins with a chapter on sending, based on the benediction, and then moves onto reflection on the word, the sacraments, and the gathering.

As beneficial as this approach may be for illuminating the theological conviction that the church is sent, his methodology, in contrast to this project's, fails to recognize the liturgy as a constitutive whole. Throughout the book, Schmit is primarily concerned with establishing the importance of what he sees as the four essential liturgical components: sent, word, sacraments, gathering. Reducing the order to these four components, however, detrimentally overlooks other elements of worship, such as confession, offerings, prayers, and passing the peace. In doing so, Schmit misses the opportunity for worship to tell the grand narrative of God's mission.[129] Moreover, and also in contrast to the thesis of this book, Schmit is not concerned with the formative capacity of the *ordo*, but only with insight as to how the content of the four movements can simultaneously communicate a call to adoration and a call to action.

Moving in a different direction from Webber and Schmit, Frost, in "Exiles at the Altar," contrasts Christendom notions of institutional worship with missional prioritizations for worship as a way of life.[130] Frost contends that questions about worship gatherings convey an underlying assumption that "we are primarily defined by a weekly meeting, and that if you attend that meeting, you can see all you need to see to get an understanding of our community."[131] While contending that a public worship service "is literally the tip of an iceberg—a very small, visible part of a much larger body," Frost invites his readers to consider church from a more dynamic, interactive perspective. "Why can't we think of churching together as a web of relationships? Why are we obsessed with the singular event rather than seeking the rhythm of a community churching together?"[132]

Briefly tracing a historical shift from missional engagement to liturgical rituals, Frost concludes that the church's emphasis on liturgical gatherings is unbiblical and culturally irrelevant. He remarks:

> Even today, in our thoroughly post-Christendom world, when the essential work of the church in providing religious, liturgical services has become irrelevant, Christians (including many

---

128. Schmit, *Sent and Gathered*, 43–50.
129. Ibid., 57–70.
130. Frost, *Exiles*.
131. Ibid., 275.
132. Ibid., 276.

exiles) can't separate the idea of Christianity from the weekly Mass or worship service. Even those who have ceased attending church services have great difficulty imagining what it means for a group of believers to church together without picturing a liturgical meeting of some kind.[133]

Quipping that "[a] day in the house of the Lord is great, but so is the thousand days outside,"[134] Frost argues that God's people glorify God (in creative alignment with the Westminster Confession) through lives marked by appreciation, adoration, affection, and subjection, not simply through corporate worship services shaped by those themes.[135] After he unpacks the nuances of how these themes shape the Christian life, Frost concludes: "My view is that worship services ought to be corporate expressions of the overflow of the regular life of a community that churches together at some level every day."[136] In such a light, Frost critiques contemporary worship, indicating that "[t]rue worship (as distinct from simply singing songs) emerges from the texture of a missioning community. The idea of worshipping with fellow believers and then bidding them farewell for the week in the parking lot—'See you next Sunday'—is the very antithesis of the experience of the earliest Christians."[137]

In the end, Frost briefly suggests seven aspects to consider in forming missional worship. These aspects include the communal nature of the church so as to involve all who have gathered, the aesthetic ambiance, attention to rituals and symbolic communication, as well as songs intimately connected to daily living in the community's particular context. Frost comments with a summarizing vision: "A few songs and a long sermon won't do it. A communal, ambient space, centered around a convivial meal table, reflecting local culture, using ancient and modern rituals, and infused with spiritual singing will be a wonderful expression of the overflow of lives lived daily to please our happy, joyful, all-powerful God."[138]

While he repeatedly affirms the validity of gathering for public worship, Frost appears primarily concerned with deconstructing what is wrong with current worship practices and how the misplaced emphasis on communal

133. Ibid., 277.
134. Ibid., 281.
135. Ibid., 279–80.
136. Ibid., 286.

137. Ibid., 288. In similar ways to Webber, Frost's assertion here regarding music likely speaks to his own preferences. Without corollary studies to support assertions like this one, MCM contributors run the risk of falsely identifying the source of the inadequacies they perceive in worship.

138. Ibid., 300.

worship gatherings has distorted what it means to be church and how we are to glorify God. Most of his comments about the nature of missional worship focus on the hospitable character, inclusionary experience, and contextual integration needed within a worship gathering. Yet Frost misses the opportunity to reflect on the capacity of a worship gathering to embody the biblical narrative, to form the character of those gathered, and to participate within God's ongoing mission of making all things new.

As these three contributions demonstrate, MCM participants are asking meaningful questions about the relationship between worship and missional identity. However, while offering their diverse responses, their perspectives also highlight the absence of a clear consensus about how worship engages with the *missio trinitatis* and the sent nature of the church. More importantly for the purposes of this project, these contributions reveal a tendency in the MCM to overlook the capacity of worship gatherings to form an evangelistic character among God's people.

Worship's Role in Forming an Evangelistic Character

With that critique in mind, the third portion of this review attends to the small subset of missional church resources that reflect directly on worship's role in forming an evangelistic character among God's people. Two books engage the broader subject material of worship forming an evangelistic character pursued through this thesis: Schattauer's *Inside Out* and Kreider and Kreider's *Worship and Mission after Christendom*.[139] Other authors engage this idea through short contributions. Tizon offers a chapter titled "Worship: The Beginning and End of Mission" in his book *Missional Preaching*, and Fitch reflects on "immersive worship" in the chapter "The Production of Experience" within his *The Great Giveaway*.[140] Alongside these chapters, five articles also offer contributions to this conversation: Dawn's articles "Reaching Out without Dumbing Down: A Theology of Worship for the Church in Postmodern Times" and "Worship to Form a Missional Community,"[141] Goheen's "Nourishing Our Missional Identity: Worship and

---

139. Schattauer, *Inside Out*; Kreider and Kreider, *Worship and Mission after Christendom*.

140. Tizon, *Missional Preaching*, 24–34; Fitch, "Production of Experience."

141. Dawn, "Reaching Out without Dumbing Down." Though providing an overview of her book *Reaching Out without Dumbing Down*, Dawn wrote this article with the MCM as her audience, instead of the broader audience of her book (Dawn, "Worship to Form a Missional Community"). Dawn is interesting in that she contributed to early discussions within the MCM but, to my knowledge, has not self-identified or continued direct engagement with MCM since the late 1990s.

the Mission of God's People," Chilcote's "The Integral Nature of Worship and Evangelism," and Guder's "Significance of the Lord's Day for the Formation of the Missional Church."[142] Each of these books, chapters, and articles are considered below.

Schattauer's Inside Out

Schattauer provides editorial leadership to one the earliest engagements in the MCM with regard to the formative capacity of worship and the evangelistic character of God's people. Including contributions from ten worship professors, *Inside Out* seeks to integrate missional ecclesiology emphases with the theology and practice of worship within the Evangelical Lutheran Church of America. Though the specific Lutheran location limits the accessibility of some contributions, *Inside Out* provides important framework components regarding the role of worship in forming an evangelistic character among God's people.

Schattauer's opening essay advocates for an "inside-out" approach to the relationship between worship and mission. The typical model within Christendom has been "inside and outside," wherein worship and mission are separate activities for separate audiences. Schattauer argues that this approach unnecessarily bifurcates the Christian life, disconnecting life in worship from life on mission. The more recent trend, evident within seeker-sensitive and social justice efforts, has been "outside in." He suggests that the priority of mission in this approach either reduces worship to an occasion for direct evangelism or treats worship as a utilitarian opportunity for mobilizing God's people to respond to urgent justice issues. Instead, Schattauer commends a missional approach to worship, "inside out," that understands the gathered worship of God's people as "an integral part of God's mission,"[143] while avoiding the false dichotomy and instrumentality of the other approaches. When engaged this way, the liturgical assembly serves as a centering space in which the church discovers and engages its missional identity in relationship to the world through its eucharistic, communal, prospective and symbolic characteristics, remarking that the liturgical gathering "always points to the eschatological reality beyond itself, to the purpose of God in Christ for the world and its peoples, for the whole created

---

142. Goheen, "Nourishing Our Missional Identity"; Chilcote, "Integral Nature of Worship and Evangelism"; Guder, "Theological Significance of the Lord's Day."

143. Schattauer, "Liturgical Assembly as Locus of Mission," 2–3, 13–14.

order."[144] As such, Schattauer concludes that "[t]he liturgy sung, spoken, *and lived* is liturgy for a church in mission."[145]

This inside-out perspective continues through a series of contributions reflecting on preaching and on the sacraments of baptism and Communion. Writing about the role of the word within worship, Fullenwieder contends that "being called into the word, the church is then called out to serve Christ in the neighbor, the stranger, and the one in need before us," with the result that "preaching Christ is preaching mission to the world that Christ redeemed."[146] Teig reinforces the perspective that "[b]aptism is about being the church, not simply voluntarily choosing to associate with a church."[147] Such a baptismal identity affirms and ordains all worshipers "to priesthood in the world." Teig then contends for a wide embrace of lay leadership within worship gatherings in order "to symbolize in worship their vocation in and for the world."[148] To these perspectives, Bangert adds his reflection on the Lord's Supper, portraying the meal as the place where "worshipers learn how to recognize the mysteries of Christ's presence among" poor and rich alike. He asserts that worship always demands a lived, evangelistic response that once embraced begins to draw God's people back toward gathered worship.[149] In the end, Bangert concludes: "The meal always serves as an epiphany of God's mission and thereby strengthens and enlightens the faithful."[150]

Additional chapters reflect on liturgical time, liturgical space, the role of music in communicating the inside-out approach, the potential for ritualization to participate in the formative process, and how occasional services can participate in the *missio trinitatis*. While providing insights, such as Oldenburg's remark that the liturgical year is scandalous because it reflects the incarnation—God's self-revelation within specific time and place[151]— most of what is offered diverges from the concerns being pursued in this project. However, Aune's cautionary note regarding the romanticizing of ritual is worth acknowledging. Aune's primary concern is the tendency to overemphasize the formative capacity of ritual as if ritual were an ancient

---

144. Ibid., 9–13.
145. Ibid., 19. Emphasis original.
146. Fullenwieder, "Proclamation," 27.
147. Teig, "Holy Baptism," 47.
148. Ibid., 54.
149. Bangert, "Holy Communion," 67–69.
150. Ibid., 82.
151. Oldenburg, "Liturgical Year," 105.

antidote for all human ills, transcending cultural and historical contexts.[152] Aune argues for a more modest understanding of ritual that communicates theological reality while not demanding an operational efficacy. Rather, rituals assist God's people in discovering what God is doing in the world in such a way that they are called through worship to actively pattern their lives according to God's reconciling love.[153] Aune's caution will be revisited in chapter 4 of this project.

Kreider and Kreider's Worship and Mission after Christendom

Whereas Schattauer et al. double-down on the place of institutional worship as locus and conduit of missional identity, Kreider and Kreider deconstruct Christendom worship practices, calling for an approach to worship conducive to the post-Christendom context. Emphasizing the narrative dimension of worship, they expose ways in which the liturgy invites God's people to participate in the *missio trinitatis*. Outlining their perspective on the historical trajectory of mission and worship in relationship to pre-Christendom, Christendom, and post-Christendom contexts, the Kreiders arrive at four principles: *mission is central to theology, shalom is central to mission, missio Dei integrates all areas of life*, and *discernment is necessary*.[154] Utilizing N. T. Wright's analogy of the five act play, they suggest that worship and mission mingle together as they engage past and future in the present[155] so as to encourage "hoping the past" and "remembering the future."[156] Their emphasis on attending to a "future horizon" is a working gloss on Yoder's call for "long-sighted" Christians, which they explain as enabling "Christians to keep the Bible's big anticipation in mind" so that God's people can "follow Jesus with courage and imagination" in present circumstances.[157]

Rooting their vision for missional worship in 1 Corinthians 11–14, they explicate the Corinthian eucharist celebration in light of the Greco-Roman practice of shared meals, in order to offer the early church as a model for integrating worship and mission in the present day.[158] Moreover, the Kreiders contend that in the early church "Christian apologists did not talk about their appealing worship services. Instead they claimed that the

---

152. Aune, "Ritual Practice," 155–59.
153. Ibid., 162–73.
154. Kreider and Kreider, *Worship and Mission*, 43–54.
155. Ibid., 62–65.
156. Ibid., 77–80.
157. Ibid., 89.
158. Ibid., 91–136.

Christians behaved differently from other people." In contrast to that time, they argue that today's Christians have lost the capacity to identify lives of compassion and imagination "as reasons why non-Christians should consider becoming believers."[159]

From this perspective, the Kreiders consider several "actions" of the liturgy[160] with the expressed assumption that God's people are transformed through them to "see signs of God at work in our neighborhoods and lives and world." They contend that by actively participating in worship the church becomes a "multivoiced *ekklesia*" that "functions as a political reality" able to influence "the cultures of work and extended families, of civic organizations and political debate" and "enables the voiceless—children, the disabled, and the inarticulate—to find their voice." Contending that such missional engagement is possible only through their encounter with God in communal worship, the Kreiders suggest that this approach extends worship into the space and times when the church is scattered, establishing an apologetic focused on lived witness rather than on rational argument.[161] Intended to evoke questions from neighbors and others about the hope that is within Christians,[162] this hopeful witness is transnational, fostering interdependence among congregations. To facilitate this lived witness, the Kreiders outline practical steps for encouraging relationships of reciprocity and mutual giftedness between Christians and congregations from different parts of the world.[163]

In their concluding chapters, the Kreiders specifically raise questions about how the community's ethos is communicated through worship. They give particular attention to what this ethos reveals about who God is, what God is doing, where God is present, and whether God makes a difference in the lives of those worshiping.[164] They close by emphasizing the essential nature of hospitality, particularly in relationship to the Lord's Supper, within a post-Christendom context.[165]

This project can be distinguished from the Kreiders's efforts in at least three ways.[166] First, the Kreiders orient their understanding of God's

---

159. Ibid., 138–40.

160. Ibid., 147. They specifically list "the offering, the sermon, the readings, the visual and dramatic arts, the benedictions, the prayers for healing" as worship actions that others will need to address.

161. Ibid., 175–81.

162. Ibid., 187–88.

163. Ibid., 190–218.

164. Ibid., 233–41.

165. Ibid., 244–55.

166. Other divergent points certainly exist between the Kreiders's work and this

mission in relationship to overcoming the consequences of the fall. This project considers such a view as shortchanging the biblical narrative, which begins with the revelation of God as creator (Genesis 1–2) and ends with a new heaven and new earth, marked by ongoing, abundant fruitfulness (Revelation 21–22). In between, God's redemptive pursuit of humanity and the reconciliation of all things in Jesus Christ are central to the story of God's mission, but they serve neither as the beginning nor the end of the *missio trinitatis*. God's mission began before the fall and will extend beyond the day in which the curses and consequences of the fall are completely overcome.[167]

Second, there is a different emphasis in considering worship. This project focuses on how worship contributes with a praxis-oriented discipleship in cultivating an evangelistic character among God's people. However, *Worship and Mission* overlooks the importance of discipleship and the ways that worship can be integrated with discipleship in this formative process.

Third, the Kreiders' contribution and this project prioritize different conversations. The Kreiders are concerned with demonstrating that missional worship recovers an integrated unity between worship and mission that was lost during Christendom. In order to achieve this objective, the Kreiders provide an overview of historical developments in worship and mission from the early church into the recent past. While this effort is admirable and worthy of further consideration, such a historical undertaking pursues a different objective and audience than those associated with this project. As such, the methodology pursued here is not concerned with how missional worship relates to historical trajectories but with identifying how worship is presently understood within the MCM.

---

book, including their rootedness within the Anabaptist tradition and this project's roots within the Reformed context. Connected to these roots, other disagreements could also be considered, such as whether the goal of God's mission is best summarized as "reconciling peace" or to what extent God's people are called to be engaged in the transformation of systems and structures as an expression of God's mission. But these points of divergence are not essential to the conversation at hand.

167. As with n. 41, see my article "Confessions of a Former Skeptic," in which I argue that the fall distorted but did not remove humanity's participation in God's mission. Humanity is sent before the fall to participate with God in cultivating life throughout creation. While not addressed in that article or this project, God's redemptive work in Jesus Christ reconciles us with God, restoring our capacity to participate fully in God's mission. The Spirit provides a glimpse of the full realization of that mission (Revelation 21–22) with the kings of the earth bringing their treasures into the new Jerusalem and the leaves of the tree of life healing the nations.

Tizon's "Worship: The Beginning and End of Mission"

Tizon's contribution to this topic comes through a brief chapter in *Missional Preaching*. Tizon relies on the missionary nature of God, scripture, and the church in shaping his perspective on preaching. He asks: "if [preachers] decide to look through missional lenses when we read, study, and interpret the Scriptures . . . how would it inform or change our preaching?"[168] In this context, he affirms the *missio trinitatis* as the basis for the missional identity of the church and for the assertion that God's mission is for the whole church—all of God's people—and not just ordained clergy or professional missionaries.[169]

Tizon's third chapter, "Worship: The Beginning and End of Mission," identifies the purpose and shape of missional worship. Describing worship without mission as "nauseating" and mission detached from worship as leaving him "unfulfilled," Tizon contends for the "absolutely integral relationship between loving God (worship) and loving neighbor (mission)."[170] Relying on the unity of these two commands, he contends for an interdependence of worship and mission, wherein worship serves both as the cause and goal of mission. Tizon remarks: "To be clear: Worship inspires, motivates, and empowers mission. The church's love for God propels it outward to demonstrate love for neighbor."[171] He then turns to Revelation 7:9–12 and 19:1–8, insisting that mission engaged leads back to worship:

> The worship scenes in these two passages imply the sacrificial activities of God's people toward racial reconciliation, social justice, and evangelization, each of which plays a role in determining the ultimate worship-to-be at the end of time—a redeemed, multicultural people praising the God who has eradicated the evils of injustice, oppression, falsehood, greed, and immorality.[172]

With this perspective on worship and mission as a foundation, Tizon notes that a missional approach to liturgy calls "all churches to practice worship's oneness with God's mission. The experience of corporate worship should, in its totality, not only give glory to God; it should also clarify the *missio trinitatis* and our participation in it, even as the redeemed themselves

---

168. Tizon, *Missional Preaching*, xxiii.
169. Ibid., 8–10.
170. Ibid., 25.
171. Ibid., 27.
172. Ibid., 28.

are transformed by the worship experience."[173] In this context, each aspect of the gathering works "together to glorify God and to better understand God's purposes in and for the world." When so embedded, missional preaching takes on a formative capacity that calls God's people into a more robust discipleship:

> We preach to cultivate a church of missional worshipers and worshiping missionaries, people who understand that their experience of worship directly affects their practice of the faith in the world, and vice versa. We preach to build a church that understands that the work of compassion, justice, reconciliation, and evangelization requires a power that is derived only from a life connected to the living God.[174]

Though not as convinced of the causal relationship of worship to mission, the direction of this thesis still resonates with Tizon's assertion that worship and mission are integral to each other. Furthermore, Tizon provides a beneficial counterpoint to Schmit's approach to missional worship by insisting on the cohesiveness and interconnectedness of the entire worship gathering, rather than only a few key parts. Tizon's emphasis on the formative capacity of the whole worship gathering resonates with ideas this project will advance in chapter 4.

Fitch's "The Production of Experience"

Also reflecting on the formative capacity of missional worship, Fitch contends that the potency of missional worship is experienced through "immersive worship," which is marked by a recovery of rituals. Acknowledging a gut-level impression that "there was little correlation between what constitutes a good worshipper and the consistent living of the Christian life,"[175] Fitch argues that missional worship engages the imagination in reorienting a person's understanding of themselves, God, and the world "through the reading of Scripture, liturgy, singing praises, preaching, and partaking of the Lord's Table."[176]

Lamenting that this formation is too often overlooked by rational approaches to worship, Fitch argues that "worship must become a culture capable of forming our worshipers' imaginations faithfully toward the

---

173. Ibid., 30.
174. Ibid., 32.
175. Fitch, *Great Giveaway*, 95–96.
176. Ibid., 96.

lordship of Jesus Christ."¹⁷⁷ The necessity for such an imagination-engaging approach to worship lies in the effectiveness with which the postmodern culture shapes imaginations. Fitch writes:

> by the time a person makes it to the pew, a post-Christian culture already forms him or her six days a week, and so the person has already been formed to hear what he or she will hear. There can be no confrontation, because in a post-Christian culture, the words the preacher says will simply have no credibility without the context of life and symbol by which people can make sense of them.¹⁷⁸

Noting that worship-induced emotional highs can allow people to continue in their sins, Fitch suggests that a missional approach to worship needs to form people into a new way of living. "Christians require character shaped by communities of faith and habits of truth in order to experience truth."¹⁷⁹ He then argues that the communal worship of God's people "orders our desires, orients our vision, and livens our words through art, symbol, prayers, mutual exchanges, participatory rituals, readings of the Word, and Eucharist every Sunday morning." These practices allow God's people to "experience God as he is and live the Christian life in the world."¹⁸⁰

As such, Fitch urges evangelicals to move their proclamation beyond words: "We cannot simply say 'Jesus is Lord.' We must embody the truth and reality that 'Jesus is Lord' . . . through art, rituals, and symbols that submerge the worshiper's mind, body, and soul into the world that is Scripture."¹⁸¹ Fitch concludes that this immersive approach to worship is not about new techniques or an altered order of worship.¹⁸² Rather, the context and content of worship needs to facilitate an encounter with God that reorients the imagination of worshipers so that they live differently in the world.

Fitch's recognition that worship reimagines the world resonates with this project, though it is largely absent from the rest of the missional conversation. Only a few others within the MCM have argued for a recovery of ritual as a means for transforming the imagination of God's people.¹⁸³ While

---

177. Ibid., 97.
178. Ibid., 101.
179. Ibid., 104.
180. Ibid., 105.
181. Ibid., 110.
182. Ibid., 124.
183. This project will address this idea of formation in chapter 4 when considering how James K. A. Smith's cultural liturgy project can contribute to a missional approach to worship.

pointing to this important dimension, Fitch overlooks how the various elements of the *ordo* can participate in this transformation, instead pointing to aesthetics as a means of creating an environment conducive to this imaginative process.

Dawn's "Reaching Out without Dumbing Down" and "Worship to Form a Missional Community"

Dawn's articles are the earliest on worship within the MCM. Writing in the context of church growth movements and seeker-sensitive church efforts, Dawn challenges the ways in which churches were blurring the lines between worship and evangelism. While confronting the failure of the church to equip all of its members to live as evangelists, Dawn exclaims: "*worship is not the point of entry. You are!*"[184] With this emphasis, Dawn insists that the character of the worship content shape the formation of character among God's people. For example, she remarks: "If we continually sing self-centered songs, we become self-centered persons."[185]

As she sketches initial outlines for missional worship, Dawn comments that the church lives as a parallel culture that is formed through "biblical narratives that tell a different story from that of the world around us."[186] Dawn insists further that "[o]ur worship practices must form us to be hospitable, to welcome strangers, to provide a public space, to invite newcomers, to tell others about our faith, to care for members of the community who are missing from corporate gatherings, to value each other in the great mix of ages, social classes, races, and gifts among God's people."[187]

At the end of her article, Dawn briefly outlines three criteria for missional worship:

- that worship focuses on the biblical God as both subject and object of worship;
- that worship forms believers to be Jesus' disciples, committed to God's mission, which she defines in terms of "peace, justice, and salvation in the world";

---

184. Dawn, "Reaching Out without Dumbing Down," 271. Emphasis original.
185. Ibid., 278.
186. Ibid., 279.
187. Ibid., 279–80.

- that worship form congregations to be an inclusive Christian community rooted in the community of God's people through time and space.[188]

Adapting her second article from *A Royal Waste of Time*, Dawn writes with a pointed focus on the necessity for worship to form the identity of God's people as an "altarnative" people among the current cultural context—that is, their identity is to be shaped by their worship. This missional identity forms in conformity with God's image and in contrast to the idolatry present around God's people. Throughout, Dawn insists that "corporate" worship not only reflects the missional identity of God's people, but also cultivates an evangelistic character among them. Dawn writes:

> The word *church* does not mean a place one "goes to"; instead, it signifies what God's people *are*. We are called away from the idolatries of the world to gather with our fellow believers in worship and fellowship and education, and then we are called out from that gathering, having been equipped and empowered by it, to go back into the world to serve it. When we participate in corporate services, we *worship God*, because God is infinitely worthy of our praise—so the focus is not on "attracting" anybody. In the corporate encounter with God that the worship service provides, those participating are formed more thoroughly to *be like God* and formed more genuinely to *be a community*. The result will be that all of us reach out to our neighbors in loving care and service and witness (evangelism), with the result that they might perhaps want to come with us to worship the God to whom we have introduced them.[189]

This extended quote reveals Dawn's conviction that the church's responsibility is to be a faithful witness through "loving care and service and witness" to their neighbors. Offering some initial reflections on Lindbeck and a postliberal emphasis on linguistic constructs, Dawn concludes that the goal of missional worship is "to practice the language of faith" through scripture, song, and prayer "until we know the truth so well that we can go out to the world around us and invite it to participate with us in the reign of God."[190] Thus, for Dawn, "We must understand that the work of the Church is to teach people the language, the habits, the practices of Christianity, so that people are both formed by the canonical texts of Scripture at the heart

188. Ibid., 281.
189. Dawn, "Worship to Form a Missional Community," 140.
190. Ibid., 149.

of the language of faith and then also sent out to bear the fruit of the discipleship thus nurtured."[191]

Dawn expresses the relationship between missional identity and worship as well as anyone in the MCM, while insisting that God is the primary actor in the church's communal worship. Yet Dawn's insistence on the formative nature of worship can lead to an impression that communal worship will automatically result in an evangelistic character among God's people. Discipleship beyond the worship gathering is not mentioned. Despite this oversight, Dawn's three points (God as subject and object of worship, worship forming believers as Jesus' disciples for mission, and worship forming congregations as inclusive communities) provided initial paths for exploring a missional approach to worship.

Goheen's "Nourishing Our Missional Identity"

Reflecting on how the Psalms nourished Israel's missional identity, Goheen seeks to identify priorities for the role of worship in the missional church. Goheen frames his article within Schattauer's language of an "inside-out" relationship of worship and mission, asserting that "[t]he church's worship is directed outward toward the world, not by transforming worship into evangelism or social action, but by celebrating the mighty deeds of God especially as revealed in Jesus Christ in the midst of the world as a witness to what God has done and is doing for the sake of the creation."[192]

Turning his attention toward the Old Testament, Goheen suggests that Israel was supposed to be a light as an alternative community among the idolatrous nations around them, but too frequently became "part of the problem."[193] He roots Israel's problem in assumptions they made about their identity as God's people—that their election and covenant justified "an insular and introverted sense of privilege that is forgetful of missional responsibility." Countering these assumptions, Goheen argues that the Psalms functioned as an antidote to "contend against such exclusivity,"[194] primarily through their declaration that God is "the one true God who is creator and lord of all nations," which reoriented "Israel's attention to the nations as the ultimate horizon of their existence."[195] From this analysis, Goheen insists that missional worship today "must witness to the real world, the true

191. Ibid., 147.
192. Goheen, "Nourishing Our Missional Identity," 34.
193. Ibid., 41.
194. Ibid., 44–45.
195. Ibid., 42.

story, the living God as revealed in Jesus Christ, and thereby form a people ready for a missionary encounter in their various callings."[196] Briefly sketching how this formative story-telling emphasis impacts the sacraments, preaching, and other elements of a worship gathering, including singing, Goheen concludes: "our worship will nourish us to be a certain kind of people—of that we can be sure! May it be a people whose lives are given for the sake of the world."[197]

Goheen's emphasis on worship narrating the biblical story as the true story of the world aligns with the trajectory of this project. In this light, missional worship is shaped by recognizing that the sovereignty of God extends over all creation and that God continues to gather a people as witnesses of God's great deeds throughout creation. However, Goheen does not address the complex relationship God's people have with their contexts. A brief acknowledgement that lament can serve as a fitting response to the sin and brokenness that God's people experience in their own lives and in their surrounding cultures would have strengthened his argument for missional worship. The absence of lament in his description of missional worship is surprising given that Goheen anchored his argument in the Psalms.

Chilcote's "The Integral Nature of Worship and Evangelism"

Engaging the conversation through a brief reflection on the Wesleyan roots for integrating worship and evangelism, Chilcote contends that worship "is a grateful surrender of all we are and all we have."[198] Through this lens, Chilcote contends that "[i]t is not too much to say that the evangelistic ministry of the community of faith and the worship of the assembly—and specifically the liturgy—shape us in such a way that we believe in God (faith), desire nothing but God (love), and glorify God by offering our lives fully to Christ (holiness)."[199] As he considered various Wesleyan hymns, Chilcote further suggested that the Wesleys "viewed the liturgy of the church—doxological evangelism, if you will—as the primary matrix in which this nurture raised and restored the children of God, both those inside, and potentially those outside the household of faith."[200]

This "doxological evangelism" consists of five elements: adoration, confession, forgiveness, proclamation, and dedication. Through further

196. Ibid., 47–49.
197. Ibid., 50–53.
198. Chilcote, "Integral Nature of Worship and Evangelism," 249.
199. Ibid., 250.
200. Ibid., 251.

consideration of each of these elements, Chilcote argues for at least five aspects of missional worship. First, both true worship and faithful evangelism begin in wonder and praise for who God is. Second, healing comes through acknowledging and confessing sins such that "[f]orgiveness liberates people from enslavement to sin through the power of God's love in Jesus Christ."[201] Third, evangelism and worship are essential for all of God's people, not just a select few. Fourth, as God's people imitate Christ in response to God's living word, "we learn to woo others into the loving embrace of God," and in doing so "help them to see that their mission in life, in partnership with Christ, is to be the signposts of God's reign in this world."[202] Fifth, in worship God's people "repeatedly participate in the Eucharistic actions of offering, and thanking, and breaking, and giving" so that, being conformed into the image of Christ, they "become truly eucharistic" and images of Christ in the world.[203]

In his argument, Chilcote consistently speaks of God's people being "conformed" to the image of Christ through worship so that they become evangelistic in their engagement with others. The emphases on confession and forgiveness, on evangelism being for all of God's people, and on God's people being shaped by Christ's character encountered in worship are all concepts that merge with emphases in this project. However, Chilcote's analysis is also limited in terms of this conversation on account of its particular focus on how Wesleyan hymns integrate evangelism and mission. As is the case with several other MCM authors, Chilcote presents this approach to worship with almost a deterministic implication, as if God's people will automatically become evangelistic if they adhere to this approach. References to the relationship between worship and discipleship are also noticeably absent.

Guder's "Theological Significance of the Lord's Day for the Missional Church"

Finally, Guder, after rehearsing a missional understanding of the church, proposes an understanding of the Lord's Day as "God's gift for our formation" through which the church is sent "to practice the life of witness and return to our gathering for ongoing formation for our sending."[204] High-

---

201. Ibid., 257.
202. Ibid., 260.
203. Ibid., 262.
204. Guder, "Theological Significance of the Lord's Day for the Missional Church," 117.

lighting what he sees as the development of a distorted ecclesiology during Christendom, Guder describes how "[e]veryone born within hearing range of church bells was, by virtue of birth and upbringing, Christian" and the need for mission disappeared from practice and theology.[205] Instead, he suggests that, understood through a missional lens, the Lord's Day is "a form of public witness" that carries an "evangelistic impact." Moreover, indicating that the Lord's Day forms God's people for their missional vocation, Guder asserts: "We cannot be about our mission if we are not in a process of discipline and formation."[206]

In this way, Guder treats worship as an occasion of discipleship, writing that "[d]iscipleship is a biblical way of talking about the gathering of the church" and that "[d]iscipleship was not an end in itself; the disciples were not drawn to Jesus in order to meet their own religious needs. Their formation was for their mission: they were discipled in order to be sent out." As such, Guder sees worship as a time of discipleship where Jesus' followers practice "being with Jesus so we can be sent by him."[207] In this gathering, disciples celebrate baptism as an act of "God's faithfulness in building his community to continue its witness, one by one." In Communion, "the Risen Lord at his table continually implements that calling through the giving of himself, the equipping power of his word proclaimed, and the hearing and responding of the community to his apostolic charge." This discipling vision of the formative capacity of worship leads Guder to lament clergy/laity divisions and call for the whole community of God's people to take up the missional vocation.[208]

Similar to the instrumentality of an "outside-in" approach to worship and mission against which Schattauer cautioned, Guder subsumes the purpose of worship within the priority of discipling God's people for mission. Without providing more details regarding what Guder means by "being with Jesus so we can be sent by him," Guder's approach is in danger of conscripting worship as merely a discipling event. The integrity of a worship gathering that leads into a praxis-oriented discipleship is almost entirely absent. In a parallel way, one could also conclude that Guder has limited discipleship to the occasion of the worship gathering, prompting the question: How are worship and discipleship different from each other within a missional context?

---

205. Ibid., 109.
206. Ibid., 114–15.
207. Ibid., 115.
208. Ibid., 116.

Identifying Gaps in the Conversation

In considering resources related to this thesis, this review reveals the presence of two worship related lacuna within MCM conversations. The first gap, pertaining to the role of worship in forming an evangelistic character among God's people, is evident both in the comparative scarcity of relevant resources and in the expressed recognition of the gap from several missional leaders. Multiple sources considered above reflect extensively on the formation of a missional identity among God's people while including very little dialogue related to the role of worship. For example, Bartholomew and Goheen assert that "worship of God is what Israel is all about" and that Israel "has been given an ethical shape and a liturgical shape" through the Exodus story.[209] Yet, they do not reflect on the nature of that worship or how worship participates in forming God's people. If worship is central to their identity, why not include worship as a central theme in the unfolding story of the biblical drama? When reflecting on how the church today continues the mission of Israel, they do not mention worship at all.[210] Van Gelder also appears to avoid considering worship. His description of a Spirit-led, missional congregation does not include worship.[211] Though he refers to worship in listing core missional practices, he does little to explicate the practice and appears to overlook the place of worship and prayer in the early church.[212] In another place, Van Gelder seems to sideline worship even while declaring its centrality: "While preaching needs to be central to worship, and while worship needs to be central to local church life, the Bible calls the church to engage in other important functions as well, such as fellowshipping, discipling, serving, and witnessing."[213] This posture begs the question: If worship is central, then why not show how it is central to the MCM?

As noted in the first chapter, Guder, among others, has urged the MCM "to explore how our gathering for worship, for sacramental celebration, for mutual encouragement and edification, can serve to equip us for our 'sent-outness,' for our apostolate as the church dispersed."[214] Yet Guder's own attempt at entering this conversation devoted only one third of the article to worship, in comparison to the other two thirds focusing on rehears-

209. Bartholomew and Goheen, *Drama of Scripture*, 71.
210. Ibid., 198.
211. Van Gelder, *Ministry of the Missional Church*, 63–67.
212. Ibid., 147–57.
213. Van Gelder, *Essence of the Church*, 57.
214. Guder, "Worthy Living," 424–32.

ing the development of a missional ecclesiology. It is as if many within the MCM conversation are uncertain with how to consider the role of worship in forming God's people for mission.

The second lacuna involves the absence of an articulated approach to missional worship. One could argue that there are multiple viewpoints within the MCM related to worship. Some, like Schattauer and Fitch, clearly advocate for communal worship gatherings that draw from, deepen, and enhance the institutional, corporate worship services developed throughout the past millennia of Christianity. Others, such as Frost, remain highly skeptical of institutional worship practices and structures due to a perceived disconnect between Christendom worship and the church's participation in the *missio trinitatis*. What these examples show is not merely two disparate approaches, but an underlying lack of clarity as to how communal worship gatherings are impacted by the emergence of a cohesive missional theology and ecclesiology.

Some MCM participants do raise helpful questions about a missional approach to worship in response to Christendom practices of worship. For example: What role ought clergy to play in missional worship? As Hammond and Cronshaw comment, "Part of the obstacle to standing in the gap for the mission of the whole people of God is that the way we imagine church, with clergy employed for ministry, causes us to rely too much on hired holy people."[215] The question could then be asked: Should the missional church pursue a model that embraces a laity-led approach, emphasizing the APEPT leadership gifts, or an even broader diversity of gifts instead of trained clergy? Van Gelder seems to suggest so when declaring that "[n]o one gift has the primary privilege of presenting God's truth" and remarking that "[t]he Spirit uses a variety of speaking gifts for this purpose: prophecy, teaching, exhorting, knowledge, wisdom, and pastor-teacher" so that "our understanding of the Word is enhanced" through them.[216] However, the intended audiences for Webber's and Schmit's contributions would imply that they see a place for clergy leadership within missional worship. The MCM does not have clear agreement on the role of clergy within a missional approach to worship.

Beyond differentiating itself from Christendom worship practices, other questions remain: What are the priorities of missional worship? Are there common themes present in a missional approach to worship? What role does the Holy Spirit play in forming God's people through worship? And how does a missional approach to worship relate to discipleship in

---

215. Hammond and Cronshaw, *Sentness*, 170.
216. Van Gelder, *Essence of the Church*, 145–46.

cultivating an evangelistic character among God's people? Questions like these could lead to developing a missional approach to worship on its own merits instead of as a reaction to the perceived distortions of worship practices within Christendom.

The existence of these gaps seems quite remarkable given the decidedly liturgical language in Newbigin's description of a community that serves as the hermeneutic of the gospel. The center of that quote reads:

> This community has at its heart the remembering and rehearsing of his words and deeds, and the sacraments given by him through which it is enabled both to engraft new members into its life and to renew this life again and again through sharing in his risen life through body broken and the lifeblood poured out. It exists in him and for him. He is the center of its life. Its character is given to it, when it is true to its nature, not by the characters of its members but by his character.[217]

What is evident here, but almost entirely overlooked in missional conversations so far, is that Newbigin's vision for a missional community is rooted in that community's engagement with Jesus' words and deeds and with the sacraments. In this sacrament-accompanied "remembering and rehearsing" the community has the capacity "to engraft new members" and be renewed "again and again." Formed in this way, the church "exists in him and for him," taking on Jesus' character as its own. Yet, somehow the MCM has largely missed the worship practices at the heart of a community that are capable of being "the hermeneutic of the gospel." As Newbigin's quote points out, being formed in and marked by Jesus' character is intimately related to the worship practices of the missional community.

An appropriate question to ask in light of these gaps is: How did these gaps form?[218] Two reactions against Christendom church practices likely have contributed to the formation of these gaps. One reaction, clearly present in MCM conversations, has been against the Christendom loss of a missional purpose for the church. In *A Light to the Nations*, Goheen locates the ongoing amnesia regarding missional identity within the advent of the "more hospitable cultural context" afforded Christianity through Christendom. He surmises: "The problem was not simply that the church had moved from the margins to the center, or that it had become established, but rather

---

217. Newbigin, *Gospel in a Pluralist Society*, 227.

218. Asking *how* the gaps formed is intended to communicate a degree of humility about our capacity to determine historic causality regarding *why* these gaps formed. In this sense, the responses that follow are offered with acknowledgement regarding their speculative nature.

that the church often succumbed to the seductive temptations this new social location offered."[219] Extending his analysis toward the present day, Goheen calls the Western church to critically assess "the modern, secular worldview with its roots in the Enlightenment—and then to repent of its own complicity in this worldview and return to the biblical story that gives its true identity and role as God's people."[220] The underlying assumption in this ecclesiology was that all citizens are Christians and therefore mission is not necessary.[221] In response, many in MCM conversations have sought to draw attention toward mission with a pendulum-like swing away from communal worship.

Another reaction is against the lingering impact of required worship services in past centuries. The Kreiders, as one example, contend that the Christendom church required "a large corps of religious professionals" to fulfill its tasks. "The majority of Christians, on the other hand, were non-specialists" who were compelled both to attend the clergy-organized and -led worship services and "to pay for these services by means of the clerical tithe"—a tax, imposed and collected by the government, in order to pay for those services.[222] The vestiges of this approach still exist in the church today, as some with a consumerist mindset expect church leaders to provide them with services they paid for with their offerings. As such, the MCM places a significant emphasis on the involvement of the whole people of God. From a practical standpoint, however, many have struggled to imagine how everyone can actively participate in a communal worship gathering. It is much easier to conceive of everyone being a missionary in their own backyard throughout the week.

Additionally, another contributing factor has been the attention to other church practices. Considering the five emphases outlined in chapter 1, the distinctive priorities of the MCM do not align neatly with a communal worship gathering. This recognition is not to imply that there is no place for gathered worship within the MCM. Rather, the MCM's emphases do not prioritize worship gatherings as a defining characteristic.

One more potential contribution to the formation of these gaps emerges from a cultural pragmatism within postmodernism that asks: Does

---

219. Goheen, *Light to the Nations*, 10.

220. Ibid., 13.

221. Much could be said about the Eurocentric view of the world during most of Christendom, the conflation of Christian identity with government recognized citizenship, and the use of government authority to establish and enforce cultic practices. However, pursuing those concerns would require hosting different conversations than those being entertained within this project.

222. Kreider and Kreider, *Worship and Mission*, 39.

worship work? Rooted in the disillusionment with broad claims regarding the salvific qualities of human progress, this present pragmatic approach desires to see if worship can live up to its own claims. Given the relatively recent entanglements of Christianity with colonialism and the militaristic atrocities of reportedly "Christian nations," Christendom practices of church, particularly its emphasis on worship, have been intentionally sidelined with the insinuation that they simply have not produced a better society or better people.

Though worthy of further exploration beyond the scope of this project, these potential factors help clarify that the worship-related lacuna have much to do with how the MCM understands the nature of the church, particularly in relationship to Christendom emphases on the centrality of worship practices. To this end, the next chapter engages a missional ecclesiology in preparation for proposing a missional approach to worship.

3

Missional Ecclesiology

ANY APPROACH TO WORSHIP depends, at least in part, on what is understood about the nature of the church. Within the MCM, the relationship between worship and ecclesiology is accentuated not only because of the *missio trinitatis* but also because of the perception that Christendom placed an inordinate emphasis upon the weekly worship service.[1] As such, before proposing contours for missional worship, this project first endeavors to identify the general shape of a missional ecclesiology.

In pursuing this objective, this chapter highlights how missional ecclesiology has developed both in line with the *missio trinitatis* and in reaction against liturgical prioritizations of the church's identity during Christendom. Responding to both of these elements, the MCM has consistently emphasized the sent identity of God's people over against institutional marks of the church, particularly preaching of the word and administration of the sacraments. From this context, this chapter sets out to describe a missional understanding of the church as a people gathered in Jesus Christ in order to be sent with the Spirit, embodying Jesus' character together as participants in the still-unfolding story of God's mission, throughout every dimension and moment of life and in anticipation of God's coming kingdom.

The hope with briefly exploring this description is to provide an ecclesiological frame of reference for unfolding the proposed missional approach to worship that will follow in the next chapter. As such, this chapter is not concerned with defending or critiquing a missional ecclesiology, but with describing in fairly broad strokes some of the traits readily evident in a missional understanding of what makes the church *the church*. As will be seen

1. Helland and Hjalmarson, *Missional Spirituality*, 119–20.

through this exploration, the MCM clearly emphasizes what could be called the *character marks of the church* more than the liturgically-shaped *notae ecclesia* of preaching and the sacraments.

To explore the contours of this missional ecclesiology, this chapter proceeds in three sections. The first section identifies the historical persistence of the question "What makes the church *the church*?" and describes the MCM's core response to this question in light of the *missio trinitatis*. Following this consideration, the second section locates two liturgically shaped marks of the Christendom church (preaching of the word and administration of the sacraments) with respect to their presence in sixteenth- and seventeenth-century Reformation movements. This section also conveys concerns present in the MCM with regard to defining *church* according to these liturgically based marks. Finally, this chapter concludes by exploring a description of the church from a missional perspective, recognizing how Jesus' character embodied among God's people makes the church *the church*.

What Makes the Church the Church?

A Historically Persistent Question

In a generalized sense, the MCM describes vast expressions of similar initiatives that are grappling with the church's identity in response to the *missio trinitatis*. At the heart of this wrestling rests a conviction that missiology and ecclesiology are profoundly intertwined.[2] Goheen depicts this relationship in terms of God calling and forming "a community to embody his work of healing in the midst of human history," noting how they were "to be a people who could truly say, 'I hope some day you will join us,' in manifesting the knowledge of God, and the joy, righteousness, justice, and peace of this new world that would one day cover the earth."[3] More pointedly, Hirsch asserts: "ecclesiology is the most fluid of the doctrines. The church is a dynamic cultural expression of the people of God in any given place. Worship style, social dynamics, liturgical expressions must result from the process of contextualizing the gospel in any given culture. *Church must follow mission.*"[4] In this sense then, the MCM itself has formed as a response to the question "What makes the church *the church*?"[5]

---

2. Van Gelder, *Essence of the Church*, 24.
3. Goheen, *Light to the Nations*, 3.
4. Hirsch, *Forgotten Ways*, 143. Emphasis original.
5. I appreciate efforts by Roxburgh to redirect MCM conversations away from ecclesiocentric questions and toward practical engagement with neighbourhoods. See

This kind of question certainly is not unique to the MCM. The emergent church movement has pursued a similar question, leading Jones to explain just how difficult it has been to describe the emergent church in terms that others are likely to understand, as emergent proponents call for a radical reorientation of what it means to be church.[6] Likewise, the rise of both fundamentalism[7] and the social gospel movement[8] developed from a desire to be the church in ways that others in their time were not.[9] This tendency to react against the perceived shortcomings of other churches is also evident in the numerous splinter denominations that have formed within Protestantism over the past several centuries:[10] the seventeenth- and eighteenth-century Revivalist[11] and Puritan movements,[12] the sixteenth-century Reformers,[13] and the rise of monastic orders and counterreform efforts in the Roman Catholic Church.[14] From this perspective, even the ecumenical creeds, councils, and controversies of the early church can be

---

Roxburgh, "Practices of a Missional People," where he writes: "Newbigin's 'missional' trajectory has been misdirected in several ways. First, the language of *missional* has become almost completely identified with ecclesiology, illustrated by the fact that the word is practically always a modifier of church as in the phrase *missional church*. This was an unintentional but major turning from Newbigin's framing into a default ecclesiocentric pragmatism." In the context of this project, the necessity of Roxburgh's critique reinforces the reality that the MCM has formed around the ecclesial question of the church's identity.

6. Pagitt and Jones, *Emergent Manifesto of Hope*, 12–13.
7. Marsden, "Fundamentalism as an American Phenomenon," 215–32.
8. Bryant, "Optimistic Ecclesiology of Walter Rauschenbusch," 117–35.
9. One could also add William Booth and the Salvation Army.
10. One of the more pointed examples of this splintering is seen in my denomination (Christian Reformed Church in North America), which split from the Reformed Church of America in 1857, and then changed its name in 1861 to *Ware Hollandsche Gereformeerde Kerk*, or True Dutch Reformed Church, adding the adjective *true* to the name originally chosen in 1859. The overt implication of this name change was that other Dutch Reformed churches were not *true* churches. http://www.crcna.org/pages/memorable_events.cfm.
11. For example, the lesser-known Dutch revivalist movement. See Lieburg, "Interpreting the Dutch Great Awakening," 318–36.
12. Brachlow, "John Robinson and the Lure of Separatism," 288–301.
13. See Luther's *Schmalkald Articles*, written in 1537, as an example of the self-understanding among Reformers that their work was an effort to reform the church from its then contemporary abuses.
14. I have in mind here efforts such as the Cluny monastic reform, the development of the Franciscan order, and the Council of Trent. One could also consider Vatican II, with its emphasis on an accessible liturgy and gospel engagement within the context of a pluralistic world, and the various liberation movements emerging from the global south in the middle-late twentieth century as further examples.

seen as attempts to clarify and embody what it means for the church to be the church both in theological confession and in localized practice.

The Christian scriptures tell of similar struggles related to faithfully identifying the church that were already present among Jesus' earliest disciples. For example, Mark records the disciples' anxiety over a non-disciple casting out demons in Jesus' name (Mark 9:38–41). Despite objections from his disciples and others, Jesus demonstrated that the church would include children (Matthew 18:1–9), beggars (Mark 10:46–52), women (John 4), tax collectors (Luke 19:1–10), and foreigners (Matthew 15:21–28). James and other leaders in Jerusalem grappled with how closely non-Jewish Christians needed to adhere to signatory Jewish marks of the covenant, such as circumcision, in order to be included in the church (Acts 15:1–38). Paul confronted Peter's hypocrisy around table fellowship with Gentiles (Galatians 2:11–21) and rebuked the Corinthians for embracing immoral behavior that "not even the pagans tolerate" (1 Corinthians 5). Viewed through this panoramic historical lens, the question "What makes the church *the church*?" has persisted among God's people since the time of Christ.

In all of these examples, widespread dissatisfaction with the inherited religious structure and practices mingles with a propelling vision for what the church could yet be. These expressions convey a persistent desire for the church to more fully and more faithfully *be* the church in contrast to another expression of church that was perceived to be less then fully faithful. Taken in the best light, the ongoing search for renewal is a missional impulse to understand how God's people are to be God's people in their respective contexts. In summarizing his overview of various ecclesiologies, Van Gelder concludes: "To some extent, every historical ecclesiology has functioned as a missiological ecclesiology, even if it has not defined itself as such. There are not multiple missions of God. God is one. His mission in the world is one. The church's understanding of its existence in the world, therefore, regardless of its presence in different contexts, should reflect an understanding of the mission of the Triune God."[15] The reality implicitly communicated through the multiplicity of these movements is that those who follow Jesus Christ are continually discerning what it means for the church to faithfully be the church within the nuances of their respective contexts.[16] In this regard, the MCM is no different from these other historical antecedents.

---

15. Van Gelder, *Essence of the Church*, 37–38.
16. Van Gelder, *Ministry of the Missional Church*, 63–67.

Responding to the missio trinitatis

As the MCM began to take shape in the mid-1990s, GOCN facilitated a conference around the question: "How are we to live faithfully as the church offering confident witness in a changing world?"[17] This question in the context of early theological explorations of missional priorities sparked significant, and sometimes contentious, debate. Both proponents and opponents of missional theology understood that the proposed changes did not simply adjust the way the church took up the "task of missions." Rather, the missional proposal altered the church's understanding of its own identity.[18] As Van Gelder contends, "Mission is no longer understood primarily in functional terms as something the church does, as is the case for the corporate church. Rather it is understood in terms of something the church is, as something that is related to its nature."[19] Hirsch expressed this vision by declaring that "[t]he church's true and authentic organizing principle is mission. When the church is in mission, it is the true church."[20] Summarizing this new understanding within the MCM, Wright asserts: "it is not so much the case that God has a mission for his church in the world but that God has a church for his mission in the world. Mission was not made for the church; the church was made for mission—God's mission."[21]

This axiom signifies a fundamental reorientation of the relationship between ecclesiology and missiology, with the MCM advancing a theological argument for the primacy of missiology, upon which methodological approaches to church can be reconsidered.[22] Rather than the institutional church taking up the task of missions alongside other tasks—discipleship, pastoral care, worship, and evangelism—the MCM contends that God has a mission within which the church has been gathered and sent as participants in the continued unfolding of God's mission. This mission is expressed most fully in the sending of Jesus, who embodied God's redemptive

---

17. Van Gelder, *Confident Witness, Changing World*, xvii.

18. See, for example, within my own denomination, the exchange, played out in part in the *Calvin Theological Journal*, between Bolt ("Does the Church Today Need a New 'Mission Paradigm,'" 196–208) and Van Gelder ("Church Needs to Understand Its Missionary Nature," 504–19).

19. Van Gelder, "From Corporate Church to Missional Church," 425–50. Also, Marshall, "Missional Ecclesiology for the 21st Century," 5–21.

20. Hirsch, *Forgotten Ways*, 82.

21. Wright, *Mission of God*, 62. Initial expressions of this perspective predate the formal development of the MCM. See Moltmann, *Church in the Power of the Spirit*, 64. For a summary of the historical development of this perspective, including its theological roots in Karl Barth, see Bosch, *Transforming Mission*, 372–73.

22. Marshall, "Missional Ecclesiology for the 21st Century," 8.

presence through his incarnation, life, death, resurrection, ascension, and promised return. The church therefore is gathered in Jesus Christ and sent with the Spirit as participants within the Trinitarian mission embodied in Jesus Christ. God's embodied mission in Jesus Christ reveals God's mission, which leads to the formation of the church, which exists for the purposes of God's mission. The shorthand expression of this theological progression has been stated as: "Christology determines missiology, and missiology determines ecclesiology."[23]

Reaction against Christendom Ecclesiology

As much as missional ecclesiology developed in light of the *missio trinitatis*, missional ecclesiology has also formed as a reaction against Christendom ecclesiology. Frost summarizes this rather pervasive criticism of Christendom when he remarks: "The net effect over the entire Christendom epoch was that Christianity moved from being a dynamic, revolutionary, social, and spiritual movement to being a static religious institution with its attendant structures, priesthood, and sacraments."[24] The perceived shift moves from a dynamic early church expression toward "a static religious institution" accompanied by the development of structures, roles, and practices that came to define not only the activities of the church, but the very nature of the church. Of particular concern in this regard are marks of the church as expressed by Reformation-related movements in the sixteenth and seventeenth centuries. While many marks were suggested, the adopted marks focused Christendom's attention on the preaching of the word and the administration of sacraments—two liturgically based activities—as the defining characteristics of the church. This section first locates the *notae ecclesia* of preaching and the sacraments and then articulates four concerns that emerge in response to these marks.

---

23. Hirsch, *Forgotten Ways*, 143.

24. Frost, *Exiles*, 5. As will be recommended at the conclusion of this project, a significant opportunity for further research exists in response to MCM assessments of Christendom, like this one. Are these assessments merely caricatures of Christendom that serve to validate the cultural blind spots of the practitioners? Are there examples within Christendom that would lead to a more nuanced assessment of Christendom than the MCM typically advances?

Notae Ecclesia of Sixteenth-Century and Seventeenth-Century Reformation Movements

In the midst of significant ecclesiastical upheaval during the sixteenth and seventeenth centuries, the *notae ecclesia*, or marks of the church, served as a way of locating the church *in situ*. While the literature on the marks of the church over the past two centuries has focused mostly on the fourfold attributes expressed in the Nicene Creed,[25] the conversation about the church's *notae* is historically rooted in the Reformation,[26] starting with Luther and other sixteenth-century Reformers.[27]

While offering a range of potential *notae*,[28] the early Protestants arrived at wide agreement on two marks: preaching the word and administration of the sacraments.[29] For example, Luther contended: "Wherever, therefore, you hear or see this Word preached, believed, confessed, and acted upon, there do not doubt that there must be a true ecclesia sancta catholica, a Christian, holy people, even though it be small in numbers."[30] In reflecting on the Lord's Supper, Luther later added: "By means of this sacrament [the church] exercises itself in faith, and openly confesses that it is a Christian people, as it does also by means of the Word of God and baptism."[31] With a similar emphasis, Calvin summarized: "Wherever we see the Word of God purely preached and listened to, and the sacraments administered according to the institution of Christ, we must not doubt that there is a Church."[32]

As the Reformers attempted to systematize their faith, the two marks that consistently appeared in the confessions were the preaching of the word and the administration of the sacraments. Expressing doctrines of the Reformed movement in sixteenth-century Netherlands, the Belgic Confession asserts that the "true church" can be recognized by three marks, of which

---

25. Nicene Creed: "I believe in one, holy, catholic, and apostolic church."

26. Lathrop and Wengert, *Christian Assembly*, 17–18. Also, Grenz, "Ecclesiology," 261; and Van Dyk, "Church in Evangelical Theology and Practice," 130.

27. Wengert asserts that Luther was the first to use the term *notae ecclesia*; Lathrop and Wengert, *Christian Assembly*, 19.

28. For example, Klug reviews Luther's seven suggested marks, including the offering of prayers and the presence of persecution ("Luther's Understanding of 'Church,'" 27–38).

29. Discussion of the *notae ecclesia* is admittedly more nuanced than what will be addressed in this project. See Williamson, "Marks of the Church," 24–34.

30. Luther, "On the Councils and the Churches," 271. Luther identifies seven marks of the church in this treatise. Also, Braaten and Jensen, *Marks of the Body of Christ*, vii–xii.

31. Luther, "On the Councils and the Churches," 273.

32. Calvin, *Institutes of the Christian Religion*, 4.1.9.

the first two are "the pure preaching of the gospel," and that "it makes use of the pure administration of the sacraments as Christ instituted them."[33] The Augsburg Confession articulates the Lutheran declaration that "[t]he Church is the congregation of saints, in which the Gospel is rightly taught and the Sacraments are rightly administered."[34] Additionally, the Westminster Confession teaches that the visible church is evident where "the doctrine of the Gospel is taught and embraced, ordinances administered, and public worship performed more or less purely in them."[35]

In each of these cases, the Reformers emphasized these marks as a way of submitting the church to the word of God[36] and as a means of equipping the laity to recognize the church with regard to its tangible, local expressions.[37] As Grenz asserts, "The focus on word and sacrament led to a renewed emphasis on the local church. This, in turn, set the Reformers' ecclesiology apart from the medieval Roman Catholic emphasis on the clergy, which had effectively devalued the gathered fellowship."[38] The Reformation's attention to the marks of preaching the gospel and administering the sacraments sought to shift the church's identity from the hierarchical strata of clergy, cathedrals, and basilicas into more accessible practices that would benefit the people gathering in the local churches.

---

33. The Belgic Confession, Article 29, http://reformed.org/documents/BelgicConfession.html. The Belgic's third mark is: "it practices discipline for correcting faults." Unlike other confessions of this time period, the Belgic Confession's Article 29 also describes distinguishing marks of those who belong to the church. This second portion of Article 29 is seldom included in conversations about the *notae ecclesia* and has the potential to serve as an ancillary project to the research pursued here.

34. Augsburg Confession, Article 7, http://bookofconcord.org/augsburgconfession.php#article7.1. Both Article 7 and Article 8 emphasize that the church is the "saints." However, in both instances, the church is located not by the people, but by the presence of the liturgical activities of preaching the gospel and administering the sacraments.

35. Westminster Confession, Article 25, http://reformed.org/documents/wcf_with_proofs/index.html. As with the Augsburg Confession, the Westminster Confession emphasizes the church as the people: "the elect, that have been, are, and shall be gathered into one, under Christ the Head thereof." However, the way the church is identified is again via the presence of the preaching the gospel and administering the sacraments in the context of public worship.

36. Bavinck, *Reformed Dogmatics*, 4:311.

37. Calvin, *Institutes*, 4.1.8. See Fitch, *Great Giveaway*, 20.

38. Grenz, "Ecclesiology," 261.

MCM Concerns with Liturgically Shaped Notae Ecclesia

With great appreciation for the intent of these marks, this project is concerned that expressing the church's identity only in the preaching of the word and the sacraments has fostered unintended consequences to the practice and nature of the church. Without recognizing that the marks themselves point elsewhere, the church is in danger of presenting a distorted image of what it means to be God's people. Such a distortion is problematic in that it sets God's people on a trajectory from which they only tangentially participate in God's mission.[39] While some in the MCM have attributed this distorted trajectory to the institutionalization of the church, this project's concern is not with perceiving the church as an institution. Rather, the concern lies with the diminished understanding of the church that has developed in response to locating the church's identity so exclusively within two liturgical activities.[40]

From the perspective of this project, there are at least four ways that limiting the marks of the church to the preaching of the word and the administration of the sacraments can distort and inhibit the identity of God's people within the *missio trinitatis*. While not fully expressed in these terms by the MCM, these concerns are evident within the MCM literature.

First, by focusing predominately on activities within the liturgy, the Reformed *notae* facilitates an understanding of the church as only that which occurs during the church's official liturgical gatherings. When limited to these marks, the church has little, if any, definition outside of its location within formal worship services. Commenting on the impact of the Reformers' marks, Guder writes:

> In their time, these emphases may have been profoundly missional since they asserted the authority of the Bible for the church's life and proclamation as well as the importance of making that proclamation accessible to all people. But over time, these 'marks' narrowed the church's definition of itself toward a 'place where' idea. This understanding was not so much articulated as presumed. It was never officially stated in a formal creed but was so ingrained in the churches' practice that it became dominant in the churches' self-understanding.[41]

The self-understanding of the church through its two liturgical marks opens the door for bifurcating the church between weekly worship

---

39. Kreider and Kreider, *Worship and Mission*, 64.
40. See Hirsch, *Forgotten Ways*, 23, who makes a similar distinction.
41. Guder, *Missional Church*, 80.

gatherings at a specific location and its existence as God's people scattered elsewhere throughout the rest of the week.[42] In some cases, this bifurcation even establishes implied limits as to what conversations are appropriate for which times and locations.[43]

Over the centuries, the Reformed tradition not only recognized this potential division, but embraced it, speaking of one church with two expressions: the church as institution and the church as organism.[44] From this project's perspective, the difficulty with this arrangement is that the institutional church has no means of being identified between worship services and that the organic church disappears when the community gathers for worship. The dualistic framework apparent within this approach has contributed to the inaction of the institutional and the organic expressions of the Reformed churches, with both expressions assuming that the other should confront injustice. In other words, a bifurcated church has a tendency to collapse under the weight of tangible sin-permeated circumstances, particularly those that involve the metastructures of race, politics, military, and economics.[45]

Second, under the pressure of being the only means of demarcating the church, the preaching of the word and administering of the sacraments are reduced to institutional events that are detached from the life of the

---

42. Bowen, *Green Shoots Out of Dry Ground*, 11–12.

43. Within my denomination, many congregations have a built-in resistance to holding budget-related meetings on Sundays and, where possible, hold financial discussions in rooms other than the sanctuary. Other congregational meetings, such as calling a pastor or electing elders and deacons, can occur on Sundays in the sanctuary with almost no resistance. The rationale is that there is a difference in what is appropriate for the church gathered in the sanctuary on Sunday and the church gathered at any other time—financial conversations are seen as too crass for the day and location of worship. Though beyond the scope of this paper, it would be interesting to relate the development of the Reformers' marks of the church with the development of a broader cultural paradigm of a sacred/secular divide.

44. See Bavinck for a further treatment of this distinction between church as institute and as organism (*Reformed Dogmatics*, 4:284–91). Also, Berkhof, *Systematic Theology*, 567.

45. Institutional churches in Nazi Germany, in apartheid South Africa, and in the slavery and Jim Crow–era United States—including churches associated with the Reformation—were complicit with the severe injustices perpetrated in these environments. Given that the Reformed tradition emphasizes that sin has infected every person and every aspect of life, this critique is rather striking. By limiting the marks of the church to liturgical expressions, the church has unnecessarily limited its capacity to respond to sin outside of the liturgical gatherings. See Williamson, who argues that Luther and Calvin recognized later on that the lived response of the people also had something to do with the nature of the church, but resisted adjusting the marks because of the doctrine of justification by grace alone ("Marks of the Church," 26–28).

body outside of worship. As Emil Brunner insightfully opined, "It is here that a great problem confronts theology, a problem almost totally neglected, namely, how to understand baptism and the Lord's Supper in a personal and non-institutional sense, as the means of the kind of communion with Christ which involves at the same time a true brotherhood expressed in everyday life."[46] As the principle elements defining the church within the Reformed tradition, the preaching of the word and the sacraments become the ultimate reference point to which everything else in the church is oriented. In other words, they have no obvious connection to life outside of themselves. If the marks of preaching and the sacraments define the church, what else can they point to beside themselves? Therein, the marks are limited to a kind of circular self-affirmation: the preaching of the word points to the sacraments and the sacraments point to the preaching of the word. The incapacitating side effect of the marks' circular exclusivity is that they are stripped of their capacity to engage life beyond the liturgy, thereby reducing orthopraxy to intellectual agreement with the proclaimed propositional theology and to reception of the sacraments, both of which are primarily evidenced through attendance at worship services. In this way, the confinement of the church's identity to these two marks lends to a self-induced isolation and increasing irrelevance of the church in relationship to life beyond the church building and the formal worship service.

This project's third concern with these marks is that the elevation of preaching and sacraments as the *notae* above the other elements of the liturgy necessitates their performance by professional clergy in order to maintain their purity.[47] The congregation's attention shifts from the formative capacity of these liturgical elements to the efficacy of the one delivering the sermon and administering the sacraments, which is often measured by the number of people in the pews. In turn, the pastoral identity of the clergy becomes almost inextricably linked with and reduced to the responsibility for presenting a particular liturgical product that will allow the local church to maintain a numerically evidenced purity *ad infinitum*.[48] In similar fashion, the laity are denied a place within the institutional church, which has

---

46. Brunner, "One Holy Catholic Church," 330.

47. Guder, *Missional Church*, 80.

48. Might this elevated attention to performing "sacred" tasks of preaching and administering the sacraments also prevent the church from recognizing the humanity—and particularly the broken, sinful humanity—of clergy? Bartholomew and Goheen seem to hint at as much when they remind their readers that "[t]here is shoddy worship and selfish prayer, just as there are unfaithful ministers, lazy missionaries, and dysfunctional churches, and all need God's healing, redirecting, and redeeming touch" (*Living at the Crossroads*, 65).

relegated them to roles of obligated recipients, passive observers, and, more recently, marketed consumers of official church services. Kreider and Kreider comment:

> In Christendom, worship was the responsibility of the religious professional. Non-professional Christians were expected to attend. The professionals spent a lot of their time organizing these acts of worship; liturgical theologians thought about what happened in the services of worship; and the laity—who, the clergy complained, often skipped the services put on in their behalf—spent most of their time engaged in secular activities.[49]

Within such constraints, the clergy and particular local expressions of the church are, by perceptual default,[50] vulnerable to the perpetual critiques of church members, whose places within the life of the church have likewise been reduced.[51]

Fourth, and finally, this project is concerned with the ways that these marks distort the rest of the worship gathering and inhibit the transformative capacity of the whole liturgy within the life of God's people. Simply stated, the Reformers' conception of the marks places so much weight on the preaching of the word and the sacraments that the other elements of the worship service liturgy are devalued as optional and predominately irrelevant. It requires very little to transition from identifying the preaching of the word and the administration of the sacraments as the defining marks of the church to seeing them as the only necessary components of the *ordo*. In such a light, prayer becomes a mere expression of formalized

---

49. Kreider and Kreider, *Worship and Mission after Christendom*, 25. Also Guder, who recognizes the impact of this clergy/laity division within the marketing orientation of church growth models when he concludes that church "members are ultimately distanced in this model from their own communal calling to be a body of people sent on a mission" (*Missional Church*, 83–85).

50. I am using the description of *perceptual default* here because I believe that the church's struggles tend to rise from the perception that the church is limited to liturgical events, physical locations, or institutional offices—preaching, sacraments, building, clergy, etc. In the context of this argument, the Reformers' marks point to a default posture that perceives the church as existing primarily within the boundaries of the liturgy.

51. Helland and Hjalmarson, *Missional Spirituality*, 60–68. Also Fitch, who summarizes the Anabapist objections to the limits of these two marks, suggesting that "one could merely post a doctrinal statement at the front of the church and have a priest show up to consecrate the Lord's Supper and that would constitute a faithful church. There need not even be any people in the pews" (*Great Giveaway*, 20). While certainly an oversimplification of the Reformers' ecclesiology, this critique still exposes the weakness of describing the church primarily in terms of its liturgical activities: the people have no place within the church and the church's dependency on the clergy is further entrenched.

piety in preparation of the marks, offerings are reduced to an obligation for maintaining access to the property and staff required to deliver the two institutional marks, congregational singing is tossed to and fro by the passing fancies of personal preferences, and the greeting and blessing become mere functional markers, identifying the opening and closing of a service.[52] In other words, the formative capacity of the other elements in the *ordo* is negated.

The purpose of these deconstructive critiques is not to discard the importance of the preaching of the word or of the administration of the sacraments, but to expose some of the vulnerabilities encountered by elevating these liturgical elements as the core components of what it means to be church.[53] The perceived consequence has been that these vulnerabilities foster an inhibition to communal participation in the *missio trinitatis*, with a cumulative effect that construes the church's main responsibility toward perfecting the sermon and properly administering the sacraments. Moreover, in this context, mission becomes distortedly perceived as a responsibility to increase Sunday worship attendance by persuading non-Christians to become church members.[54] In contrast, the argument arising from within the MCM is that a different ecclesiology derived from the *missio trinitatis* is needed in order for the people of God to live more faithfully as the church within God's mission.[55] As will be seen in chapter 4, the preaching and the sacraments play important roles in forming the evangelistic character of God's people within the MCM. However, those two liturgical acts are insufficient to mark the church *in situ*.

---

52. Goheen, "Nourishing Our Missional Identity," 51–53.

53. Ibid., 49–51.

54. A number of outreach events come to mind, including one I encountered where a church hosted a "sportsmen's club" dinner, featuring a motivational talk by a professional sport fisher and plenty of door prizes. Nothing on the invitation itself indicated that a gospel presentation, including an altar call, would be inserted into the middle of the evening's event. Yet, for the host church, the end goal of the night was to win converts to Christianity. But the way the night was advertised as a talk and with door prizes, however, quite literally created a "bait-and-switch" scenario. While certainly not the violent threats of conversion under the penalty of death attributed to past Christian campaigns, such approaches demonstrate the extent to which the end goal of counting conversions still seems to justify the means used to secure those conversions.

55. Goheen, "Nourishing Our Missional Idenitity," 34.

Toward Character Marks: Outlining a Missional Ecclesiology

To some extent, a different question is needed in order to develop a missional ecclesiology. As Goheen asserts, "Ecclesiology is about understanding our identity, who we are, and why God has chosen us—whose we are."[56] Rather than emphasizing particular institutional functions, these identity concerns are profoundly relational in orientation and call for ongoing discernment. As Guder contends:

> Neither the church nor its interpretive doctrine may be static. New biblical insights will convert the church and its theology; new historical challenges will raise questions never before considered; and new cultural contexts will require a witnessing response that redefines how we function and how we hope as Christians.[57]

In this light, missional critiques of the Reformers' marks offered above are occasioned by perceived limits to the question: What is the church? Ecclesiology framed through such a line of questioning is prone to assume a static answer, and therein to look for institutional activities—preaching and sacraments, for example—that are assumed to be readily transferable across cultural and historical environments.[58] Alternatively, asking identity-type questions in line with Goheen's and Guder's assertions leads toward an ecclesiology that makes room for God's people to be authentic within their particularized locations, while simultaneously expressing and enriching a universal recognition of what being church can look like. This transition moves the conversation toward dynamically describing God's people in relationship to God and God's mission.

To this end, the capacity to dynamically describe the church is increased by asking different kinds of questions. Small offers a few potential questions: "What is the character of the community of God's people? How can God's people live faithfully in the midst of a culture that may overwhelm them? What does it take for God's people to remain *God's* people?"[59] Questions such

---

56. Goheen, *Light to the Nations*, 5.

57. Guder, *Missional Church*, 12.

58. Though beyond the scope of this current research, one could also look at the pre-Vatican II mass, which utilized a uniform language and *ordo*, as an example of this tendency toward maintaining a static, supposedly supracultural understanding of the church.

59. Small, "Who's In, Who's Out?," 64.

as these reorient conversation about the church's identity toward a community's ongoing and maturing faithfulness in revealing God's character.[60]

In this regard, MCM practitioners are turning more toward images and stories to describe the church, rather than utilizing the typical terminology of systematic theology.[61] As such, the literature includes parables, analogies, and metaphors present within scripture and contemporary culture as resources for describing the church. Perhaps the most persistent of these images are variations on Newbigin's description of the church "as sign, instrument, and foretaste" of God's grace in the world.[62]

While acknowledging this trend to image the church rather than define the church, this project offers a descriptive overview of MCM ecclesiology, suggesting the church to be: *a people gathered in Jesus Christ in order to be sent with the Spirit, embodying Jesus Christ's character together as participants in the still-unfolding story of God's mission, throughout every dimension and moment of life and in anticipation of God's coming kingdom*. Each phrase of this description is briefly engaged in order to outline a missional ecclesiology that can serve as a backdrop to the rest of the project.

A People Gathered in Jesus Christ

The MCM's understanding of the church hinges on the conviction that the church is called together in Jesus Christ. This gathering is not primarily about physically gathering for worship services—that vision of gathering is too narrow for missional ecclesiology. Rather, the movement sees being gathered as integral to the identity of the community of God's people. The church has not come together on their initiative or as individuals. Instead, being gathered implies God's prior activity and initiative. Moreover, being gathered in Jesus Christ communicates that they have been gathered by means of God's mission in Jesus Christ and in conformity with God's mission in Jesus Christ. Expressed differently, the church exists because of God's mission in Jesus Christ.[63]

Hirsch insists that "Jesus the Messiah plays an *absolutely* central role. Our identity as a movement, as well as our destiny as a people, is inextricably

---

60. Such a reorientation holds promise beyond the MCM. See Van Dyke, who notes that "[i]f ecclesiology were understood to be an articulation of the character, acts, will, and purposes of God for the people of God, that would be a much broader and grander scope of discourse than the rather limited range of topics that often occupy what is assumed to be ecclesiology" ("Church in Evangelical Theology and Practice," 132).

61. Goheen, *Light to the Nations*, 15.

62. Newbigin, *Gospel in a Pluralist Society*, 232–33.

63. Kreider and Kreider, *Worship and Mission after Christendom*, 55.

linked to Jesus—the Second Person of the Trinity. In fact, our connection to God is only through the Mediator—Jesus is 'the Way'; no one comes to the Father except through him. This is what makes us distinctly Christian."[64] Likewise, Tizon remarks that "[t]he kingdom refers to a reality that is characterized by God's rule, reflected most profoundly, powerfully, and completely in Jesus Christ."[65] Fitch and Holsclaw caution the church against losing sight of Jesus Christ: "we need to start at the beginning—the beginning of the good news of Jesus, the beginning of the gospel of Jesus Christ, the Son of God."[66] For the MCM, without Jesus, there is no church.

Moreover, the centrality of Jesus and Jesus' work of gathering a people is evident in the communal nature of the church. From a missional perspective, there is no such thing as an individual Christian. Hirsch reflects on this communal identity extensively in *The Forgotten Ways*, calling for the church to see itself as *communitas* in the post-Christendom context.[67] Goheen's insight expands this communal perspective in the context of Jesus' mission, which "is to restore an eschatological community that takes up that missional role and identity again."[68] The communal identity of God's people is essential to the *missio trinitatis*. As Guder asserts: "we are a communal body of Christ's followers, mutually committed and responsible to one another and to the mission Jesus set us upon at his resurrection."[69] Each of these insights reflects an expanded version of Newbigin's insight conveyed in the opening section of this project: Jesus "did not write a book but formed a community." God is not simply out to save individuals, but in Jesus Christ God is gathering and forming a new community, a people of God.

In Order to Be Sent with the Spirit

MCM participants are quick to assert that this gathering has always been in order that God might send the community of God's people as part of the *missio trinitatis*. Hammond and Cronshaw describe the church's sent nature this way: "The church is not primarily a voluntary association, a chaplain to society or a vendor of religious goods and services. It is not intrinsically here to *sell*. Rather the church is an alternative community that witnesses

---

64. Hirsch, *Forgotten Ways*, 94.
65. Tizon, *Missional Preaching*, 16.
66. Fitch and Holsclaw, *Prodigal Christianity*, 23–26.
67. Hirsch, *Forgotten Ways*, 217–41.
68. Goheen, *Light to the Nations*, 76.
69. Guder, *Missional Church*, 108.

by living differently. The church is a body characterized by *sentness*."[70] *Missional Church* adds to this perspective: "Churches are called to be bodies of people sent on a mission rather than the storefronts for vendors of religious services and goods in North American culture."[71]

Van Gelder recognizes this orientation toward God's mission as the primary difference in ecclesiology between the MCM and other understandings of church:

> The genetic code of missional church means it is missionary in its very essence. This means that congregations exist in the world as being missionary by nature. The self-understanding of such congregations is not first of all being established (that they represent the primary location of God's activity in the world), or being corporate (that they do something on behalf of God in the world), but rather their self-understanding is missional (they participate through the Spirit's leading in what God is doing in the world).[72]

At times overtly and others more subtly, this sent nature of the church is related to Jesus' post-resurrection commissioning of the disciples as recorded in John 20:21: "Again Jesus said, 'Peace be with you! As the Father has sent me, I am sending you.'" Citing this text, Fitch and Holsclaw explain:

> We have a string of three: the disciples are sent; and whoever receives them, in some sense also receives Jesus; and not only that also receives the Father who sent Jesus. All who claim to be Christ's disciples are extensions of this sending. All Christians are by nature sent into this mission. We, all of his disciples, have been caught up in the radical prodigal mission of the Triune God.[73]

Hammond and Cronshaw add their perspective in response to this same text: "You won't die on a cross and be raised again to save the world. But you are sent as a representative or ambassador of Jesus, who did live, die and rise from the dead to transform the lives of people and nations."[74]

Yet, God's people are not sent in this way on their own. Rather, God's people are sent with the Spirit. John 21:22 declares: "And with that he breathed on them and said, 'Receive the Holy Spirit.'" The interconnectedness of these

---

70. Hammond and Cronshaw, *Sentness*, 49–50.
71. Guder, *Missional Church*, 108.
72. Van Gelder, "From Corporate Church to Missional Church," 445.
73. Fitch and Holsclaw, *Prodigal Christianity*, 30.
74. Hammond and Cronshaw, *Sentness*, 46–47.

two verses has been embedded within the MCM.[75] As in implication of being sent with the Spirit, numerous authors highlight that the Spirit is already at work in neighborhoods and communities throughout the world.[76] Rather than taking God with them on their missionary endeavors, God's people join the Spirit in the work the Spirit is already doing.[77] Frost and Hirsch clearly convey this perspective:

> The question that must drive us is the question of whether we can join with God in his mission—in whatever place we find ourselves. The evangelicalism that grips the church in the West teaches us (implicitly and explicitly) that we take God with us where we go in mission. We 'tell' people about God, assuming quite falsely that they have had no God experiences or epiphanies . . . prior to that point. This is simply unbiblical! The fact is God was already there! He was always there wooing, forever courting, constantly wowing, and acting redemptively by drawing people to himself.[78]

As such, MCM participants understand that part of their responsibility is to listen attentively within their respective contexts for how they might join with the Spirit.[79] Through this discernment process, God's people discover that, though they are sent by God, they are never the whole of God's presence, mission, or kingdom in any given context.[80]

Embodying Jesus Christ's Character Together

As God's people are sent with the Spirit, they take on Jesus' character as their own, revealing in their life together the story of God's faithfulness in the person of Jesus Christ. Without specifically defining Christ's character, the MCM highlights why embodying Jesus' character is central to a missional ecclesiology. Kreider and Kreider contend that "Jesus' involvement in God's mission

---

75. For example, Marshall cautions: "Neglect of the role of the Spirit in divine sending contributes to an overly functional, mechanistic, less organic view of the church and its mission. If we are not careful, the original conception of the Trinitarian missio can lead to a passing the baton relay-race understanding of mission whereby the Father sends the Son, who then sends the church" ("Missional Ecclesiology for the 21st Century," 12).

76. Fitch and Holsclaw, *Prodigal Christianity*, 29–30.

77. Hammond and Cronshaw, *Sentness*, 47–48.

78. Frost and Hirsch, *Shaping of Things to Come*, 161.

79. Huckins, *Thin Places*, 34. This project reflects further on the Holy Spirit and the MCM at the end of chapter 4.

80. Hunsberger, *Bearing the Witness of the Spirit*, 166–67.

embodied alertness to God's action. It was humble and compassionate to the outsider. And it rejected violence, coercion, and domination. God's missional action today has the same character as God's missional action in Jesus."[81] Similarly, Guder observes: "The church displays the firstfruits of the forgiven and the forgiving people of God who are brought together across the rubble of dividing walls that have crumbled under the weight of the cross. It is the harbinger of the new humanity that lives in genuine community, a form of companionship and wholeness that humanity craves."[82] Relying on Marshall McLuhan's famous adage, "The medium is the message," Frost and Hirsch argue further that "[w]e need to take seriously the fact that the medium—our lives—conveys very different messages, ones that are being read all the time by the people around about us."[83] As such, the character of Jesus Christ, embodied by the community of God's people, is integral to the gospel proclamation. In this light, Fitch and Holsclaw state quite succinctly: "Through our transformed lives, the world sees something it did not know was possible: it sees the kingdom breaking in."[84]

Yet, it is not the character of God's people in and of itself, but as their character is reoriented toward and coheres with the character of Jesus Christ, that the gospel becomes an embodied reality. *The New Parish* authors illuminate this character focus: "The church exists as Christ's body to form us as people who are faithfully present to God, one another and creation, even as Christ was and is faithfully present."[85] This reorientation toward Jesus' character fits well with the MCM's emphasis on the *missio trinitatis* revealed in the unfolding of the biblical narrative.[86] To be God's people is to embody God's character in God's mission. As Grenz recognizes, "At the heart of the

---

81. Kreider and Kreider, *Worship and Mission after Christendom*, 55.
82. Guder, *Missional Church*, 103.
83. Frost and Hirsch, *Shaping of Things to Come*, 154–56
84. Fitch and Holsclaw, *Prodigal Christianity*, 62.
85. Sparks, Soerens, and Friesen, *New Parish*, 90.

86. The biblical injunctions for God's people to live in accord with God's character are plentiful. "You are to be holy to me because I, the LORD, am holy, and I have set you apart from the nations to be my own" (Lev 20:26). "For the LORD your God is God of gods and Lord of lords, mighty and awesome, who shows no partiality and accepts no bribes. He defends the cause of the fatherless and the widow, and loves the foreigners residing among you, giving them food and clothing. And you are to love those who are foreigners, for you yourselves were foreigners" (Deut 10:17–19). "Dear friends, let us love one another, for love comes from God. Everyone who loves has been born of God and knows God. Whoever does not love does not know God, because God is love" (1 John 4:7–8). Additionally, see Bowen, who reflects on Leviticus 19:2 and how the commands that follow it reveal God's character in the lives of God's people (*Evangelism for "Normal" People*, 31).

biblical narrative is the story of the triune God bringing humankind to be the *imago Dei*, that is, to be the reflection of the divine character—love . . . the church is to be a people who reflect in relation to each other and to all creation the character of the Creator and thereby bear witness to the divine purpose for humankind."[87] In essence, a focus on embodying the character of Jesus shifts the ecclesiological conversation toward the way the community of God's people engages with God, with each other, and with the world around them in response to the *missio trinitatis*.

Therefore, the ecclesiological concern within the MCM is primarily about the faithful embodiment of God's character. Hirsch adds:

> Discipleship, becoming like Jesus our Lord and Founder, lies at the epicenter of the church's task. It means that Christology must define all that we do and say. It also means that in order to recover the ethos of authentic Christianity, we need to refocus our attention back to the Root of it all, to recalibrate ourselves and our organizations around the person and work of Jesus the Lord.[88]

In a similar way, Guder highlights the ethical implications of this recalibration, contending that God's people are "called and sent to be the unique community of those who live under the reign of God" in the same manner that Jesus did.[89] Thus, for the MCM the marks of the church are rooted in how God's people embody Jesus' character throughout their relationships and the various activities in which they engage together.

As Participants in the Still-Unfolding Story of God's Mission

Yet the MCM recognizes that this embodied character is not a replacement of Jesus Christ, as if God's people could somehow fully imitate Jesus' redemptive role. Rather, as the church embodies Jesus' character, the church does so as a sign, foretaste, and instrument of God's mission.[90] Guder notes how the church is a sign by speaking "boldly and often so that the signs of

---

87. Grenz, "Ecclesiology," 267.

88. Hirsch, *Forgotten Ways*, 94.

89. Guder, *Missional Church*, 103.

90. The language of "sign, foretaste, and instrument" draws from Newbigin. See Newbigin, *Gospel in a Pluralist Society*, 232–33; and Newbigin, "What Is a Local Church Truly United," 115–28. While these terms (sometimes with *servant* substituted for *instrument*) appear widely within missional literature, few people cite Newbigin directly. Hunsberger notes how Newbigin utilizes several other metaphors as well in order to highlight the church's identity within the mission of God (*Bearing the Witness of the Spirit*, 167).

the reign of God in the Scriptures, in the world's history, and in the present may be clearly seen. It speaks so that the signposts to the reign of God evidenced in the church's own deeds will not be misunderstood."[91] In their life together, God's people are also a foretaste of God's kingdom. As Frost writes, "The very planet yearns for renewal. It joins us in that chorus of expectation. Just as snow-capped mountains and raging rivers and lush fields are reminders or foretastes of the renewed planet to come, so should our communities of faith, hope, and love be similar examples of the shape of things to come."[92] The people of God are also an instrument. Bartholomew and Goheen explain that this metaphor reveals three dimensions of the church's participation in God's mission: "As the church takes up the mission of Jesus, it becomes an instrument of God to make his kingdom known, to proclaim the good news, and to challenge opposition to God's gracious rule."[93] Taken together, these metaphors exemplify ways in which God's people embody Jesus' character as participants in the *missio trinitatis*.

While the broad strokes of God's mission have been identified through scripture, the church today is living between Pentecost and Jesus' promised return with the new heavens and new earth. Bartholomew and Goheen contend that this space can be helpfully understood as an improvised act within a broader drama, where the previous scene and the final scene are already known. The story of God's mission is therefore still unfolding in the present through the faithfulness of God's people as they seek to follow the Spirit along the trajectory of God's mission, which stretches from creation, through the fall, along the long road of redemption in Jesus Christ, and anticipates the flourishing life of the new heaven and new earth in Christ's return.[94]

Because the church knows how the story will finally unfold, God's people participate within their current contexts with a bold confidence. Hirsch contends that the church "is by far and away the most potent force for transformational change the world has ever seen. It has been that before, is that now, and will be that again."[95] This transformational change is not rooted in the church's own efforts, but comes about through their coherence within the still-unfolding nature of God's mission.

Yet the MCM recognizes that God's people are called to be aware of their own sinfulness and their own continual need for further maturity.

---

91. Guder, *Missional Church*, 109.

92. Frost, *Road to Missional*, 31.

93. Bartholomew and Goheen, *Living at the Crossroads*, 59.

94. Bartholomew and Goheen, *Drama of Scripture*, 25–27, 198–206. Also, N. T. Wright, *New Testament and the People of God*, 139–42.

95. Hirsch, *Forgotten Ways*, 17.

So while confidently participating in the continuing story of God's cosmic reconciliation and restoration in Jesus Christ, God's people seek to do so with a humble posture. As Guder reminds his readers, "What the church identifies as true about itself because of Christ, it also knows to be far from true about itself in its present experience."[96] The reality of ongoing human sinfulness in God's people leads Huckins to state: "How easy it is to say we know God's will for our lives, when in reality we may simply be manifesting our personal agenda?"[97]

Throughout Every Dimension and Moment of Life

Relying heavily on Jesus' incarnation, missional theologians and practitioners have consistently emphasized the need for the church to actively engage within their respective geographic neighborhoods. As Helland and Hjalmarson comment, "Apart from the incarnation, there would be no mission of God in the world, no redemption, and no meaning to the prayer 'May your kingdom come on earth.'"[98] In advocating for this incarnational grounding, Frost and Hirsch contend that "the missional church disassembles itself and seeps into the cracks and crevices of a society in order to be Christ to those who don't yet know him."[99]

This disassembly, or scattering, is not the disintegration of the church, but integral to the church's identity and embodiment of Jesus' character, and particularly in line with Jesus' incarnation. Fitch argues that Jesus' incarnation is the basis for understanding that the people of God are still God's people as they engage in their respective families, neighborhoods, vocations, and other communities, and not only when gathered in worship.[100] This engagement happens in rather ordinary ways because God is at work in the mundane, common moments of the world. Bowen remarks on how the times beyond gathered worship, when the leadership of professional clergy is less visible, is "when some of the hardest assignments have to be done." He continues:

> Church members go as Jesus' apprentices "into all the world" as representatives of his kingdom, to speak his truth and to act his love. A Christian bank teller turns down a promotion in order

---

96. Guder, *Missional Church*, 103.

97. Huckins, *Thin Places*, 31. Though not grammatically necessary, the question mark appears in the original text.

98. Helland and Hjalmarson, *Missional Spirituality*, 57.

99. Frost and Hirsch, *Shaping of Things to Come*, 12.

100. Fitch, *Great Giveaway*, 229.

to continue giving her attention to those the bank consider little people—retired people with scant savings, the working poor, teenagers trying to save for college. A Christian businessman sets up a laundromat as a safe place for mentally challenged young people to find their first employment. A Christian professor is surprised at her students' comment that she is the only teacher who remembers their names.[101]

Likewise, Roxburgh insists, "God is present and acting in the ordinary, in the everyday realities of people's lives in the neighborhoods where we find ourselves," which leads God's people to engage with their neighbors in the ordinary moments and life of their neighborhoods in order to discover how God is already there.[102]

Such a posture emphasizes the priesthood of all believers. Helland and Hjalmarson encourage churches to see that the priesthood of all believers is primarily "spiritual and missional, not institutional."[103] Frost adds: "I am not suggesting that there is anything inherently wrong with seminaries, denominations, church buildings, and the rest of the massive infrastructure that the church in the West has at its disposal. What I'm saying is that our reliance on them is limiting our spiritual growth."[104] Insisting that this priesthood is really for every believer, Wright explains: "we find that an essential part of the mission of God's people is nothing other than to be what they are—by living out the holiness of God in practical everyday living. Mission is not something that happens when you go somewhere else. It starts in your own home and neighborhood. That is where we are called to be holy."[105] For the MCM, then, the incarnation is not about going to church, but about being God's people, being the church, in the ordinary moments of life, an emphasis that shifts attention toward the people and away from clergy.

This incarnational emphasis on the ordinary moments leads to an ecclesiological emphasis of equipping every follower of Jesus Christ to engage God's mission by living more faithfully in their daily lives.[106] Hirsch and Hirsch clarify the purpose of this equipping emphasis: "One of the biggest shifts needed is to de-professionalize the ministry/clergy class and give ministry back to the people of God. This does not mean that we don't have leaders: any movement that makes any impact has definite leadership. They simply

---

101. Bowen, *Green Shoots Out of Dry Ground*, 12.
102. Roxburgh, "Practices of a Missional People."
103. Helland and Hjalmarson, *Missional Spirituality*, 64.
104. Frost, *Exiles*, 139.
105. Wright, *Mission of God's People*, 125–26.
106. Harder, "New Shoots from Old Roots," 56–58.

don't confuse leadership with ministry. Not all are leaders, but all are ministers. Leadership is a calling within a calling."[107] From this perspective, the primary role of church leadership is therefore transitioned from facilitating worship services to empowering all disciples to be the church at all times.[108]

While recognizing Marshall's caution regarding the potential for missiologically equivalent heresies to Docetism or Arianism via underapplying or overapplying the incarnation to the church's own efforts,[109] missional ecclesiology understands Jesus' incarnation as essential to the MCM's own engagement with the world and, particularly, in clarifying the equipping role that clergy and other church leaders take in relationship to the rest of the church.[110] Simply stated, the incarnation serves as a paradigm for the MCM's engagement within the world.

In Anticipation of God's Coming Kingdom

Bartholomew and Goheen assert: "If we recognize that we have been called to provide our world with a preview of God's coming kingdom, the hope of that kingdom's coming will shape all that we say and do in the here and now."[111] This eschatological vision permeates the missional vision. Highlighting the present implications of this coming kingdom, Frost argues:

> [God] gave us these gifts so that we might breathe shalom throughout the world, that we might bring reconciliation and joy, peace and justice to a broken world yearning for redemption. He gave us gifts so that we might design beautiful buildings, produce beautiful art, defend and protect this beautiful earth. He gave us these gifts so that we would defend the oppressed and protect the widow and orphan, and so that we might announce the beautiful message that through Christ our God reigns and that he has defeated sin and death and the devil and that he has come to your house offering you relationship with him and citizenship in a brand-new world that is here and still coming.

In these ways, the church becomes a living anticipation of God's coming kingdom and the kingdom of God becomes tangibly present even now.[112]

---

107. Hirsch and Hirsch, *Untamed*, 144.
108. Woodward, *Creating a Missional Culture*, 91–96.
109. Marshall, "Missional Ecclesiology for the 21st Century," 18–20.
110. Frost and Hirsch, *Shaping of Things to Come*, 35.
111. Bartholomew and Goheen, *Drama of Scripture*, 206.
112. Frost, *Road to Missional*, 120.

While looking forward to the fullness of God's coming kingdom, the MCM also recognizes that God's people will encounter tension and hostility because the kingdom they are called to embody conflicts with the power structures and values within the present culture. Guder comments that "[i]n every cultural context, no matter how benevolent or hostile the governments and societies around it may be, the church is called to demonstrate an alternative culture."[113] Goheen contends further that this counterculture posture is essential to the witness of God's people: "Only when the church is a faithful embodiment of the kingdom as part of the surrounding culture yet over against its idolatry will its life and words bear compelling and appealing testimony to the good news that in Jesus Christ a new world has come and is coming."[114] Yet, this tension and the church's own ongoing struggles to faithfully embody Jesus' character do not negate the eschatological hope that shapes the missional church's vision. Rather, as Bowen writes:

> Is this just pie in the sky when you die? No. Christian hope for the future is anchored securely in an event in the past, the resurrection of Jesus Christ from the dead. The restoration of all things in the future is just as certain as the resurrection of Jesus in the past. Indeed, God's past is also a foretaste of God's future. In the resurrection, God has lifted a corner on the veil that hangs over the end of time and given us something to hope for that is not dependent on us and our ups and downs, but is dependent on the God of Jesus Christ, who is faithful and therefore may be trusted.[115]

Implications of a Missional Ecclesiology Relevant to This Project

While there are certainly more nuances to a missional ecclesiology than what has been briefly described here, the broad strokes of how the MCM perceives the church are evident. The church's identity is rooted in God's act of gathering a people in Jesus Christ in order to send them into the world with the Spirit. This gathered and sent people is marked by their communal embodiment of Jesus' character. As they embody Jesus' character in their everyday lives, God's people do so with hope, anticipating God's coming kingdom.

This ecclesiological vision carries far more implications than will be enumerated within this project. However, in preparing to outline a missional approach to worship in the next chapter, three implications of the missional

---

113. Guder, *Missional Church*, 119.
114. Goheen, *Light to the Nations*, 5.
115. Bowen, *Green Shoots Out of Dry Ground*, 19.

ecclesiology sketched above need to be mentioned here. First, immersion in the story of God's mission is critical to the nature of the church. As Goheen, Wright, Guder and other have consistently emphasized, the *missio trinitatis* shapes the gathering and sending of the church as participants in God's mission in agreement with the grand narrative of scripture. The identity of the church, therefore, is made known through and caught up in the unfolding story of God's mission. The way the church worships, therefore, needs to engage and immerse God's people in the biblical narrative.

Second, the ecclesiological vision is directed toward sending God's people as participants in the *missio trinitatis*. As contributions like *Thin Places, Sentness, Missional Spirituality*, and *The New Parish* have emphasized, the ecclesiological shift here moves attention toward tangible engagement within the neighborhoods and communities in which they participate on a daily basis. In this context, worship gatherings are not the culminating moments of the community's life together. Instead, worship gatherings are bent toward equipping God's people to embody Jesus Christ's character within and for the world.

Third, the primary calling of church leaders is to cultivate and equip the rest of the church to live as God's people throughout the week, and indeed, throughout their whole lives. As has been evident in contributions from Breen, Van Gelder, Woodward, and others, local church leaders are called to cultivate a community of disciples who will in turn make more disciples. In this missional ecclesiology, this role clarification means the primary task of a leader is to come alongside the people of God and equip them to live more fully and more faithfully as God's people in the contexts of their daily living. The goal of forming God's people for missional living, whether through worship or in other contexts, becomes the driving purpose for everything that church leaders do.

With these three implications in mind and with the broader missional ecclesiology explored throughout this chapter as a back drop, chapter 4 proposes a missional approach to worship. As will become evident through that chapter, the story of God's mission, the sent nature of the church, and the equipping role of leadership all contribute to the shape of missional worship and strengthen the capacity of communal worship gatherings to participate in cultivating an evangelistic character among God's people.

4

A Missional Approach to Worship

THE PURPOSE OF THIS chapter is to propose a missional approach to worship, with a particular focus on how worship participates in cultivating Jesus' character among God's people. In pursuing that purpose, this chapter engages MCM conversations regarding the Holy Spirit, particularly on seeing the Spirit as the primary actor within worship. Emerging from these pneumatological considerations, the proposal engages Smith's reflections on the formative capacity of Christian worship, thereby attending to one of the worship-related gaps identified at the outset of the project. After attending to these foundational matters, the chapter provides a two-part proposal for a missional approach to worship, identifying thematic priorities shaping missional worship and providing an example of how these priorities can shape a local worship gathering. The chapter then concludes with brief commentary on why missional worship needs a praxis-oriented discipleship. Because this chapter engages several gaps within MCM conversations, the project utilizes several external voices as a means of navigating the conversations that follow. While MCM contributors are included throughout the chapter, they more frequently appear in supporting rather than leading roles in this proposal.

The Transformative Presence of the Holy Spirit[1]

The foundational conviction regarding a missional approach to worship is that God is the primary actor within worship.[2] In affirming this conviction, the MCM points to the transformative presence of the Holy Spirit with God's people. For example, Fitch insists that worship spaces need to "be places for the Holy Spirit to reorder our imaginations and shape our characters into his holiness."[3] Affirming this holiness as highly missional, Hirsch and Hirsch assert that "[o]ne of the key roles of the Holy Spirit is to oversee the change process by which we become holy."[4] Likewise, Wright concludes that the Holy Spirit makes available "the same transforming power that energized the life and ministry of Jesus and raised him from the dead."[5] Each of these perspectives affirms ways in which the Spirit is actively at work among God's people in worship.

At least four other perspectives on the Holy Spirit can be identified within MCM conversations. First, the Spirit is integral to the formation and direction of the church. Van Gelder insists that "the church is the creation of the Spirit," adding that the church can be renewed "only by developing discipline in discerning the leading of the Spirit."[6] Second, the Spirit heals God's people, equipping them to participate in God's mission. As Kreider and Kreider note, "the Holy Spirit bestows gifts to heal our wounds, restore broken relationships, and empower us to participate in God's mission."[7] Third, the Spirit unites God's people in Jesus' death and resurrection, which becomes a template—perhaps *the* template—upon which the Spirit forms God's people through the confession of sin and the extension of forgiveness. Huckins contends:

> we allow his Spirit to transform and move freely through the life of our community as we continually put to death the ways of old, step fully into the mystery and conviction of life in Jesus, and live lives that reflect the transformation of Jesus's resurrection. It is only with the Spirit's leading that we can then set off

---

1. I first encountered the language of "transformative presence" in reference to the Holy Spirit within Smith, *Desiring the Kingdom*, 150.

2. Dawn, "Reaching Out without Dumbing Down," 281; and Schattauer, "Liturgical Assembly as Locus of Mission," 14.

3. Fitch, *Great Giveaway*, 109.

4. Hirsch and Hirsch, *Untamed*, 92.

5. Wright, *Mission of God's People*, 43.

6. Van Gelder, *Essence of the Church*, 42–43.

7. Kreider and Kreider, *Worship and Mission after Christendom*, 32.

on the holy pilgrimage of Jesus discipleship as participants in the mission of God.[8]

Fourth, the Spirit strengthens God's people for mission. Helland and Hjalmarson summarize this when they write: "The Spirit fosters a lively missional *Spirit*-uality in which corporate worship is a gathering point from which God's people emerge, directed by Jesus, strengthened by the Spirit, to join the Father's mission throughout the week."[9]

While this brief summary reveals some attention by MCM contributors to the person and presence of the Holy Spirit, MCM conversations would benefit in at least two ways from further reflection on the Holy Spirit, particularly with regard to the Spirit's role in transforming the character of God's people. First, a robust engagement would assist the MCM with recognizing the Holy Spirit as the third person of the Trinity. The Spirit is more than an impersonal force or power by which God the Father accomplishes the mission of God in Jesus Christ. The Nicene Creed teaches that the Holy Spirit "with the Father and the Son is worshiped and glorified"; to which the Athanasian Creed adds that the Holy Spirit is coequal, uncreated, immeasurable, eternal, almighty, God and Lord with the Father and the Son. Second, focused engagement on the person of the Holy Spirit would invite attention to the transformative presence the Spirit has with the people of God. MCM contributors refer to the Spirit's power, the Spirit's gifts, the Spirit's revelation, the Spirit's work in the world, and the Spirit's leading into mission, but seldom acknowledge the Spirit's ongoing transformative presence with the people of God.[10]

Recognizing the Holy Spirit in this way—as the third person of the Trinity, who relates with God's people—is essential for understanding how missional worship participates in cultivating an evangelistic character among God's people. Two challenges encountered in creating a missional approach to worship illustrate this perspective.

Both of these challenges become clear when taking a closer look at Schattauer's analysis of the relationship between worship and mission. As explained in the literature review, he suggests that an "inside-and-out" understanding of this relationship depicts worship and mission in separate

---

8. Huckins, *Thin Places*, 36–37.
9. Helland and Hjalmarson, *Missional Spirituality*, 123.
10. One of the few exceptions within the MCM is Hirsch and Hirsch, who urge their readers to experience the Holy Spirit, though they do so without direct connections to communal worship settings (*Untamed*, 82–103). Rather surprisingly given their topic, Helland and Hjalmarson, *Missional Spirituality*, dedicate very little space to talk directly about the person of the Holy Spirit or the relationship the Spirit has with God's people, despite a strong emphasis on spiritual disciplines within their project.

spheres as distinct activities of the church. He also describes an "outside-in" approach, which subsumes the activities of worship for the purposes of mission. An additional approach, not included in Schattauer's description, could be an "outside-for-inside" approach, wherein mission exists for the sake of gaining more worship participants. In the end, Schattauer recommends an "inside-out" approach within which worship retains its internal integrity while its very occurrence is an expression of God's mission. The relationship between worship and mission is not marked by instrumentality or isolation.

The first challenge is that Schattauer's recommendation makes sense in theory, but has been much more difficult to realize in practice. The MCM has displayed tendencies toward both the isolation of worship and mission and the instrumentality of worship for mission. Van Gelder, for example, separates worship and mission by declaring worship to be central to the MCM without offering direction as to how a worship gathering participates in the *missio trinitatis*.[11] Frost displays an instrumental approach to the relationship by insisting that communal worship has no value if it cannot produce people who treat their neighbours better than the rest of the world.[12] Moreover, even those who would agree with Schattauer's inside-out approach show a tendency to slide toward an instrumental relationship of worship serving mission. For example, Dawn, who emphasizes that God ought to be the "Infinite center of worship," assesses worship based on the outcomes of how congregations conduct their worship gatherings with the goal of practicing the language of faith in worship "until we know the truth so well that we can go out to the world around us and invite it to participate with us in the reign of God."[13] While affirming Schattauer's desire for inside-out worship, the implementation of his vision appears to be quite challenging.

This difficulty with moving from theory into practice exposes a second and more critical challenge in proposing a missional approach to worship. A closer look at Schattauer's model reveals that the Holy Spirit is not included in the conversation about how worship and mission relate with each other or in how an inside-out approach leads to the transformation of God's people for their participation in God's mission.[14] The challenge for this conversation is that the MCM has largely neglected the Holy Spirit and the Spirit's presence with the people of God in worship; and in doing so the MCM has accepted a view of worship within which God's people are

---

11. Van Gelder, *Essence of the Church*, 151–52.
12. Frost, *Exiles*, 287.
13. Dawn, "Worship to Form a Missional Community," 148–50.
14. Schattauer, "Liturgical Assembly as Locus of Mission," 4–13.

responsible for constructing their own transformation, either by abandoning worship as ineffective or by adjusting the content, style, and format of their worship gatherings in an attempt to produce the desired capacity to love their neighbours.

Within this viewpoint, MCM participants have frequently considered Christendom worship approaches as detrimental to the missional identity of God's people, concluding that worship has failed to produce people who love God or their neighbors. Citing a disproportionate relationship between worship-related resources and mission engagement within Christendom, some in the MCM appear to have concluded that worship does not work,[15] with at least one author labelling the attention to institutional worship as "unbiblical."[16] Fitch summarizes this point of view, noting the perception that there has been "little correlation between what constitutes a good worshipper and the consistent living of the Christian life."[17]

A thorough response to this perspective would include an engagement with MCM treatments of Christendom—a topic that is worthy of a separate research project.[18] For instance, how might localized community engagement through convents and monasteries during Christendom relate to the MCM's more recent attention to parish as a model of incarnational ministry? Or, how do Bucer's and Calvin's emphases on caring for the poor in the 1500s relate to the MCM's depiction of Christendom as insular?[19] These brief examples highlight a tendency within the MCM to dismiss the whole of Christendom as a monolithic departure from biblical ecclesiology—a conclusion that calls for further, more nuanced assessment than the MCM has thus far provided.[20] While not directly engaging MCM critiques of Christendom, this project is concerned by approaches to worship that neglect the Holy Spirit's involvement, thereby rooting the transformation of God's people within their own capacity to construct and conduct communal worship.

---

15. Kreider and Kreider, *Worship and Mission after Christendom*, 23–25; Hirsch, *Forgotten Ways*, 43–44; Breen, *Building a Discipling Culture*, 12; and Huckins, *Thin Places*, 71–73.

16. Frost, *Exiles*, 275–77.

17. Fitch, *Great Giveaway*, 95–96.

18. While beyond the scope of this project, such research could bend into sociological, ethnic, and economic values as well as what kinds of practices would have been contextually appropriate within Christendom contexts.

19. See Bucer, *Instruction in Christian Love*; and Calvin, *Institutes of the Christian Religion*, III.vii.6.

20. MCM dialogue with Leithart, *Defending Constantine*, could provide a beneficial starting place for nuancing the MCM assessment of Christendom.

These approaches are problematic because they assume that when a person attends worship they should exit worship with a distinct ethical behavior and responsiveness to the world. In other words, worship services are expected to function as assembly lines that manufacture a particular type of person as their desired product. In this case, a conclusion that worship does not work measures worship's value by whether or not that worship produces people who are effective at loving others.[21] Frost's critique of Dawn's hope for liturgical formation is representative of this perspective:

> It is Dawn's assumption that when a community of believers, churching together, meets to worship, they are formed more deeply into the people of God. And when this happens, they are more likely to impact their neighborhood by the quality of their lifestyles and relationships. She believes that good worship forms a people whose way of life is a warrant for belief. I'd like to think so, but I'm not convinced. I cannot buy the assumption that the corporate encounter with God that the worship service provides forms people to be more like God and therefore to be more genuinely a missional community. I think that it is debunked by the thousands of church services from which Christians emerge to carry on with their lives as thoughtlessly and as selfishly as any nonbeliever.[22]

For Frost, worship does not work because thousands of worship services have had the outcome of Christians living "as thoughtlessly and selfishly as any nonbeliever." Such a conclusion reveals an assembly line view of worship that has no room to account for or respond to the presence and transforming activity of the Holy Spirit in the midst of the worship gathering.

One potential avenue for considering a missional approach to worship that is rooted in the person and work of the Holy Spirit is the relationship between orthodoxy, orthopraxy, and orthopathy. Within an assembly line view of worship, a transactional relationship exists between orthodoxy (understood as right doxology and doctrine) and orthopraxy (understood as right living). God's people enter worship to receive instruction regarding the proper understanding of who God is, who they are, what condition the world is in, and how God intends to fix it (orthodoxy).[23] After responding to this declaration of reality through prayers and songs, and with offerings inside of the worship gathering, the people of God are sent out to live in accordance with this described reality in relationship to their spouses,

---

21. Schattauer, "Liturgical Assembly as Locus of Mission," 2–3.
22. Frost, *Exiles*, 287.
23. See Walsh and Middleton, *The Transforming Vision*, 35.

children, neighbors, government, etc. (orthopraxy). The assumption in this model is that the orthodoxy imparted in worship must lead to an engaged orthopraxy outside of worship.

Yet this assembly line approach to worship completely overlooks orthopathy (right affections). Woodbridge describes the importance of including orthopathy in an understanding of formation: "We need not only right beliefs and practices, we need a right heart; we need not only to think and do what is faithful, we need to be faithful persons."[24] Orthopathy, therefore, serves as the locus of relational experience: one's desires, motives, orientation, affections, and movement in relationship to God and others. In other words, as Woodbridge writes, "orthopathy does not primarily refer to a warm heart, but to a heart formed, governed and motivated by love."[25] This perspective is not suggesting that orthopathy is the missing ingredient in an assembly line approach to worship, as if incorporating orthopathy with orthodoxy and orthopraxy will suddenly allow the church to produce transformed lives. Rather, the absence of attention to the heart of God's people—to their motivations and desires—is symptomatic of the overall neglect of the Holy Spirit, and the Spirit's transformative presence, within communal worship.

While a variety of ways could facilitate recognition of the connection between orthopathy and the Holy Spirit, this relationship is visible by stringing together a number of Calvin's insights regarding the Holy Spirit from his *Institutes of the Christian Religion*. Calvin contends that the Holy Spirit creates in God's people a longing for that which is good,[26] uniting them to Christ so they can enjoy his benefits.[27] Moreover, by arousing faith within God's people,[28] illuminating their minds and hearts so they can comprehend scripture as God's word,[29] the Holy Spirit assures God's people of their salvation,[30] which empowers them to deny themselves in love for their neighbors.[31] Furthermore, the Spirit calls the people of God to live in freedom, making them capable of joyfully serving God,[32] therein leading God's

---

24. Woodbridge, "Living Theologically."
25. Ibid.
26. Calvin, *Institutes*, II.ii.27.
27. Ibid., III.i.
28. Ibid., III.i.4.
29. Ibid., III.ii.33–34.
30. Ibid., III.ii.38–39.
31. Ibid., III.vii.
32. Ibid., III.xix.2, 5.

people to trust God in prayer.³³ Uniting God's people with each other,³⁴ the Spirit binds them together as the communion of saints across time and culture,³⁵ administering grace to them through the sacraments,³⁶ equipping them to live in righteousness with each other, and in generosity toward all who bear the image of God and for the benefit of creation, through both the church and the civic government.³⁷ Additionally, Calvin remarks that even the desire to seek God and to pray is evidence of the Spirit's regenerative work in a person,³⁸ that the Spirit is the source of faith,³⁹ and that the Spirit makes God's word efficacious in the lives of God's people.⁴⁰ From Calvin's perspective, the Holy Spirit, who is present with and working in God's people in worship, transforms their affections (orthopathy) so that they joyfully choose to serve God and others (orthpraxis) in response to God's word (orthodoxy). In other words, God the Spirit transforms not simply the minds and behaviors of God's people, but their hearts and souls as well.

Therefore, in agreement with Calvin, and counter to an assembly line understanding of worship, the missional approach to worship proposed in this project is rooted in dependency on the person of the Holy Spirit and will flourish only because of the transformative presence of the Spirit among God's people. Without this reliance on the Holy Spirit, worship will fall into a works-righteousness trap, limited by the imagination of an assembly line, where God's people are bound to work harder at perfecting their worship in order to become the type of people they think God wants them to be. Thus, this project contends that missional worship participates in cultivating an environment that encourages God's people to be attentive to the Holy Spirit's transformative presence among them.

Smith's Reflections on the Formative Capacity of Christian Worship

As a bridge between reflecting on the Holy Spirit's transformative presence within worship and the proposal for a missional approach to worship, this section attends to James K. A. Smith's argument for the formative capacity

33. Ibid., III.xx.
34. Ibid., IV.i.3.
35. Ibid., IV.vii.
36. Ibid., IV.xiv.
37. Ibid., IV.xx.
38. Ibid., II.ii.27.
39. Ibid., III.i.4.
40. Ibid., III.ii.33.

of worship in his *Desiring the Kingdom*.[41] Admittedly, Smith is not the only one to advance such considerations;[42] yet, his insights provide a theological and philosophical framework around which a missional approach to worship, especially regarding the role of worship in cultivating an evangelistic character among God's people, can gain clarity and coherence. Moreover, Smith's attention to the Holy Spirit throughout his project heeds Aune's caution against "overromanticizing" a missional liturgy as a panacea for the ills of the church.[43]

In *Desiring the Kingdom*, Smith sets out to "raise the stakes of Christian education, which will also mean raising the stakes of Christian worship," by cultivating a deeper appreciation for "what's at stake in both—nothing less than the formation of radical disciples who desire the kingdom of God."[44] By attempting to articulate "the shape of a Christian 'social imaginary' as it is embedded in the practices of Christian worship,"[45] Smith argues that humans "are lovers before and above all else, and that the people of God is a community marked by a love and desire for the kingdom of God."[46]

Demonstrating how liturgies "shape and constitute our identities by forming our most fundamental desires and our most basic attunement to the world," Smith emphasizes throughout the book that "liturgies make us certain kinds of people, and what defines us is what we *love*."[47] He develops this argument on the basis of a liturgical anthropology contrasted against what he perceives to be deficient understandings of humanity as either thinking or believing beings.[48] Smith offers that humans are first and foremost lovers—ones who are shaped by affective, and therefore precognitive, desires.[49] Smith writes:

---

41. I am aware of critiques regarding Smith's project, including Turley, who, while affirming Smith's project, contends that Smith did not allow ritual meaning to stand on its own, but validated ritual meaning with appeals to intellectualism ("Practicing the Kingdom," 131–42). See also Galbreath, who suggests Smith's analysis lacks attention to the cultural development of worship practices and to power dynamics involved with determining who shapes liturgies ("Desiring the Kingdom," 432).

42. For example, Saliers, "Liturgy and Ethics," 173–89; Schmemann, *For the Life of the World*; and Chan, *Liturgical Theology*.

43. Aune, "Ritual Practice," 155.

44. Smith, *Desiring the Kingdom*, 19.

45. Ibid., 11. Smith readily attributes the impetus for his reflections on the formative capacity of Christian worship to Taylor, *Modern Social Imaginaries*.

46. Smith, *Desiring the Kingdom*, 15.

47. Ibid., 25.

48. Ibid., 40–46.

49. Ibid., 53.

we are not primarily *homo rationale* or *homo faber* or *homo economicus*; we are not even generally *homo religiosis*. We are more concretely *homo liturgicus*; humans are those animals that are religious animals not because we are primarily believing animals but because we are liturgical animals—embodied, practicing creatures whose love/desire is aimed at something ultimate.[50]

Moving from this anthropology toward worship, Smith offers a gloss on the *lex orandi–lex credendi* axiom, arguing that "we pray *before* we believe, we worship before we know—or rather, we worship *in order to* know."[51] Looking to broad cultural liturgies, Smith explains how liturgies form people to inhabit the world in certain ways. As such, asking a question about "what kind of person is this habit or practice trying to produce, and to what end is such practice aimed" becomes vitally important.[52] Moving from cultural liturgies toward Christian worship, Smith contends that in worship God's people open themselves up to the Spirit's transformative power.[53] Smith then provides an extended overview of affectual dimensions present within the liturgy, briefly addressing the need for personal disciplines and a daily experience of community with other Christians.[54] Returning to his consideration of Christian education, Smith concludes that a Christian education is foundationally an ecclesial education because its primary calling is the formation of disciples and not merely the impartation of information.[55]

For this project, Smith's chapters on the formation of desire through Christian worship and particular practices within the liturgy are the most relevant.[56] In considering the formative character of the liturgy, Smith provides a more established means of engaging the missional church's worship-related lacunae than what is currently accessible within MCM conversations related to worship and forming an evangelistic character.

Relying on Charles Taylor's work with social imaginaries, Smith suggests that "Christianity is a unique social imaginary that 'inhabits' and emerges from the matrix of preaching and prayer. The rhythms and rituals of Christian worship are not the 'expression of' a Christian worldview, but are themselves an 'understanding' implicit in practice."[57] This perspective

50. Ibid., 40.
51. Ibid., 34.
52. Ibid., 83.
53. Ibid., 138.
54. Ibid., 208–14.
55. Ibid., 215–30.
56. Ibid., 133–214.
57. Ibid., 69.

shapes Smith's approach to the scriptures, seeing them "as a means of grace, as a conduit of the Spirit's transformative power, as part of a pedagogy of desire," rather than through the lens of Hodges' view that scripture is merely a "storehouse of facts."[58] Contending that Christian worship preceded "the formation of the biblical canon," he argues that participating in Christian worship comes before Christian doctrine and worldview can be formed.[59] Affirming the materiality of creation—"it is charged with the presence and glory of God"[60]—he further argues that the Christian liturgy and the sacraments in particular have a sacramental intensity not found elsewhere. "The Spirit's presence is intensified" through the rituals of the sacraments and the liturgy, so that "Christian worship is nothing less than an invitation to participate in the life of the Triune God."[61]

Throughout his project, Smith frequently contrasts a Christian liturgy with "secular liturgies that are fixated on the novel and the new," contending that "Christian worship constitutes us as a people of memory."[62] Moreover, he writes: "We are constituted as a people who live between times, remembering and hoping at the same time. Each week this between-ness is performed in the Eucharist, which both invites us to 'Do this in remembrance of me' and by doing so to 'proclaim the Lord's death until he comes.'"[63] In such a way, "The temporality of Christian worship—macrocosmically expressed in the Christian year, microcosmically expressed in particular elements each Sunday—trains our imagination to be eschatological, looking forward *not* to the end of the world but to 'the end of the world *as we know it*.'"[64] Yet as Smith notes, the transformative power of such an experience of Christian worship rests not in the ritual elements themselves. Rather, "the church's worship is a uniquely intense site of the Spirit's transformative presence" because these practices "bring us face to face with the living God."[65]

Smith's insights here assist this conversation in three ways. First, Smith affirms that the Holy Spirit is the one transforming the people of God. Though practices engaged in Christian worship might be powerful conduits through which God's people encounter the Holy Spirit, the practices

---

58. Ibid., 135.

59. Ibid., 136. This perspective expresses Smith's conviction that *lex orandi* leads into *lex credendi*.

60. Ibid., 143.

61. Ibid., 144–50.

62. Ibid., 191.

63. Ibid., 158. This theme will be addressed again in chapters 5 and 6.

64. Ibid., 158.

65. Ibid., 150.

themselves are not what transforms God's people. The Spirit transforms God's people. Second, Smith contends that practices are embodied, engaging the material reality of God's people in the process of them becoming attuned with the Spirit's transformative presence. In this way, liturgical practices reveal God's presence among the people of God and throughout creation. Third, Smith points to how gathered worship, while necessary, is insufficient on its own as a location for fully transforming God's people. The Holy Spirit's transformative presence leads God's people from worship into personal and communal discipleship practices throughout the week.

Proposing a Missional Approach to Worship

While some MCM participants have offered insights that resonate with Smith,[66] few have attempted to work out their vision for worship with regard to the particular movements of a worship gathering in a parallel manner to Smith's efforts in *Desiring the Kingdom*.[67] Though not attempting as ambitious of an undertaking as Smith's, this section proposes a missional approach to worship. Encouraging attention to the transformative presence of the Holy Spirit and drawing from Smith's reflections on the formative capacity of worship, the proposal briefly outlines priorities for missional worship and then provides an example of what a missional approach to worship could look like *in situ*.

Distinctive Priorities of Missional Worship

This proposal briefly identifies four distinctive priorities for a missional approach to worship. These priorities relate to several of the emphases noted in the opening description of the MCM and take into consideration some of the perspectives on the formation of an evangelistic character as encountered in the literature review.

---

66. For example, Huckins, *Thin Places*, 154; and Fitch, *Great Giveaway*, 97.

67. Kreider and Kreider, *Worship and Mission After Christendom*, 147–74, comes the closest to engaging the liturgy in a manner similar to Smith, *Desiring the Kingdom*, 155–207.

Missional Worship Immerses God's People in the "Grand Narrative" of God's Mission

The MCM argues that the story of God's mission forms the foundational reality within which the church, and indeed all of creation, lives.[68] Congruent with this reality, missional worship immerses God's people within the grand narrative of God's mission. In the context of the literature review, particularly with Goheen and Wright, this immersion in the *missio trinitatis* involved three components: ongoing rehearsal of the story, submission to the story's authority, and a lived response to the story.

The purpose of immersing God's people within the narrative of God's mission is so that the people of God might be attentive to how the triune God, revealed in scripture, is the primary actor not only in the worship gathering but also in the whole world, across the entire expanse of time. To this end, Goheen contends that missional worship "needs to tell the true story of the world" in such a way that God's people are invited "to come live in the real world it narrates."[69] Van Gelder sees this connection as pivotal for the formation of the church's identity:

> A trinitarian understanding shifts the focus such that the Spirit-led missional church participates in God's mission in the world. In doing so, it becomes a *sign* that God's redemption is now present in the world, a *foretaste* of what that redemption is like, and an *instrument* to carry that message into every local context and to the ends of the earth.[70]

As God's people respond to this comprehensive redemptive story, they are called to abandon other narratives that proclaim alternative visions of reality.[71] Turning from these competing narratives, God's people begin to yearn for the future promised within the story of God's mission.[72] Fitch clarifies how the desire for this still-to-come future is rooted in worship practices that immerse God's people within the narrative of God's mission:

> We unconsciously hunger for an alive body of Christ we can be immersed into, an encultured organism that orders our desires,

---

68. Wright, *Mission of God*, 43–44.

69. Goheen, "Nourishing Our Missional Identity," 47–48. Also Webber, *Ancient-Future Worship*, 44.

70. Van Gelder, *Ministry of the Missional Church*, 18–19. Emphasis original.

71. See Huckins, *Thin Places*, 67–68; and Dawn, "Worship to Form a Missional Community," 141. Also Roxburgh, *Missional*, 80–82; Dawn, "Reaching Out without Dumbing Down," 278; Hirsch, *Forgotten Ways*, 97–100; and Frost, *Road to Missional*, 70–72.

72. Bartholomew and Goheen, *Drama of Scripture*, 26.

orients our vision, and livens our words through art, symbol, prayers, mutual exchanges, participatory rituals, readings of the Word, and Eucharist every Sunday morning. Only through immersion can our 'selves' be ordered doxologically so as to experience God as he is and live the Christian life in the world.[73]

In ways like these, missional worship immerses God's people within the *missio trinitatis* so that the desired character of God's people becomes conceivable and accessible.[74] While the full story of God's mission might not be recalled in every worship gathering, by continually immersing God's people within this narrative, missional worship cultivates an environment in which the Spirit, as the primary actor within worship and throughout creation, transforms the people of God.

Missional Worship Orients God's People through Liturgical Rhythms of Remembering and Anticipating[75]

The second distinctive priority of missional worship is evident in Webber's declaration that "in worship we remember God's story in the past and anticipate God's story in the future."[76] Though possible to interpret such actions as static events, missional worship perceives liturgical remembering (*anamnesis*) and anticipating (*prolepsis*) as dynamic patterns that orient God's people toward a particular way of living.[77] Webber explains further:

> When worship remembers the past, it praises God for God's work in history whereby he has already begun the restoration of the world. When worship anticipates the future, it looks for the culmination of all God's works in the complete transformation of the world, the consummation of God's work in Jesus Christ by

---

73. Fitch, *Great Giveaway*, 105.

74. Though not referenced in missional literature related to worship, this line of reasoning seems to resonate with—and would certainly benefit from direct engagement with—conversations surrounding Berger's plausibility structures and Taylor's social imaginaries. Sire, *Naming the Elephant*; and Smith, *Desiring the Kingdom*, both of which are included as external sources impacting this project, could serve as beneficial entry points into these broader conversations regarding worship and evangelism in the MCM.

75. I have been utilizing the language of *remembering and anticipating* since 2006 during my ThM program. See Schoon, "Unveiling God's Face," 52–83. I later encountered this concept in Webber, *Ancient-Future Worship*, 41–66, and have continued to discover other examples among liturgical theologians who reflect on the importance of the anamnetic and proleptic aspects of communal worship.

76. Webber, *Ancient-Future Worship*, 23.

77. Kreider and Kreider, *Worship and Mission after Christendom*, 90.

the power of the Spirit, whereby worship witnesses to the victory of Christ over all the powers and principalities and proclaims he now rules over all creation as the Lord of the universe.[78]

At times, the anamnetic rhythm is viewed against the MCM's perception that remembering in Christendom worship merely meant preserving traditional forms as idyllic expressions of how worship should be done.[79] Yet, contrary to this perceived entrenchment in nostalgia, a missional approach to worship seeks to remember God's past deeds as setting a paradigmatic trajectory, rather than a static location, for moving toward a promised future. Moreover, missional worship recognizes that this promised future has not yet been realized; and, therefore, God's people need the proleptic dimension of worship to orient God's people with regard to how they are to live today. As Kreider and Kreider contend, "God's promises beckon us to the future," neither by avoiding nor attempting to control the future, but by calling God's people to live in conformity with how the grand narrative describes that future.[80] In this regard, Bartholomew and Goheen point out that the biblical story "culminates in the restoration of the entire creation to its original goodness. The comprehensive scope of creation, sin, and redemption is evident throughout the biblical story and is central to a faithful biblical worldview."[81] This anticipated comprehensive restoration in the culmination of the biblical narrative provides a baseline with which God's people are to align the patterns of their daily living in the present.

As such, liturgical *remembering* calls God's people to live in the present as both a visible response to and a faithful continuation of the story of God's engagement in the world, particularly through Jesus Christ. Likewise, liturgical *anticipating* beckons God's people, through the Spirit, to become a continually more tangible embodiment of the flourishing life that one day will characterize all of creation. Liturgically speaking, then, within missional worship *remembering* is never a merely static commemoration of past historical events and *anticipating* is substantively more than proclaiming a naïve idolization of a utopic future. With both rhythms working together, missional worship consistently orients God's people toward how they will engage their present circumstances in response to what God has already done and what God has promised yet to do.

---

78. Webber, *Ancient-Future Worship*, 61.
79. Frost, *Exiles*, 9, who relies on Brueggemann, *Cadences of Home*, 11.
80. Kreider and Kreider, *Worship and Mission after Christendom*, 87.
81. Bartholomew and Goheen, *Drama of Scripture*, 12.

Missional Worship Locates God's People in Their Respective Heres and Nows

The third distinctive priority is that missional worship locates God's people within their respective heres and nows. This priority is intimately connected with—and could even be said to flow out of—the first two priorities. Webber describes the connection this way: "here is what biblical worship does: It remembers God's work in the past, anticipates God's rule over all creation, and actualizes both past and future in the present to transform persons, communities, and the world."[82] Essentially, this priority provokes a response to the question: Since we live inside of the still-unfolding narrative of God's mission, how will we live right here, right now?

Moreover, the priority to locate God's people within their particular contexts is a direct application of the MCM emphasis on incarnational mission dynamically expressed in locally contextualized ministry, as described in the first chapter. Within worship, this dynamic contextualization means that local circumstances shape prayers, testimonies, responses to scripture, and the experience of the sacraments, as well as the greetings and blessings that gather people into and send people from communal worship. In this regard, Hirsch and Hirsch state succinctly that worship "must involve and include all elements of life and spirituality, not just religious practices—as if politics, economics, sexuality, and such are somehow excluded from God's insistence of wholeness before him."[83] Frost adds to this perspective, contending that missional worship also "involves a serious incarnational attempt to enter, know, love, and enjoy the culture that you have been sent into."[84] In other words, missional worship locates God's people within their respective circumstances in order that they might experience God's presence with them and participate with God in extending God's presence through them. As such, a missional approach to worship engages a diversity of participants and cultural expressions that reflect the particularities of those within the community, the cultural influences impacting those gathered as well as those in the surrounding communities, and other peculiarities of their present circumstances. Being located is not only about experiencing God's presence but also about becoming God's presence with and among their neighbors.

---

82. Webber, *Ancient-Future Worship*, 43.
83. Hirsch and Hirsch, *Untamed*, 76.
84. Frost, *Exiles*, 295.

Missional Worship Sends God's People as Participants within the Missio Trinitatis

Admittedly, the MCM has wrestled with how to tangibly enact this priority on missional worship sending God's people as participants within the *missio trinitatis*. Guder's *Missional Church* states bluntly: "We need to learn how worship concretely calls and sends us into Christ's service, and how it is a facet of our mission itself."[85] In similar fashion, Goheen remarks that through worship "we must be continually directed to the unbelieving world as the ultimate horizon of our calling."[86] Hammond and Cronshaw also agree, commenting that "God's call on our lives is more than attending a Sunday show and listening to someone chat. God's call is to serve God in the world. We need the gathering of church to empower us for that."[87]

Rather than simply a distinct moment of commissioning, a call to holy living, or charge to the congregation, missional worship returns frequently to three themes that send God's people as participants within the *missio trinitatis*. These motifs intertwine with each other—in other words, they are in no way mutually exclusive—to express recognizable patterns within the practice of missional worship.

One sending theme, *blessed to be a blessing*, recognizes how God has blessed the people of God so that they might become a blessing to others. Guder, in one of the earliest statements about the need for a missional approach to worship, points to this theme.

> We meet the missionary God who is shaping God's people for their vocation, namely, to be a blessing to the nations. For this to happen, the people constantly receive the blessing that makes them a blessing. The people hear the word of forgiveness, experience their own continuing healing, and find the comfort that they need in order to function as Christ's witnesses.[88]

In developing this theme, the MCM perceives God's blessing of Abraham in Genesis 12:1–3 as paradigmatic for how God's people are called by God in order to be sent in God's mission. Wright contends that "the blessing of Abraham becomes self-replicating. Those who are blessed are called to be a blessing beyond themselves—and this is one feature that makes it so profoundly missional. For if we see ourselves as those who have entered in the blessing of Abraham through faith in Christ, then the

---

85. Guder, *Missional Church*, 242.
86. Goheen, "Nourishing Our Missional Identity," 49.
87. Hammond and Cronshaw, *Sentness*, 178.
88. Guder, *Missional Church*, 242.

Abrahamic commission becomes ours also—'be a blessing.'"[89] Remembering that God is the primary actor within worship and that the church's very identity is as those who are sent, this thematic emphasis treats the worship gathering as a microcosm of God's mission. God, who is at work reconciling and restoring all of creation, gathers a people that they might be reconciled, restored, and sent as participants within God's ongoing mission to reconcile and restore creation.

The theme of *lament and celebration*[90] forms the second motif connected with the sending priority in missional worship. As God's people are immersed within the unfolding of God's mission in their particular contexts, missional worship forms them to respond in one of two ways. When they encounter aspects in which their daily realities—whether in themselves, the people around them, creation, or the structures and circumstances they are experiencing—that do not cohere with the reality of God's mission, God's people are ushered into a posture of lament. This lament includes sorrow and repentance over sin, as well as intercession in imitation of the Spirit and Jesus, both of whom scripture depicts as interceding with the Father (Romans 8:26, 34). At the same time, as God's people witness ways in which their own lives, the people around them, the societal structures, and even creation itself align with the unfolding of God's mission, missional worship calls them to celebrate. In this way, missional worship encourages God's people to be attentive to how they and the world around them are (or are not) responding to the presence of the Holy Spirit. As Fitch helpfully points out, the emphasis on lament and celebration is not for the sake of emotional catharsis. Rather, they empower God's people to participate with the Spirit in God's mission as it continues to unfold in contexts that both resist and embrace the good news of Jesus Christ in frequently unexpected ways.[91]

Finally, the third common theme emerging within the sending priority of missional worship is that there are always personal and communal elements within worship.[92] Guder frames the communal aspect in contrast to a postmodern perception of worship "as the private, internal, and often arcane activity of religionists who retreat from the world to practice their mystical rites." As God's public assembly, "the walls and windows of churches need to become transparent."[93] Huckins presses this idea further, contending:

89. Wright, *Mission of God's People*, 67–68.

90. I explored these themes of lament and celebration in the closing plenary address, "Lamenting and Celebrating in the Still Unfolding Story," at the 2014 Edifide Educators Convention.

91. Fitch, *Great Giveaway*, 114.

92. Schattauer, "Liturgical Assembly as Locus of Mission," 11.

93. Guder, *Missional Church*, 243.

it is important to differentiate between being a sent person and a sent people. God's mission wasn't designed to advance with a set of sent individuals. It was designed to advance through a faithful people living as advocates of the missio Dei. This is why we can't live as a sent people alone. It just doesn't work and isn't sustainable. It runs counter to our design and to the ultimate goal of God's redemption project to restore communion with him, his people, and the whole cosmos.[94]

Thus, a missional approach to worship offers a counternarrative to what the MCM has perceived to be an overindividualized gospel within the North American church.

Yet missional worship also insists that personal engagement within God's mission and within worship is necessary for everyone among God's people.[95] Dawn calls for a wide diversity of musical expressions within worship instead of conformity to a particular musical style, so as "not to divide the community according to the false idolatry of personal taste in musical style,"[96] but to make room for all to participate. This attention to how each person can contribute to worship also recognizes the need for polycentric leadership advocated by Woodward[97] and Guder's insistence that a missional identity rooted in Sabbath practices calls for the inclusion of all of God's people, not just professional clergy, in leading the church.[98] The Spirit did not gift only one or two credentialed people, but has given gifts to everyone within the body of Christ in order that the whole body might grow into the fullness of Christ.[99] Worship that is personal and communal encourages the full participation of all of God's people by engaging the gifts entrusted to them through the Spirit for the continued unfolding of God's mission.

94. Huckins, *Thin Places*, 135.

95. Frost, "Exiles at the Altar," 291. While agreeing with his basic point, I disagree with the "anything-goes" approach that Frost later advocates. Frost extends this perspective to the point of "allowing ordinary Christians to mix and match practices from a variety of traditions and eras" ("Exiles at the Altar," 297). By advocating for this "mix-and-match" selection of practices, Frost has opened the door to dismiss the original cultural contexts of worship practices on utilitarian grounds of what appeals to whomever is planning a particular worship gathering. In doing so, Frost ignores the locational rootedness that shapes much of the MCM and imitates in part the cultural appropriations associated with colonialism for which Christendom has been frequently criticized.

96. Dawn, "Worship to Form a Missional Community," 142.

97. Woodward, *Creating a Missional Culture*, 60.

98. Guder, "Theological Significance of the Lord's Day," 116.

99. Ephesians 4:7–16.

Applying Missional Worship Priorities to a Local Worship Gathering

A beneficial question in response to these priorities is: So what does this missional approach to worship look like in the context of a worship gathering? Recognizing that the MCM places a high emphasis on dynamic, locally contextualized ministry, there are no preconstructed templates for something that could be called a "missional order of worship." Moreover, a missional approach to worship is intended to be applicable to a variety of worship settings, stretching across denominational, ethnic, and other cultural contexts. Rather than advocate for one *ordo* to be preferred over others because it is more "missional" in its structure, a missional approach to worship is concerned with finding ways to recognize and express the priorities of missional worship within each particular worship gathering. Therefore, rather than construct a universalizing order of worship to be applied to all missional churches, this project offers an example of how these missional priorities have been expressed within one worship gathering of a particular congregation, with the hope that such an illustration will encourage imagination of how these priorities can live within other worship contexts.

The annotated order of worship that follows is offered as a particularly situated worship gathering from First Hamilton Christian Reformed Church, an urban congregation in the Durand and Kirkendall neighbourhoods within Hamilton, Ontario. I have been involved with this congregation since 2009 and have served as senior pastor since 2011. Our congregation has deliberately focused on being a missional church for the past seventeen years, starting when Michael Goheen served as the preaching pastor in 1998.

To provide a few other contextual markers, our church started in 1929 as a Dutch immigrant congregation. Worship services and official church business were conducted in the Dutch language until the mid-1940s. Serving as the "mother church" for many post-World War II Dutch immigrants, the congregation swelled to around a thousand members in the 1950s and participated in launching several church plants from then through the 1970s. In the 1980s and early 1990s the congregation's membership aged and declined rapidly, prompting conversations about whether to close the doors, buy property south of town, or commit to staying in the community. In the mid-1990s, the congregation chose to stay and become a "neighbourhood church," though most admitted they did not know what that would look like. Along with our denominational identity, we are covenant members of TrueCity Hamilton, a movement of churches participating in God's mission together for the good of the city.[100] We currently have just over 260 adult members, with approximately another 30 adult adherents. There are presently 115 children under the age of 18 in our congregation.

The particular order of worship included below comes from November 22, 2015. In that worship gathering we celebrated the Lord's Supper, which we typically do once a month. That particular Sunday concluded a six-week sermon series during which we journeyed through Ephesians 1–3. We also recognized that day as "Christ the King Sunday" according to the liturgical calendar. The worship bulletin for the morning contained the following introduction:

Christ the King Sunday

Welcome to worship at First Hamilton CRC. Whether you are here for the first time today or if you have been engaged with this community for more than 50 years, we are delighted to join with you in responding to God's grace this morning as we worship together. Following the worship service, all of us are invited to stay around for a cup of coffee and conversation in the gathering room, just outside of the sanctuary.

During October and November, we have been journeying through a six-week series Ephesians 1–3, called *God's Great Plan*. (We'll pick up Ephesians 4–6 in January.) These messages highlight God's lavish grace in the presence of powers and principalities that stand opposed to God and the life God calls us to. This morning we conclude our series, looking at Ephesians 3:14–21: "That Christ May Dwell in Your Hearts." As part of our worship this morning, we will celebrate the Lord's Supper together.

Though not part of the liturgy, we frequently utilize short introductory notes in the bulletin both to extend a hospitable welcome to those who have gathered and to locate some of the context related to the worship gathering.

The liturgy that morning consisted of a prelude and six movements. In order, these movements are titled: *God Gathers His People*;[101] *God Calls Us to Confess Our Sins and Receive His Forgiveness*; *God Invites Us to Respond*

---

100. http://truecityhamilton.ca.

101. Our denomination mostly utilizes male personal pronouns when referring to God. While there has been some movement toward gender inclusivity, particularly through an increased use of newer Bible translations, gender-specific pronouns in reference to God are still part of the cultural context.

with *Our Offerings*; *God Speaks to Us through His Word*; *God Welcomes Us to His Table*; and *God Sends Us Out by His Grace*. As a means of reminding ourselves that God is the primary actor within worship, each of these movements is structured with God as the subject. While this particular gathering did not have a baptism within it, when baptisms occur the title for that movement is typically *God Extends His Covenantal Faithfulness through Baptism*. Additionally, for gatherings that do not celebrate the Lord's Supper, the offerings are typically included immediately prior to God sending out the people.

> Prelude:
> Song: *Lift Up Your Hearts (LUYH)*[102] #538, "Holy, Holy, Holy, Lord God Almighty"
> Welcome and Announcements

Before the worship gathering formally begins a few activities occur that contribute to the worship environment. There are teams of people near the main entrance and in the sanctuary welcoming people to worship, introducing themselves to people they do not recognize, and providing assistance as needed regarding directions to nursery, washrooms, and other spaces within the building. Also, a few elders and deacons from the church gather with the pastor in the prayer room to pray. A different elder or deacon leads this prayer time each week, which can take a variety of formats. Additionally, the music team leads the congregation in a prelude song or two. Most weeks, the chosen song is one that is quite familiar to the congregation and has some thematic connection to the sermon.

After the prelude song, the pastor welcomes everyone to worship and facilitates the announcement time. Typically, the welcome begins with one of two call and response refrains.

> Pastor: The Lord be with you.
> People: And also with you.
> Or
> Pastor: God is good.
> People: All the time.
> Pastor: All the time.
> People: God is good.

These refrains are offered for the purpose of reminding those gathered that they are there in response to God's presence and on account of

---

102. Borger, Tel, and Witvliet, eds., *Lift Up Your Hearts*, is the primary hymnal for the CRCNA.

God's character.[103] A variety of people participate in the announcements. The pastor typically introduces them with a comment like, "Though we are gathered as God's people for worship this morning, we realize that the life of our congregation stretches well beyond this worship time and building. These announcements highlight some of the upcoming opportunities we have to live together as God's people." During these announcements, the pastor or an elder also acknowledge milestones in terms of anniversaries, births or deaths, and significant prayer concerns within the congregation.

> God Gathers His People:
> Call to Worship: Colossians 1:15–20; Philippians 2:5–11; Revelation 1:12–18
> * Song: *LUYH* #224, "Rejoice, the Lord Is King"
> * Prayer
> * Greetings: Revelation 1:4–6
> * Song: *LUYH* #821, "Let All Mortal Flesh Keep Silence"

In recognition of Christ the King Sunday, the worship began that morning with three scripture readings that revealed Jesus Christ's reconciling work, his servant heart, and his majesty. The readings were done by three members of the congregation, who were spread across the front of the stage. On this occasion, we had two women and one man reading, each doing so as if they were a herald bringing good news. The intent of the call to worship is to have scripture, the story of God's mission, be the first words of the formal worship time. The song that follows provides the congregation with an opportunity to add their voices in praise and affirmation of God as the primary actor in the world and among God's gathered people. The pastor offers a prayer petitioning God, through the Spirit, to receive and bless the worship, to form those gathered through scripture, prayer, forgiveness in Jesus, message, and offering, and to send them as God's people to participate in God's mission. The greetings that follow utilize scripture to bless those gathered (typically reminding God's people of God's gifts of grace, mercy, and peace) and then invites them to turn and pass Christ's peace to those around them. In this way, at the beginning of worship God's people practice the pattern of being sent by God to bless others with the blessing that God has extended to them.[104]

---

103. Schattauer writes that the church's purpose in being gathered is "to make present the One in whom all things are at their *end*, and all things are at their *beginning*" ("Liturgical Assembly as Locus of Mission," 11).

104. Hammond and Cronshaw, contend that the gathering reveals and embodies "a dangerous story of sentness" (*Sentness*, 179). Also Cosper, who asserts that such an

The song that concludes this section typical serves to draw attention to God's character or to God's mighty deeds in creating or providing for all that God has made.

> God Calls Us to Confess Our Sins and Receive His Forgiveness:
> Call to Confession:
> Leader: Ephesians 2:1–2
> Scripture: 1 John 1:8—2:2
> Song: *LUYH* #615, "Softly and Tenderly Jesus is Calling"
> Prayer of Confession
> Assurance of Pardon:
> People: Ephesians 2:4–5
> * Our Communal Profession of Faith: Nicene Creed

During this series in Ephesians, the confession time each week began with the pastor reading Ephesians 2:1–2. This passage continues immersing God's people within the *missio trinitatis* both by rehearsing another part of the story and by encouraging God's people to submit to the authority of the story, allowing the story to narrate the reality of their lives. The second scripture reading served as an invitation to a personal confession of sins.[105] The song "Softly and Tenderly Jesus Is Calling" was chosen as a means of preparing the hearts of those gathered for the prayer of confession. The prayer of confession opened with a simple prayer voiced by the pastor, acknowledging that "we frequently create noise in our lives so that we don't hear you calling to us." The pastor then invited the Holy Spirit to reveal to those gathered the ways they have sinned against God, against each other, and against the rest of God's creation. This invitation was followed by a full minute of silent prayer. The prayer ended with the pastor expressing gratitude to God for hearing their prayers of confession and for releasing God's people from their sins. Throughout this series, those gathered responded to the prayer of confession by reading Ephesians 2:4–5 as the assurance of pardon. This text continues to orient God's people through remembering that God has forgiven their sins by grace in Jesus Christ. On this particular week, the congregation responded to the good news of God's forgiveness in Jesus Christ by standing together to communally profess their faith as they read the Nicene Creed together.

---

approach is paradigmatic for Christian living. (*Rhythms of Grace*, 150).

105. Chan, *Liturgical Theology*, 132; and Smith, *Desiring the Kingdom*, 181.

A MISSIONAL APPROACH TO WORSHIP 135

> God Invites Us to Respond with Our Offerings:
> Offerings
> Offertory Prayer
> Children Enter Children's Worship and Sunday School
> Prayer of Thanksgiving and Intercession

One of the deacons introduces the offerings each week. On this occasion, the deacon also announced that the congregation would be participating with several other TrueCity congregations to assemble and distribute Christmas hampers. Members were invited to sign up for times they could personally participate in this communal initiative. The deacon then explained briefly one of the ministries that the offering for the general ministry fund supports and indicated that the second offering plate would serve to support the Ontario Christian Gleaners.[106] Along with inviting the congregation to give generously, the deacon also encouraged people to consider volunteering.

Following a brief offertory prayer, the pastor invited the children to gather at the front. Each week, as the children prepare to enter Children's Worship and Sunday School, they participate in a call and response with the congregation. Often times, these calls and responses are rooted in traditional greetings or affirmations of the church. For this morning, the children declared, "He is risen!," to which the rest of the congregation replied, "He is risen indeed!" The pastor then offered a prayer of thanksgiving for the children and those leading them, asking the Holy Spirit to reveal Jesus Christ to them that they might desire to follow Jesus with their whole hearts.

After the children left the sanctuary, one of the elders led the prayer of thanksgiving and intercession. The prayer moves between lament and celebration, locating the prayer in the local context as the elder specifically names people and situations directly impacting the congregation. Additionally, this weekly prayer always includes requests for God to bless two other congregations: one from a list of local CRCNA congregations and another from among our TrueCity partners or other neighboring congregations. The elder will also typically wrap broader national and global issues of injustice, political and environmental concerns, and notable world events into this prayer.[107]

---

106. See http://ontariogleaners.org. They identify themselves as "an Interdenominational Christian organization that seeks to visibly demonstrate God's love and grace by working with volunteers to collect, process, and make available surplus agricultural produce for the relief of the hungry in overseas nations."

107. Wright argues: "Prayer is participation in that ultimate victory and in the struggle that leads to it. For this is the mission of God, and the mission of God's people

God Speaks to Us through His Word:
Scripture Reading: Ephesians 3:14–21
Leader: This is the word of the Lord.
People: Thanks be to God!
Message: "So that Christ May Dwell in Your Hearts"
Prayer
* Song: *LUYH* #251, "The Church's One Foundation," vs. 1, 2, 4, 5

The focus of this movement is on the preaching of the word. The scripture is read by a different congregation member each week, followed by the declaration, "This is the word of the Lord," to which, the people respond, "Thanks be to God!" The message is typically presented with a narrative style and in line with the four-page method.[108] The emphasis of this particular message was on Paul's intercessory prayer for the Ephesians, expressing God's desire to dwell in the hearts of God's people. Given the images of God as a holy judge and unapproachable that many in the congregation grew up with, the message invited the people to receive the good news of God's immeasurable love for them in Jesus Christ and to believe that God really desires to dwell with them. In this way, the message was bent toward an affective encounter with God. The song of response served as a transitional affirmation from the story of God's love in the message to the celebration of the Lord's Supper. Since children are welcomed to the Table, the congregation waits for them to return from Children's Worship and Sunday School before beginning the Communion litany.

God Welcomes Us to His Table:
Institution
Pastor: The Lord Jesus, on the night he was betrayed, took bread, and when he had given thanks, he broke it and said, "This is my body, which is for you; do this in remembrance of me." In the same way, after supper he took the cup, saying; "This is the new covenant in my blood; do this, whenever you drink it, in remembrance of me."
People: For whenever we eat this bread and drink this cup, we proclaim the Lord's death until he comes.
Teaching

---

is to be coworkers with God in the field that is God's world" (*Mission of God*, 260).

108. Wilson, *Four Pages of the Sermon*.

Pastor: In the beginning, God created all things very good. He filled creation with the capacity and opportunity to mutually flourish in God's presence.

People: However, we refused to do our part in cultivating life within God's creation, choosing instead to take creation's abundance for our own purposes.

Pastor: But God refused to abandon us or his creation to the death and decay we had chosen and instead set out on the long road of restoring us and all of creation to his abundant life.

People: In the midst of the chaos we created, God raised up a people through whom the whole world would be blessed.

Pastor: When they, too, turned away from their role among the nations, grasping God's blessings as their exclusive possessions, God moved in with us in the person of Jesus Christ—the uncreated God became part of God's own creation!

People: In doing so, God revealed his salvation in Jesus Christ and, through his death and resurrection, reconciled us to himself.

Pastor: In this reconciliation, the Spirit is also at work: gathering us together as the people of God, sending us as servants of God's reconciliation among all people, and, equipping us to cultivate life throughout God's creation—in anticipation of Jesus Christ's return and the renewal of all things.

People: This good news is not only for us, but also for our children and for all who are far off from God.

Pastor: Therefore, though undeserving, we receive the bread and cup from the Lord. In doing so, we remember and believe that in Jesus Christ, God has wrapped us into the still-unfolding story of God's redemptive love and has sent us to joyfully extend his covenantal faithfulness throughout the world.

Prayer of Consecration

Pastor: Heavenly Father, show forth among us the presence of your life-giving word and Holy Spirit, to sanctify us and your whole church through this sacrament. Grant that all who share the body and blood of our Savior Jesus Christ may be one in him and may remain faithful in love and hope. As this grain has been gathered from many fields into one loaf and these grapes from many hills into one cup, grant, O Lord, that your whole church may soon be gathered from the ends of the earth into your kingdom. In Jesus Christ, we hope and pray. Amen.

Invitation

Pastor: All those who have been baptized in the name of the one true God—Father, Son, and Holy Spirit—are invited to the table of the Lord. The gifts of God's grace through Jesus Christ for the people of God gathered and sent by the Spirit.

Distribution Song: *LUYH #627*, "Just As I Am, Without One Plea"

Sharing of the Bread and Cup

Pastor: Take, eat, remember and believe, the body of Jesus Christ has been broken for the complete forgiveness of all of our sins.

Pastor: Take, drink, remember and believe, the blood of Jesus Christ has been poured out for the complete forgiveness of all of our sins.

Prayer of Celebration

The celebration of the Lord's Supper typically unfolds through the above litany. This litany has been adapted from traditional CRCNA liturgical forms[109] so as to include an extended section on telling the gospel story leading into the acclamation. As the invitation indicates, the Table is open to all who have been baptized. When inviting the people to come forward to receive the elements, the pastor acknowledges that not everyone in attendance is at a place in life where they can participate in this meal in good conscience. Those who are not prepared to participate are still invited to come forward and to receive a blessing from the elders who are serving. Accommodations are made for those with mobility challenges and gluten free bread is available at each serving station. While the congregation receives the elements, the musicians played "Just as I Am, without One Plea," which resonated both with the Ephesians passages from the confession and assurance movement as well as from the message in Ephesians 3. Before leading the congregation in partaking of the elements, the pastor asks: "Has everyone who would like to participate this morning been served?" Following the bread and the cup, the pastor leads the congregation in a brief prayer of celebration, which ordinarily includes thanksgiving for the Spirit nourishing us with this small taste of the abundant life that awaits God's

---

109. The traditional forms and some additional adaptations are available on the CRCNA's website: http://crcna.org/resources/church-resources/liturgical-forms-resources/lords-supper/lords-supper-1994.

people in the new heaven and new earth and quite often concludes with the plea, "Come, Lord Jesus. Come quickly!"

> God Sends Us Out by His Grace
> * Charge to the Congregation: Colossians 3:12–14
> * Call to Holy Living:
> People: Ephesians 2:10
> * Blessing:
> Pastor: "God go before you to lead you, God go behind you to protect you, God go beneath you to support you, God go beside you to befriend you. Do not be afraid. May the blessing of God the Father, Son, and Holy Spirit be upon you. Do not be afraid. Go in peace to love and serve the Lord. Amen."[110]
> * Song: *LUYH* #608, "Salvation Belongs to Our God"

As the final movement of the worship gathering, the sending commissions God's people to live into the fullness of God's mission in response to the grace they have just received. Typically, the pastor gives a charge to the congregation that builds on or responds to the theme of the message. Throughout this particular series on Ephesians, the congregation voiced a call to holy living each week by reading Ephesians 2:10 together, which again rehearses their missional identity and sends them to live in response to the *missio trinitatis* they have experienced through the worship gathering. The final word is a blessing, reminding the people that God remains with them as they leave worship and will continue to equip them for their participation in God's mission.[111] The people then respond with a song, usually declaring God's love, sovereignty, and faithful provision not only for the people of God, but for the whole world. Following the song, a couple elders and the pastor remain in the sanctuary to pray with those who wish to receive personal prayer.

This particular worship gathering highlights ways in which First Hamilton CRC has attempted to express the four priorities within their worship. However, a couple significant elements that shape the overall approach were not present within this particular gathering. Notably, there was no baptism this week. When engaged, the baptismal litany includes a telling

110. The story of this blessing can be found on the Calvin Institute for Christian Worship website: http://worship.calvin.edu/resources/resource-library/neal-plantinga-on-his-god-go-before-you-blessing.

111. Kreider and Kreider: "God may send some people to the other side of the world; but God sends all of us into our own lives—our lives of work, leisure, community life, and retirement" (*Worship and Mission after Christendom*, 52).

of the gospel story that is similar, but not identical, to the one utilized with the Lord's Supper. The baptism litany also moves between the personal and communal and includes congregational vows along with those vows being made by the person being baptized or, in the case of an infant baptism, by their parents.

Additionally, First Hamilton Christian Reformed Church frequently engages paintings, drawings, and other visual arts within worship. Some of these are created by members of the art team. At other times, the art team encourages those who are gathered for worship to create art that will enhance the worship gathering. As an example, one September the art team invited congregation members to submit photographs taken from their front porch, on their commute to school or work, or in another location that they regularly spent time during the week. Around forty households participated, with more than one hundred pictures being submitted. For a couple months, several pictures were displayed on the projection screen as a preface to the prayer of thanksgiving and intercession. At Advent that year, as the congregation focused on John 1:14, the art team removed several pews and installed a tent in the sanctuary. Around the tent, they hung copies of the same photographs with a sign indicating that Jesus had moved into their neighborhoods.

As indicated at the opening of this section, this annotated order of worship is offered as an illustration of how one congregation is engaging these priorities for missional worship. The intent is not to universalize the experience at First Hamilton Christian Reformed Church, but to encourage other congregations to creatively consider how they might live into these priorities within their respective contexts.

Missional Worship Needs a Praxis-Oriented Discipleship

Before turning to the next chapter, two final thoughts regarding why missional worship needs a praxis-oriented discipleship are beneficial. One of the consistent themes in MCM conversations with regard to the Holy Spirit is that the Spirit is already at work outside of worship. Roxburgh contends that churches are called to pay attention to the Spirit's boundary-breaking presence in the world around them, not just in gathered worship, and join the Spirit in the work the Spirit is doing.[112] In other words, gathered worship is only one context of practices through which the Spirit transforms the

---

112. Roxburgh, *Missional*, 112–14, 150. Also, Sparks, Soerens, and Friesen, *New Parish*, 26–30.

character of God's people. As such, a worship gathering—even one shaped by the missional priorities expressed in this chapter—is insufficient on its own. Missional worship must be integrated with the Spirit's work elsewhere in order to fully cultivate an evangelistic character among God's people.

Returning to an earlier conversation in this chapter, the idea of an assembly line approach to worship falls short not only because it ignores the Holy Spirit and the Spirit's transforming presence, but also because that approach assumes that worship can be detached from the rest of the Christian life, particularly from discipleship.[113] This isolative assumption can be enacted both by depreciating and also by elevating worship. While the broad critique of worship's failures can lead to a diminished emphasis on communal worship, others in the MCM, like Van Gelder, have declared that gathered worship is central to the missional church. Yet, in doing so, they have frequently failed to articulate how participation in communal worship contributes to the life of God's people beyond the worship gathering. Without identifying ways that worship extends into other aspects of Christian living, Van Gelder has effectively isolated worship as a separate activity of God's people, somehow detached from their formation and participation within the *misso trinitatis*.[114] This disconnection from the rest of a missional way of life makes it easy to conclude that "worship does not work" in forming a missional identity.

Therefore, on account of the Spirit's transformative presence in and beyond gathered worship and because worship cannot be separated from the rest of the life of God's people, this project is persuaded that a missional approach to worship needs a praxis-oriented discipleship, through which God's people can learn to live into their sent identity. The next chapter attends to ways in which missional worship can be integrated with a praxis-oriented discipleship in cultivating an evangelistic character among God's people.

---

113. See Hauerwas, "Worship, Evangelism, Ethics," 205–14. This brief reflection served as one of the launching points for the considerations being developed throughout this project.

114. Van Gelder, *Essence of the Church*, 151–52.

5

Missional Worship and a Praxis-Oriented Discipleship

THE PROJECT NOW TURNS its attention to how the missional approach to worship presented in the previous chapter can be integrated with a praxis-oriented discipleship in order to more fully cultivate Jesus' character among God's people. The movement from a worship gathering into discipleship practices considered here is guided by recognition that missional approaches to worship and discipleship share a common vision. As seen previously, the proposed approach to worship cultivates an environment within which God's people are encouraged to be attentive to the Holy Spirit's transformative presence, leading to the formation of God's people for their participation within the *missio trinitatis*. Likewise, the MCM perceives missional discipleship not as "add-on or byproduct of the Christian life," but in such a way that "[m]ission is the essence of discipleship."[1] Thus, missional worship and missional discipleship converge around a common concern for the formation of God's people for mission.

Rather than merely recognizing this shared concern, this chapter contends that the formation of God's people occurs more fully through the integration of worship and discipleship within the MCM. Retaining the previous chapter's underlying concern of how to encourage God's people to be attentive and responsive to the Holy Spirit's transformative presence, the consideration of discipleship below also resists a temptation to treat discipleship practices as the missing ingredient that will produce mature and faithful disciples if engaged properly. Associating this temptation with a lingering Christendom, Guder contends that the contemporary North

---

1. Maddix and Akkerman, *Missional Discipleship*, 21.

American church believes they "are still capable of designing and building the Kingdom of God, as we assumed we were doing during the centuries of an overtly Christian social structure."[2] While asserting that a praxis-oriented discipleship can contribute to the formation of God's people, this project is not suggesting that such an approach will automatically produce disciples. As Ashlin-Mayo argues, discipleship needs to be understood in organic and relational terms rather than through the metaphors of the industrial mass production methodology prevalent in North American culture.[3]

This chapter explores the integration of a missional approach to worship with a praxis-oriented discipleship in three conversations. Drawing from Hauerwas and Wells' liturgical approach to ethics in their editorial work with the *Blackwell Companion to Christian Ethics*, the opening conversation considers how liturgical rhythms of remembering and anticipating contribute to integrating worship and discipleship. The second conversation examines three contours of a praxis-oriented discipleship: the need for a praxis-oriented discipleship, apprenticeship in the character and ways of Jesus, and an overview of personal and communal practices that encourage attention to the Spirit's transformative presence. The final conversation in this chapter focuses on hospitality and compassion as practices that cultivate Jesus' character among God's people through the integration of missional worship and a praxis-oriented discipleship.

Integrating Worship with Discipleship: Remembering and Anticipating

While beginning with an overview of how each of the worship priorities identified in chapter 4 extend beyond the worship gathering, this particular conversation will focus primarily on how the rhythms of remembering and anticipating can extend into a praxis-oriented discipleship within the MCM. Because this conversation directly engages the MCM lacuna regarding the formative capacity of worship, several outside sources, including Hauerwas and Wells' *Blackwell Companion to Christian Ethics*, will assist with facilitating this particular reflection.

---

2. Guder, "Evangelism and Justice," 17.

3. Ashlin-Mayo, "You Are NOT a Machine," http://bryceashlinmayo.com/2012/07/you-are-not-a-machine-post-industrial-discipleship.

Worship Priorities Extend Beyond Worship Gatherings

By briefly observing some of the ways that missional worship priorities extend beyond a worship gathering, this conversation focuses on the MCM recognition that what happens in worship is not intended to stay within worship.[4] For example, this project's literature review recognized that one aspect of being immersed in God's story is that God's people are called into a lived response to the story. Cosper provides a helpful summary of how immersion in the biblical narrative of God's mission extends beyond worship:

> Rehearsed regularly, the gospel becomes part of our way of thinking, seeing, feeling, loving, and being in the world. It's a weekly heartbeat gathering us in and scattering us back out to our homes and workplaces, to children's soccer games and board meetings, to chemotherapy sessions and evenings around the dinner table. From there, we return to the gathered church, once again rehearsing the story, remembering who God has made us, singing and celebrating that identity. Liturgy that immerses the people of God in the rhythms of grace doesn't merely train them for gospel-centered worship; it trains them for gospel-centered lives.[5]

Similarly, Hammond and Cronshaw contend that worship's call toward God's shalom "is a spirituality of everyday life" that "encourages us to engage our 'worldly' responsibilities with attentiveness to God's purposes for the world. It helps us live for the Messiah seven days a week."[6] In this way, the MCM sees that the communal worship priority on locating God's people within their respective heres and nows leads into their participation with God's mission "seven days a week."

Additionally, one can observe that the sending priority of missional worship ushers God's people into their new identity as participants in the *missio trinitatis*, through which they learn to see "every experience, conversation, and interaction as an opportunity to participate with God in his restoration project."[7] More specifically, Kreider and Kreider argue that "[w]e who have learned to make peace in our worshipping communities bring special skills to our jobs, acute intuitions of what might be possible,

---

4. Also Helland and Hjalmarson remark: "Christian spirituality is both relational and ethical, inward shaping for outward expression. The theater of this spirituality is missional as it both forms and feeds mission" (*Missional Spirituality*, 30).

5. Cosper, *Rhythms of Grace*, 124.

6. Hammond and Cronshaw, *Sentness*, 90.

7. Huckins, *Thin Places*, 135.

and a deep conviction that what we are doing is an expression of the *missio Dei*."[8]

Rather than extensively reference the ways that each of the missional priorities is developed, a more substantive engagement with one priority—how missional worship orients God's people through the rhythms of remembering and anticipating—is provided here. This particular priority serves the thesis and the objectives of this project well because the anamnetic and proleptic liturgical rhythms emerge in MCM conversations as well as in conversations among liturgical theologians and Christian ethicists. As such, the next section continues the argument that a missional approach to worship is intended to extend into the life of God's people beyond their gathered worship by taking a closer look at how the rhythms of remembering and anticipating can integrate missional worship with discipleship.

A Closer Look at the Rhythms of Remembering and Anticipating

The missional worship priority of orienting God's people through the liturgical rhythms of remembering and anticipating serves to integrate worship and discipleship within the MCM. By way of summary, the communal rhythms of remembering and anticipating contribute to the formation of the people of God so that they become marked by the character of Jesus Christ through the Holy Spirit. Therein, these rhythms are bent toward the cultivation of Jesus Christ's character among the people of God in such a way that God's people amplify throughout their lives their encounter with God's transformative presence within their worship gatherings. This recognition resonates with Newbigin's perspective quoted in the opening of this project, in which he argues that through its liturgical practices the church gains its true identity by "sharing in [Jesus'] risen life through the body broken and lifeblood poured out."[9] In this formation, the church's character is received from and formed by the character of Jesus Christ. Therefore, as God's people remember and anticipate the story of God's mission made known in Jesus Christ, revealed and encountered in gathered worship, they are sent out as a community of God's people to embody that story within the world.

As considered in the previous chapter, rather than urging an escape from present circumstances, the liturgical rhythms of remembering and anticipating continually form God's people to more fully engage their present circumstances. The *missio trinitatis* encourages neither a nostalgic view of

---

8. Kreider and Kreider, *Worship and Mission after Christendom*, 167–70.
9. Newbigin, *Gospel in a Pluralist Society*, 227.

the past nor a utopic view of the future. Instead, by remembering and anticipating the full story of God's mission, God's people are oriented toward living faithfully in their present contexts.

The priority on remembering and anticipating leads to the creation of a community of God's people who will faithfully embody the good news of Jesus Christ in their respective contexts.[10] Goheen sees this emphasis as an imperative for missional worship leading into discipleship: "Liturgy today must witness to the real world, the true story, the living God as revealed in Jesus Christ, and thereby form a people ready for missionary encounter in their various callings."[11] When engaged this way, the unfolding of redemptive history through Jesus Christ, remembered and anticipated in the liturgy, is intended to be remembered and anticipated through the body of Christ in a robust engagement with the specific cultural contexts of its localized expressions.[12] As such, anamnetic and proleptic rhythms serve not simply as liturgical accents within worship; rather, they serve to infuse the entire life of God's people with the character of Jesus Christ.

Again, the emphasis on this connection is not intended to establish or reinforce an idea of an assembly line through which God's people are manufactured into a certain type of people. In response to this implied mechanistic output that motivates much of the desire for concrete examples for replication,[13] a praxis-oriented discipleship focuses instead on cultivating ongoing faithfulness as opposed to numeric outcomes.[14] By focusing on faithfulness, a praxis-oriented approach calls for different measurements—qualitative observations about relationships in community instead of individual-to-standardized-aggregate comparisons focused on quantitative inventories—that allow personal and communal practices to be observed.[15] The anamnetic and proleptic rhythms are not the missing link in worship by which effective disciples can now be produced.

Rather, a more holistic response to the desire for discipling examples can be accomplished through a dialogue of practitioners sharing their responses to questions such as: "What rhythms give shape to your community's

10. Ibid., 189.

11. Goheen, "Nourishing Our Missional Identity," 49.

12. Goheen identifies a tension in this engagement between "how it can be an alternative community that is critical of the idolatrous status quo without becoming a ghetto or parallel community that attempts to withdraw from culture" ("Missional Church," 486).

13. Roxburgh and Boren address this propensity while explaining the difficulty with defining "missional church" (*Introducing the Missional Church*, 27–45).

14. Fitch, *Great Giveaway*, 27-46.

15. Ibid., 44–45, proposes a list of five qualitative questions that would assist in this discernment process.

discipleship and lend to your community's capacity to embody the character of Jesus Christ?"[16] A question along these lines would allow a community's faithfulness to be expressed without isolating the community as the only or as a primary example for replication. The model of shared stories around an open question of practices and faithfulness allows not only for strengths to be shared, but also ongoing struggles, failures, and contextual questions. Moreover, such an interchange broadens a view of discipleship that encourages and celebrates multiple ways for a community of God's people to faithfully embody Jesus' character among them.[17]

The extension of these rhythms from worship into the daily living of God's people reveals the transformative presence of the Holy Spirit, who is at work among God's people both within and outside of a community's worship gatherings. As Bowen argues:

> The Holy Spirit whom we invoke at the heart of the service is not only the Spirit of Christ, but by the same token the Spirit of mission, who empowers and directs the people of God in the same way that he directed the Lord Jesus during the years of the Incarnation—the way of the *missio dei*. We dare not invoke the Spirit unless we are prepared to follow the Spirit into mission.[18]

One avenue for considering the Spirit's transformative presence more closely is to consider the remaining missional worship priority—to orient God's people through the rhythms of remembering and anticipating—with regard to how it extends from worship into discipleship. The liturgical rhythms of remembering and anticipating, particularly as they press the character formation of God's people into the relationships, places, and structures of community life outside of worship, will be considered through dialogue with Hauerwas and Wells' editorial work in the *Blackwell Companion of Christian Ethics*.

---

16. In the same spirit, Guder asks: "How shall we prepare one another for our work as witness when we are gathered for worship, nurture, and fellowship?" ("Worthy Living," 431).

17. While these types of gatherings can be found in local and denominational specific settings, a couple broader initiatives are worth noting for their efforts in this regard. See, for example, Missio Alliance (missioalliance.org), Inhabit Conference (inhabitconference.com), and Praxis Gathering (thepraxisgathering.com).

18. Bowen, "Liturgical and Missional."

Hauerwas and Wells' Liturgical Ethics

Hauerwas and Wells' editorial work in the second edition of their *Blackwell Companion of Christian Ethics* is perhaps the most ambitious project recognizing the integral relationship of worship and the formation of the character of God's people. Yet, to date, this contribution has remained outside of the MCM conversation regarding the capacity of worship and discipleship to form God's people for mission. Their evocative project roots Christian ethics within the Christian liturgy, calling God's people to embody the gospel. They contend:

> The liturgy offers ethics a series of ordered practices that shape the character and assumptions of Christians, and suggest habits and models that inform every aspect of corporate life—meeting people, acknowledging fault and failure, celebrating, thanking, reading, speaking with authority, reflecting on wisdom, naming truth, registering need, bringing about reconciliation, sharing food, renewing purpose. This is the basic staple of corporate Christian life—not simply for clergy, or for those in religious orders, but for lay Christians, week in, week out. It is the most regular way in which most Christians remind themselves and others that they are Christians. It is the most significant way in which Christianity takes flesh, evolving from a set of ideas and convictions to a set of practices and a way of life.[19]

Among the assembled essays shaping the book, Kenneson offers the opening reflection on elements of the *ordo* itself. Focusing on the significance of the gathering, he remarks:

> priority is given to the community at worship not because the actions practiced there are in themselves *inherently more important* than the actions engaged in outside of the liturgy, but because the actions of the community at worship are taken to be *paradigmatic* for all other actions. That is, the community of disciples gathered for worship seeks to have its imagination so shaped by these formative liturgical actions that its entire life outside the liturgy will itself be a powerful expression of the worship of this God.[20]

With similar contributions throughout this volume, Hauerwas and Wells' editorial work accomplishes much of what the MCM has struggled

---

19. Hauerwas and Wells, *Companion to Christian Ethics*, 7.
20. Kenneson, "Gathering," 60–61.

to do on its own: demonstrate the integral relationship between communal worship and discipling God's people for life outside of a worship gathering.

Drawing from Hauerwas and Wells, then, this conversation considers four implications of the liturgical rhythms of remembering and anticipating, with particular attention to how they can be integrated with a praxis-oriented discipleship. The four aspects mentioned here point to a discipleship that is *Eucharist-centered*, marked by an *eschatological humility*, reliant upon *abundance in community*, and serves as an *embodied apologetic*. By turning a momentary spotlight on these implications, this project shows how the anamnetic and proleptic rhythms present in the liturgy are in fact rhythms that animate the whole communal life of God's people. The intention here is not to provide an exhaustive analysis of each implication but to sketch a picture that more clearly identifies ways in which the rhythms of remembering and anticipating serve to integrate worship and discipleship in their common concern with forming the character of Jesus Christ among God's people.

Eucharist-Centered

The first implication of these communal rhythms is that discipleship will be Eucharist-centered.[21] In *With the Grain of the Universe*, Hauerwas observes: "Christians betray themselves as well as their non-Christian brothers and sisters when in the interest of apologetics we say and act as if the cross of Christ is incidental to God's being. In fact, the God we worship and the world God created cannot be truthfully known without the cross."[22] Wells picks up on this idea in *God's Companions*, noting how ecclesial ethics believes that "God's call turns the world upside-down, but that that subversion finds its power not in numbers or guile but in running with the grain of the universe, that is along the contours of the cross and resurrection, remembering God's surprises and anticipating God's transforming future."[23]

On a certain level, this cruciform attention makes sense simply because the liturgical rhythms of remembering and anticipating are prevalent within the Eucharist celebration. Yet, the implication for a Eucharist-centered

---

21. Admittedly, in my own tradition the emphasis on celebrating the Eucharist has been occasional rather than weekly. The CRCNA Church Order, Article 60, requires that the Lord's Supper be served at least once every three months. First Hamilton CRC, where I currently serve, celebrates the Lord's Supper at least once per month, with several additional celebrations during the year. That said, there is a growing movement within the denomination to celebrate the Eucharist weekly.

22. Hauerwas, *With the Grain of the Universe*, 17.

23. Wells, *God's Companions*, 4.

discipleship is more fully evident when recognizing how such attention focuses on Jesus Christ. The celebration of Jesus' death and resurrection in the Eucharist reminds God's people of the embodiment of God's character in the person of Jesus Christ, emphasizing the historical narrative of redemption. Hauerwas and Wells write:

> For God's people, if Jesus is the person they remember, he is also the person they look forward to. They look back to the one crowned on the cross, and forward to the one enthroned in judgment. They thus perceive that those in distress and agony are by no means outside God's purposes now, and that those who have been trodden down and abused may look forward to vindication on the great day.[24]

Therefore, a Eucharist-centered discipleship that participates in the liturgical rhythms of remembering and anticipating takes on a narrative focus that seeks to encounter God through the redemptive history made known in Jesus Christ, anticipating a fullness of life not yet received. As Hauerwas writes, "In the sacraments we enact the story of Jesus and in so doing we form a community in his image. We could not be the church without them. For the story of Jesus is not simply one that is told; it must be enacted. The sacraments are means crucial to shaping and preparing us to tell and hear that story."[25]

Hauerwas and Wells' attention to this Eucharist-centered vision provides a framework for locating insights from several MCM authors and other liturgical theologians who have also recognized the integral way in which the celebration of the Lord's Supper forms the character and posture of discipleship among God's people. Webber writes:

> Because God is the subject who acts upon me in worship, my participation is not reduced to verbal response or to singing, but it is living in the pattern of the one who is revealed in worship. God, as the subject of worship, acts through the truth of Christ remembered and envisioned in worship. This truth forms me by the Spirit of God to live out the union I have with Jesus by calling me to die to sin and to live in the resurrection.[26]

Chilcote recognizes how God's people "repeatedly participate in the Eucharistic actions of offering, and thanking, and breaking, and giving" so that, being conformed into the image of Christ, they "become truly

---

24. Hauerwas and Wells, eds., *Companion to Christian Ethics*, 17.
25. Hauerwas, "Servant Community," 383.
26. Webber, *Ancient-Future Worship*, 111.

eucharistic" and images of Christ in the world.[27] While reflecting on the practice of the Eucharist in the early church, Moore-Keish asserts:

> The eucharistic meal attempted to transform the social status quo by emphasizing the common humanity of all the table guests. This intention has been carried by the practice over time. Even when participants are not aware of it and even when structures are not immediately affected, the eucharistic practice bears within itself the challenge to social hierarchy, a challenge that has periodically been realized by Christian communities throughout history.[28]

Reflecting further on the impact of remembering Jesus' history during the Eucharist, McKenna draws attention to how liberation theologians have emphasized the Eucharist as a pattern for life:

> Could one announce in the Eucharist that the risen Christ gives himself in food and drink for *our* nourishment and have no concern for millions who die for want of nourishment? Could one proclaim that Christ's presence in the Eucharist is a microcosm of his presence throughout the *whole* material universe and be totally insensitive to the use men and women make of that material universe? Could one celebrate the extension of the risen Lord's presence in people, as well as in bread and wine, and be blind to the need many people still have for peace and justice? One could, but not without violating the essential link between "orthodoxy" and "orthopraxy."[29]

McKenna's concluding insight, namely, that orthodoxy and orthopraxy are violated when the people of God do not extend the Eucharist into the ways they live among the poor, reveals how closely worship and discipleship are integrated. In this light, a Eucharist-centered discipleship trains God's people to see, embrace, and serve those who are marginalized within society in similar ways to how Jesus Christ engaged with those living on the margins of his society.

Discipleship that is Eucharist-centered assists God's people in remembering that "[a]ll that Christians do and do not do thus finds its intelligibility in the worship of God,"[30] even as it trains them to anticipate the fullness of the resurrection life by embodying Jesus' love here and now. A praxis-

---

27. Chilcote, "Integral Nature of Worship and Evangelism," 262.
28. Moore-Keish, *Do This in Remembrance of Me*, 105.
29. McKenna, "Liturgy," 302.
30. Hauerwas and Wells, eds., *Companion to Christian Ethics*, 50.

oriented discipleship then attends to the Eucharist—and the revelation of God's love in Jesus Christ through it—not merely as a memorial celebration within worship, but as a paradigmatic posture for God's people in the way they engage their neighbours throughout the week.[31]

Marked by an Eschatological Humility

Discipleship shaped by anamnetic and proleptic rhythms can also be identified by an eschatological humility. Such humility involves recognizing that significant contours of reality—creation, reconciliation, new creation—have come and will come about by God's engagement in the world, and not by the self-initiated efforts of God's people. This emphasis echoes the contention from the last chapter that missional worship is rooted in the person and transformative presence of the Holy Spirit.

Such an eschatological humility emerges from remembering the fullness of God's storied engagement with sinful humanity. Hauerwas writes: "We need a story that not only provides the means to acknowledge the blunders as part of our own story, but to see ourselves in a story where even our blunders are part of an ongoing grace, that is, are forgiven and transformed for 'our good and the good of all the church.'"[32] Wells furthers this thought, writing: "If the overcoming of sin is God's word on perversity, the fulfillment of potential is God's word on lack of imagination. And if God's people realize that in the overcoming of sin, a great deal of that sin is their own, then they likewise have to acknowledge that in the fulfillment of potential, a great deal of the kindled imagination in the world lies beyond them." He continues by contending that God is at work throughout the world, so that "[t]he signs of the kingdom in the world are a constant challenge to the Church to renew its practices and to keep its heart open to receiving new gifts from God."[33]

Such recognition develops anticipation of God's coming kingdom among God's people, cultivating a humble patience in the present. In connection with the liturgy, Kenneson emphasizes this relationship:

> The coming of God's reign is not driven by human initiative; however, God is capable of sanctifying human action in ways that extend God's purposes. The *ekklesia* has not been given the task of engineering a future of its own devising, but instead

---

31. Goheen, "Nurturing Our Missional Identity," 50.
32. Hauerwas, "Character, Narrative, and Growth in the Christian Life," 249.
33. Wells, *God's Companions*, 33–34.

one of recognizing, announcing, welcoming, and "midwifing" a future that God is bringing. The *ekklesia* gathers both to honor and praise the One who promises that future, and to be shaped and formed for its part within that future.[34]

Remembering and anticipating orients the *ekklesia*, God's people, to recognize with humility that, though they are participants within God's mission, the *missio trinitatis* is neither dependent upon them nor limited to them. Rather, God's mission is engaged as the Spirit works in and through God's people.

A discipleship marked, then, by this kind of eschatological humility will emphasize at least three things. It will be a discipleship that practices confession, owning up to the ways that the church—in practice and theology—has fallen and continues to fall short of fully embodying the good news of the gospel.[35] This aspect of discipleship will also value both the history of the church and its promised future, not as ways of escaping the present, but as means of living more fully into the present circumstances into which God has sent them.[36] Moreover, this remembering-and-anticipating discipleship trains God's people to listen attentively for the Spirit, particularly with regard to how they can serve others. Such discipleship, rather than violently demanding its own way, recognizes and trusts that God is at work whether God's people are on the margins or in the center of society's power structures. This posture nurtures a free and dependent obedience among God's people. As Hauerwas and Wells write: "True freedom comes by learning to be appropriately dependent, that is, to trust the one who wills to have us as his own and who wills the final good of all. In more traditional language, for the Christian, to be perfectly free means to be perfectly obedient. True freedom is perfect service."[37]

Reliant upon Abundance in Community

A discipleship shaped by the anamnetic and proleptic rhythms emerging from within communal worship also teaches God's people to be reliant upon abundance in community. In this light, Hauerwas and Wells point to how the church's ethics aspire to a political vision "that discerns the best use of the unlimited gifts of God." Such a view of God's people as a community

---

34. Kenneson, "Gathering," 67.
35. Goheen, "Nourishing Our Missional Identity," 49.
36. Frost and Hirsch, *Shaping of Things to Come*, 141–44.
37. Hauerwas, "Character, Narrative, and Growth in the Christian Life," 224.

that seeks the mutual benefit of others in God's abundance "regards the contrast between public and private as yet another binary distinction that misrepresents the call of the Gospel and the nature of the Christian life."[38] Moreover, this attention to abundance in community shifts the central focus of discipleship from mastering a defined set of personal knowledge about God and God's kingdom to engaging an ongoing, lifelong encounter with God as revealed by the Spirit and expressed through the community of God's people. To this end, Hauerwas and Wells comment: "Thus growth in the Christian life is not required only because we are morally deficient, but also because the God who has called us is infinitely rich. Therefore, conversion denotes the necessity of a turning of the self that is so fundamental that the self is placed on a path of growth for which there is no end."[39] As such, discipleship that relies on abundance in community teaches that following Jesus involves continually being formed more faithfully and more fully into the image of Christ within community.

This communal discipleship, rooted in ongoing growth in Jesus Christ, bends toward discovering God's generosity and abundance together. Hauerwas and Wells point to this aspect of discovery as they challenge the separation of beauty, truth, and goodness between the academic disciplines of worship, philosophy, and ethics, arguing instead for an integration of all three in God's abundance so that amplifying one does not come at the cost of another.[40] Remembering and anticipating God's beauty, truth, and goodness, created but lost in the opening chapters of Genesis and raised to new life in the closing chapters of Revelation, helps cultivate an environment in which a praxis-oriented discipleship makes sense as a means of God's people discovering that their flourishing comes about as they contribute to the flourishing of others.

Chester and Timmis echo this communal understanding of discipleship, contending that "most character formation and discipleship takes place through informal and ad hoc conversations," requiring "relationships, time, and gospel intentionality" in lived community.[41] Goheen contends that this communal identity, in opposition to our bent toward understanding communities as a conglomeration of individuals, is foundational to a biblical understanding of the church as God's people.[42] Not only is the abundance found in their communal identity, but it is also evident in the priesthood

---

38. Hauerwas and Wells, eds., *Companion to Christian Ethics*, 6.
39. Hauerwas, "Character, Narrative, and Growth in the Christian Life," 226.
40. Hauerwas and Wells, eds., *Companion to Christian Ethics*, 5–6.
41. Chester and Timmis, *Total Church*, 115.
42. Goheen, *Light to the Nations*, 157–62.

in which all believers share. Woodward calls on church leaders to create a thriving environment that "helps the congregation to live out her calling in the world for the sake of the world," so that "[p]eople begin to link Sunday with Monday, and their work transforms from a job into a sacred vocation. They learn to bring God's power to bear on human need."[43] The liturgical rhythms of remembering and anticipating lead into a discipleship where the abundance of God's presence is encountered and learned through the shared life of God's people outside of worship.

Serves as an Embodied Apologetic

Finally, the liturgical rhythms of remembering and anticipating can be integrated with a praxis-oriented discipleship through a concern for the people of God to become an embodied apologetic.[44] Kenneson argues that "[e]very human life is an embodied argument about what things are worth doing, who or what is worthy of attention, who or what is worthy of allegiance and sacrifice, and what projects or endeavors are worthy of human energies. In short, every human life is 'bent' toward something. Every human life is an act of worship."[45] Recognizing that Christians are formed in community, a discipleship shaped by remembering and anticipating will emphasize that the community of God's people as a whole becomes an embodied apologetic of God's love. Hauerwas and Wells hold both the personal and communal dimensions together when they write: "Above all, worship trains God's people to be examples of what God's love can do. Worshiping God invites God to make the life of the disciple the theater of God's glory. Worshiping God together invites God to make the body of believers the stage of God's splendor."[46] In this way, a people who worship together are also called to live together, so that God's character might become evident in their shared life as the people of God.

Locating the embodied argument of the gospel within the life of the community in this way lends to a discipleship that is concerned with continually growing in faithfulness to the character of Jesus Christ as revealed through the grand narrative of God's mission. Kenneson writes: "it

---

43. Woodward, *Creating a Missional Culture*, 53.

44. The embodied apologetic concept, briefly introduced here as an aspect of integrating missional worship with a praxis-oriented discipleship, owes its vantage point to Newbigin's idea of the people of God as the hermeneutic of the gospel. Chapter 6 will return to this concept as the culmination of this project's thesis.

45. Kenneson, "Gathering," 56. This argument resonates closely with Smith's *homo liturgicus* anthropology in *Desiring the Kingdom*, 40–46.

46. Hauerwas and Wells, eds., *Companion to Christian Ethics*, 26.

is precisely *because* the *ekklesia* believes that its embodied life is part of the gospel that it must ask about the *shape* of that life, asking hard questions about how it might more faithfully devote its entire life to the right worship of the triune God."[47] Such a discipleship refuses to be placated with simple or static answers but lives with a dynamic tension that is perpetually discerning how to be more faithful in its current circumstances than it already is. Moreover, in forming the community as a more faithful expression of God's love, this kind of discipleship attends to the contours of the community's life together not merely with securing assent to particular articulations of orthodoxy. As Hunsberger writes: "Every church everywhere will embody a local, particular expression of the gospel. God intends this to be so to give variegated witness to the salvation given in Christ. But each local expression is valid as an incarnation of the gospel only as it is faithful to the gospel's version of what is good, true, and beautiful."[48]

Finally, a discipleship bent toward becoming an embodied apologetic will invite others into the story of God's mission. This invitation comes not simply because of what God's people offer the world, but because the people of God trust that the Spirit will enrich both the church and the world through their interactions with each other.[49] As will be explored further in chapter 6, such an invitation operates with an approach to evangelism that blends centered-set and bounded-set understandings of belonging among God's people,[50] recognizing that belonging to the community of God's people frequently precedes a personal commitment to theological expressions of who Jesus is and the biblical narrative of God's mission. To this end, the good news, and the embodiment of that good news, is not limited to the people who already believe and belong. Rather, the invitation to belong among God's people becomes an entry way into believing that the good news of God's mission in Jesus Christ is for all people. Such a discipleship, rooted in the liturgical rhythms of remembering and anticipating, cultivates Jesus' character more fully among the people of God.

While not an exhaustive consideration, this overview of the liturgical rhythms of remembering and anticipating provides ample opportunity to recognize ways in which missional worship can be integrated with discipleship to more fully cultivate the character of Jesus Christ among God's people. Thus, relying on this integration of worship and discipleship, the

---

47. Kenneson, "Gathering," 68.
48. Hunsberger and Van Gelder, *Church between Gospel and Culture*, xvi.
49. Huckins, *Thin Places*, 65–83; and Wright, *Mission of God's People*, 128–47
50. Frost and Hirsch, *Shaping of Things to Come*, 47–51.

next section attends more specifically to the MCM's view of discipleship as being praxis-oriented.

Three Contours of a Praxis-Oriented Discipleship

Rather than occurring in a classroom or other institutional setting, the MCM locates discipleship within the shared life of God's people. As Helland and Hjalmarson have contended, "We must ground a missional spirituality in practices and people, not merely in ideas and information."[51] This discipling emphasis on practices and people reflects the intended purpose of a missional discipleship, which is to enable the people of God to embody the good news of Jesus Christ.[52] This conversation unfolds in three sections: the need for a praxis-oriented discipleship, apprenticeship in the character and ways of Jesus, and an overview of personal and communal practices.

The Need for a Praxis-Oriented Discipleship

One of the weaknesses apparent among MCM contributions to a missional approach to worship is gravitation toward an inexorable logic that worship *must* lead to a certain way of life. For example, Dawn posits that if worship forms God's people to dwell in God's reign, "then we *will* carry God's kingdom wherever we go—and we *will* be equipped to reach out to the culture around us with words of gospel truth and deeds of gospel faithfulness."[53] Likewise, Fitch contends that "worship *must* become a culture capable of forming our worshipers' imaginations faithfully toward the lordship of Jesus Christ."[54] Guder states: "The gathered life of the church *must* flow into the scattered and sent-out life of the church."[55] Goheen adds: "Liturgy today *must* witness to the real world, the true story, the living God as revealed in Jesus Christ, and *thereby* form a people ready for missionary encounter in their various callings."[56] While most of these examples could be understood with an imperatival urging behind them (i.e., "Let's make sure that worship leads into the way we live"), the multiple occurrences by multiple authors of what *must* or what *will* occur as a result of worship raises a concern.

---

51. Helland and Hjalmarson, *Missional Spirituality*, 41.
52. Fitch, *Great Giveaway*, 62.
53. Dawn, "Worship to Form a Missional Community," 149–50. Emphasis added.
54. Fitch, *Great Giveaway*, 97. Emphasis added.
55. Guder, "Worthy Living," 429. Emphasis added.
56. Goheen, "Nourishing Our Missional Identity," 49. Emphasis added.

These arguments appear to move straight from worship to mission, as if worship is all that is needed to effectively form disciples who faithfully embody the good news of Jesus Christ. Frequently these assertions regarding the impact worship must have upon the life of God's people leave unanswered the question of how God's people transition from gathered worship into this missional way of life. This project contends that a praxis-oriented discipleship serves to usher God's people from worship toward mission, equipping them to embody in their daily living the good news they encountered in worship.

Smith speaks to this very concern at the conclusion of his reflections on embodied worship practices.[57] He wonders: "Isn't it a bit of a naïve overestimate to think that the practices of Christian worship, formative though they may be, could really function as sufficient counter-formation to the power and ubiquity of the secular liturgies" prevalent in the contemporary North American context? Recognizing that "we don't seem to be a people that looks very different from our neighbors" apart from Sunday church attendance, Smith advocates for a recovery of monastic practices outside of Sunday worship that abstain from competing liturgies in the world and from a "triumphalist project of changing the world," while also "embracing habits of *daily* worship."[58] Though only briefly identifying a few of these practices, Smith's attention to them acknowledges that the formation of Christ's character among God's people calls for ongoing formation through worship and discipleship, indicating that neither worship nor discipleship is sufficient on its own. By rooting the formation of God's people both in worship and in communal practices of discipleship, Smith further signifies the integrated nature of worship and discipleship.[59]

Therefore, contrary to the apparent MCM temptation to skip over discipleship and in line with Smith's advocacy for discipleship enacted through communal practices, this project contends that a missional approach to worship needs a praxis-oriented discipleship in order to fully cultivate the character of Jesus Christ among God's people. The next section frames discipleship as apprenticeship in the character and ways of Jesus.

Apprenticeship in the Character and Ways of Jesus

The discipleship described through this chapter is bent toward assisting the people of God in their journey of becoming what they already are: the body

---

57. Smith, *Desiring the Kingdom*, 207–14.
58. Ibid., 211. Emphasis original.
59. Ibid., 212–13.

of Jesus Christ here and now. In line with Kreider and Kreider's observation that the early church "offered the world a way of living rooted in Christ,"[60] the praxis-oriented discipleship described here encourages God's people to attend to the Spirit so their capacity to faithfully embody the character of Jesus Christ in every area of life might increase.

Within this perspective, Frost draws attention to the cruciform shape of such a discipleship, remarking that "[t]he cross is more than a metaphor or a symbol of Christian discipleship; it is a paradigm by which we can view Jesus as our example for life. When we speak about Jesus being the exemplar of missional living, we must not ignore the cross-shaped nature of that example."[61] But Jesus was not merely an example for God's people to follow. Bowen asserts:

> His amazing life—what he did, what he said, and the way he did and said it—was part of it, but only a part of it. The achievement of his life cannot be separated from the achievement of his death. It is strange to think of someone's death "achieving" anything, but Christians have always believed that Jesus' death was more than just an unfortunate martyrdom, the untimely death of a beautiful young life. Instead, it was the Creator striking a deadly and accurate blow at the heart of evil from which it would not recover.[62]

Yet the death of Jesus would simply be "an unfortunate martyrdom" if Jesus had not also risen from the dead. Bowen offers: "The resurrection is not a hopeful clue to the search for personal survival after death. It is much bigger than that, much bigger. This is the first demonstration of the reality of the new world that God has in mind."[63] Bauckham adds to this perspective that "the gospel is that in Christ Jesus the curse has been set aside and God's creative purposes for the blessing of his creation is established beyond any possibility of reversal."[64]

With confidence in what God has already accomplished and what God has begun to do in Jesus' death and resurrection, discipleship calls God's people to live in response to this new reality as a follower of Jesus Christ. Bowen offers that this understanding of discipleship—as a follower or disciple of Jesus—could be better perceived through the metaphor of apprenticeship. "Jesus is like a master craftsman in the work of the kingdom, and

---

60. Kreider and Kreider, *Worship and Mission*, 139.
61. Frost, *Road to Missional*, 91.
62. Bowen, "Why Mission? Why Now? Why Here?," 4.
63. Ibid., 4–5.
64. Bauckham, *Bible and Mission*, 36.

the disciples are his apprentices, learning kingdom trades by watching him at work, asking him questions, and gradually being initiated into the work themselves."[65]

While not often utilizing the language of apprenticeship, others in the MCM employ this concept in relationship to discipleship. Rooting the apprenticeship model in Jesus' pattern of discipling the apostles,[66] Breen emphasizes the need for leaders to be accessible to the people they are discipling. He contends that leaders "are inviting people into our lives and asking them to imitate the parts of our life that look like Jesus."[67] In other settings, the identity of God's people as coapprentices of Jesus Christ becomes central to the conversation. For example, Huckins emphasizes how their community participates together in discerning how God is inviting a particular member to participate with the Spirit in God's mission.[68] Whether as an apprentice learning to imitate Jesus through the life of a leader or as a member of a community of coapprentices, God's people are invited to live into the ways and character of Jesus Christ through a praxis-oriented discipleship. As Bowen remarks, to be Jesus' apprentice is "to learn from him what it means to live as God's people in God's world in God's way."[69]

An Overview of Personal and Communal Practices

A natural question at this point could well be: What are the practices that contribute to a praxis-oriented discipleship? Or, what does it look like "to live as God's people in God's world in God's way"? Because of the MCM's rootedness within particular contexts, there are likely more practices across the spectrum of the MCM than can be considered in a project like this one. Therefore, the practices identified below are intended to highlight potential practices to stir the imagination as to what practices could participate in cultivating Jesus' character among God's people.

As has been indicated a couple times previously in this project, God's people come to embody God's character through the transformative presence of the Holy Spirit. As such, these practices are not intended to be seen as a magic key by which Jesus' character is automatically formed among God's people. Rather the practices identified below assist God's people to

---

65. Bowen, "Why Mission? Why Now? Why Here?," 5.
66. Breen and Cockram, *Building a Discipling Culture*, 37.
67. Ibid., 47.
68. Huckins, *Thin Places*, 37–39.
69. Bowen, "Why Mission? Why Now? Why Here?," 7.

"keep in step with the Spirit" (Gal 5:25), through whose presence they are transformed.

The practices identified here are expressed within two groups: practices that encourage personal attentiveness to the Spirit and practices that encourage communal attentiveness to the Spirit. While utilizing these categories, this project also recognizes that there are many creative ways that personal practices can be adapted for use in communal settings; and, in similar fashion, communal practices can be personalized. In fact, this project is hopeful that the lists below would contribute to such imaginative, crossover adaptations of these practices.

Personal Attentiveness

A number of traditional spiritual disciplines can be engaged in ways that increase personal attentiveness to the Spirit's transformative presence and lead toward personally embodying the character of Jesus Christ with others and in creation. For example, the discipline of daily scripture reading can be engaged through a set of four questions that serve to immerse one more fully in the story of God's mission: (1) Where in God's mission does this story take place? (2) How does this text anticipate or respond to God's reconciliation of all things in Jesus Christ? (3) How does this passage show God's people embracing or resisting their identity as a sent people within the *missio trinitatis*? (4) Is there one way that I can participate in this part of God's mission in the way I live today? In similar fashion, the discipline of silence can encourage greater attentiveness to the Spirit by creating space that abstains from the counternarratives in the broader culture and creates room to listen and watch for the Spirit's transformative presence. Rather than retreat or withdrawal from normal life rhythms this practice can be engaged in the midst of life through a variety of adaptations, like not speaking except in response to others, turning off news and entertainment sources when commuting, or restricting one's time to engage with emails and social media to a specific time of day. While engaging these means of entering into silence, a simple prayer such as, "Holy Spirit, open my eyes and ears to your transformative presence today; please show me how to join you in the work you are already doing," can encourage one to be more attentive to the Spirit.

Two other personal practices can encourage apprentices to more faithfully embody the character and ways of Jesus Christ. One is the practice of "parish presence." The essence of this discipline is to find a public space within one's neighborhood to be consistently present. In a culture that frequently celebrates mobility, privacy, and detachment,[70] this discipline seeks to personally emulate Jesus' incarnation by becoming rooted within a specific community. While there is a communal nature to this discipline—being present with others in the community—the emphasis of this discipline is on an apprentice being present within the neighborhood without an agenda beyond being present with their neighbors.[71] This parish presence can take on a wide variety of applications, including sitting in a local park at the same time each week, stopping by a local barber shop, walking a pet, joining local artists or a theatre troupe, and even the ubiquitous frequenting of a local coffee shop. The discipline trains God's people to personally embody Jesus' character and actions in line with his identity as "God with us."

Another practice that encourages personal attentiveness to the Spirit is a *lectio* reading of a local newspaper. This practice is an adaptation of *lectio divina*, a traditional practice through which one engages scripture through rhythms of repeated readings of the same passage and spaces of silence between each reading.[72] The intent is to see if a particular word or phrase from that reading catches the reader's attention and then to reflect on what the Spirit might be saying through that word or phrase. In a similar way, a *lectio* reading of a local news source reads a page or two of local news stories watching for a story or situation to catch one's attention. Then, through repeated readings and the silence between readings, the apprentice reflects on the Spirit's transformative presence in their neighbourhood in order to discern how the Spirit might be inviting their personal participation in God's mission.

Communal Attentiveness

Other practices can encourage communal attentiveness to the Spirit's transformative presence and cultivate Jesus' character among God's people. One example is the practice of neighborhood storyboarding, which emerges from insights within "asset-based community development" conversations.[73] The idea of a neighborhood storyboard practice is for a team of apprentices to

---

70. Bouma-Prediger and Walsh, *Beyond Homelessness*, 1–28.

71. Huckins, *Thin Places*, 135, argues that the *missio trinitatis* cannot be engaged only as an individual, but requires communal engagement in order to be congruent with God's mission of restoring relationships between God, others, and creation.

72. For a brief description of this practice, see the website for Ignatian Spirituality: http://ignatianspirituality.com/ignatian-prayer/the-what-how-why-of-prayer/praying-with-scripture.

73. McKnight and Block, *Abundant Community*. Also, http://abcdinstitute.org.

listen to people within the surrounding community tell the neighborhood's story from their perspectives.[74] Then, with people in the community, apprentices depict those stories on a time line or map of the neighborhood. While there can be a one-time-event nature to storyboarding, implementing this practice facilitates an ongoing discipline of listening with neighbors and storyboarding relationships in the community as those relationships continue to grow and change along with shifts in community demographics and circumstances.

While a variety of storylines will emerge through this process, one particular narrative thread that God's people can attend to through this process comes through questions like: How does the neighborhood perceive their relationship with God's people who gather there? How has that relationship changed over the years? And, what future does the neighborhood desire from those who gather to worship within the neighborhood? Questions like these, inside a practice of listening to and with their neighbors, assist God's people with discerning how the Spirit is at work around them, with identifying spaces of lament and celebration, and with collaboratively imagining how they might embody Jesus' character in ways that their neighbors would see and understand as God's presence with them.

Finally, the communal practice of sharing meals together encourages greater attention to the Spirit and tangible embodiment of Jesus' character and actions. Noting that shared meals are "at the heart of the Christian story," Heuertz and Pohl suggest that God's people need to consistently pay attention to who they are and to who they are not eating with as a measure of how their lives are aligning with patterns Jesus set. They assert: "Our meals become kingdom meals especially when people who are usually overlooked find a place—a place of welcome and value."[75] This practice trains God's people not only to be present with their neighbors, but to affirm God's image in the other—and therefore, the other's inherent value. Attending to the Spirit's transformative presence in the lives of others through shared meals like these can also serve to whet one's own appetite for the promised banquet feast of the new heaven and new earth in which the reconciliation of all people and all creation will be fulfilled in Jesus Christ.

As indicated at the outset of this section, this brief consideration of practices that can increase personal and communal attentiveness to the Spirit

---

74. Roxburgh contends that this listening posture is absolutely necessary as Jesus' disciples engage in their neighborhoods (*Missional*, 123–27).

75. Heuertz and Pohl, *Friendship at the Margins*, 81. With a similar emphasis, a former mentor of mine, Rev. Dante Venegas, would frequently say: "Reconciliation is not about who you sit next to on Sunday morning, but who you hang out with on Friday night."

among God's people and their embodiment of Jesus' character is intended to be illustrative of myriad potential practices. These practices encourage immersion in the story of God's mission, increase awareness of how the Spirit is working in one's particular neighborhood, and train God's people to embody Jesus' character through being present with their neighbors and listening well to them. With a desire to consider more closely the character and shape of these practices, the final conversation in this chapter turns its attention to hospitality and compassion as paradigmatic expressions of the praxis-oriented discipleship considered here.

Hospitality and Compassion

While the previous conversation sought to describe a praxis-oriented discipleship with rather broad strokes, this chapter's third conversation turns toward two practices—hospitality and compassion—as examples of how the liturgical rhythms of remembering and anticipating can integrate a missional approach to worship with a praxis-oriented discipleship. Though not often utilizing the language of remembering and anticipating as a foundation, a significant number of MCM sources have pointed to the practices of hospitality and compassion as being essential to the church's identity as a sent people of God and to the ways these practices relate to worship and the discipleship of God's people.[76]

Hospitality

The practice of hospitality has a rich tradition within Christian history. As Pohl has argued, from the earliest days of the church, the extension of a warm welcome even to those perceived as enemies has been of significant importance.[77] The Christian scriptures speak clearly to this practice being rooted in God's character,[78] expressed by Jesus Christ,[79] and called for among

76. For example, Fitch, *Great Giveaway*, 60–61; Roxburgh and Boren, *Introducing the Missional Church*, 188–90; and Helland and Hjalmarson, *Missional Spirituality*, 185–88.

77. Pohl, *Making Room*, 16–58.

78. For example: Psalm 23 speaks of God as "you prepare a table before me in the presence of my enemies." Deuteronomy 10:18 describes God as one who looks after the fatherless and the widow and who loves the foreigners. Isaiah 56:7 shows God extending his hospitality to the foreigner and the eunuch, assuring them of a place in God's house. Revelation 7:9 points to the multitudes who are welcomed around God's throne in anticipation of the new heaven and new earth.

79. For example: Matthew 19:13–15, where Jesus welcomes little children with a declaration that "the kingdom of heaven belongs to such as these"; Mark 7:24–30,

God's people.[80] By extending hospitality to the stranger, particularly to orphans, widows, and immigrants, Christian communities remember God's gracious hospitality in creating humanity in the first place[81] and in welcoming them into table fellowship through Jesus Christ's death and resurrection.[82] Moreover, by extending hospitality to others, God's people anticipate God's coming kingdom, where there will be people "from every nation, tribe, people, and language."

The opportunities for the practice of hospitality to shape the life of God's people are numerous. A tangible expression of this hospitality can be seen in North American churches facilitating opportunities for their members to learn the languages of immigrants and refugees entering their communities. Particularly in neighborhoods that lack access to public space, a church that opens up its property for community gardens and its building for community gatherings and functions deepens their own memory and anticipation of God's character through extending hospitality. Even liturgical settings can be transformed by the practice of hospitality, by offering alternative worship times for those who work first shift on the weekends, through the inclusion of visual and kinetic arts within worship to express the gospel in a variety of learning styles, or by creating accessible worship spaces where people with physical and cognitive impairments are integrated throughout the sanctuary. Maddix remarks that in his community hospitality "is our way of being Christ in the city. Our church's embrace of immigrants and refugees, the sexually exploited and the marginalized, the mentally handicapped and the mentally ill, hard-to-employ people and children from broken families, all flows from the love of God shed in our hearts, moving us toward friends and neighbors."[83]

---

where Jesus welcomes a Syro-Phoenician woman; Luke 5:27–31 and 15:1–2, which both describe Jesus' table fellowship with "sinners"; and John 3–4, where Jesus extends hospitality to Nicodemus and then to the Samaritan woman.

80. For example: the repeated laws in Leviticus and Deuteronomy to care for foreigners, widows, and orphans; Matthew 25:31–46 calls for the extension of hospitality to the least of these through the parable of the Sheep and the Goats; church leaders are to be known as hospitable people (1 Timothy 3:2; Titus 1:8); Romans 12:13 conveys the command to "Share with God's people who are in need. Practice hospitality"—a command that is echoed in Hebrews 13:2 ("Do not forget to show hospitality to strangers") and in 1 Peter 4:9 ("Offer hospitality to one another without grumbling"); and James goes so far as to define "religion that God our Father accepts as pure and faultless" with a call to "look after orphans and widows in their distress."

81. Pohl, *Making Room*, 61–88.

82. See Frost who, reflects on the potency of table fellowship for disciples in exile (*Exile*, 158–76).

83. Maddix, "Missional Communities," 30.

These expressions create an environment where God's hospitable character is not only relayed through words but also seen and touched through the diverse gifts that God entrusts to the people of God. In this way, the church becomes an embodiment of God's self-giving character.[84] Keifert remarks: "In the church, showing hospitality to a stranger is less a matter of making the stranger feel at home and more a matter of opening one's private world to the stranger. In fact, it is a matter of opening one's private world to a public one, of gaining the competence to participate in the customs of public life, of learning to enjoy life among strangers."[85] Therein, the communal practice of hospitality extends the rhythms of remembering and anticipating so as to facilitate the ongoing discipleship of God's people as they put God's hospitable character into practice.

Compassion

In similar fashion, communal practices of compassion also participate in the rhythms of remembering and anticipating. By engaging in issues of justice and mercy, God's people remember that each person participates in the *imago dei*,[86] that the history of God's mission includes releasing God's people from the impoverishment of slavery to foreign kings and to sin, and that God has had a pattern of releasing God's people into places "flowing with milk and honey." These patterns within redemptive history hold together through Jesus Christ's compassion in laying down his life to release people from their sins.[87] Moreover, practices of compassion also anticipate the day when God will make all things new, thereby removing everything that is opposed to the flourishing life of God's kingdom.[88]

Attention to issues of justice and mercy through practices of compassion has been a strong suit within the MCM. The centrality of incarnational theology within the MCM is closely intertwined with perspectives on compassion, expressed through acts of justice and mercy. Roxburgh and Boren observe that "the call to be a sign, witness, and foretaste of God's dream is a call for us to be a contrast society." Among other things, the church is to exemplify God's love in its relationships with one another[89] and to engage

---

84. Meyers, "Missional Church, Missional Liturgy," 47.
85. Keifert, *Welcoming the Stranger*, 8.
86. Keller, *Generous Justice*, 82–88.
87. Ibid., 92–100.
88. Revelation 21:1–5, 22:12–16.
89. Roxburgh and Boren, *Introducing the Missional Church*, 103–10.

with those who are on the margins of society.[90] Such engagement takes on practical dimensions that include restructuring patterns of responding to need,[91] developing work ethics and priorities shaped by righteousness and bent toward the good of others,[92] entering into the poverty of others,[93] and advocacy.[94] While recognizing a tendency to be involved in justice from a distance,[95] the MCM places a strong emphasis on expressing practices of compassion within the life of the local church.[96] Such practices can take the form of financial assistance, but are more often expressed through listening carefully to neighbors, being present with others in their suffering,[97] and a commitment to reconciliation.[98]

As this chapter has argued, missional worship priorities extend into the daily living of God's people, making it possible for God's people to faithfully embody the character of Jesus Christ. This formative context is aided by a variety of practices that encourage personal and communal attention to the Spirit's transformative presence. Paradigmatic practices, like hospitality and compassion, disciple God's people into their identity as an embodied apologetic of God's good news in Jesus Christ. As will be argued more directly in the next chapter, becoming an embodied apologetic through these practices is not merely about discipleship for God's people. Rather, through them God's people become evangelistic.[99]

---

90. Heuertz and Pohl, *Friendship at the Margins*, 47–67.
91. Keller, *Generous Justice*, 104–47.
92. Frost, *Exiles*, 177–200.
93. Bessenecker, *New Friars*, 58–84.
94. Haugen, "Integral Mission and Advocacy," 187–200.
95. Fitch, *Great Giveaway*, 61.
96. Ibid., 163.
97. Bessenecker, *New Friars*, 89–97.
98. Claiborne, "Marks of New Monasticism," 23.
99. Maddix and Akkerman, *Missional Discipleship*, 21

6

Communally Embodying the Gospel of Jesus Christ

THUS FAR, THIS PROJECT has identified lacunae in MCM conversations related to worship and the formation of an evangelistic character among God's people, recognized basic contours of a missional ecclesiology, proposed a missional approach to worship, and argued for the integration of missional worship with a praxis-oriented discipleship. With those considerations in mind, this final chapter attends to how an integrated approach to worship and discipleship can cultivate an evangelistic character among God's people by forming communally embodied expressions of the gospel of Jesus Christ.

In pursuing this objective, the chapter unfolds through five conversations. The first one looks at MCM insights regarding how Jesus Christ's character is perceived to be evangelistic. Returning briefly to the practices of hospitality and compassion, the second conversation considers two missional ideas related to evangelism: why prepositions matter and how belonging and believing are related. The third conversation gives particular attention to Stone's *Evangelism after Christendom* and to a discussion on embodied apologetics, highlighting how dialogue related to post-Christendom evangelism supports this project's trajectory. Concluding this book's argument, the fourth conversation considers the idea of communally embodied expressions of the gospel. Serving as an afterword of sorts, the final conversation in this chapter provides a few closing remarks regarding implications of this project and suggests potential contours for further research related to this project.

Jesus Christ's Evangelistic Character

So far, the argument advanced in this project has focused on how a missional approach to worship integrated with a praxis-oriented discipleship contributes to forming the character of Jesus Christ among the people of God. The attention now shifts to showing how the MCM understands Jesus Christ's character, and therefore the desired character of God's people, as evangelistic.

The Evangelistic Nature of Jesus' Character and the Character of God's People

In outlining a missional ecclesiology in chapter 3, this project emphasized the centrality of Jesus within the MCM. As quoted in that chapter, Hirsch insists: "For authentic missional Christianity, Jesus the Messiah plays an *absolutely* central role. Our identity as a movement, as well as our destiny as a people, is inextricably linked to Jesus—the Second Person of the Trinity."[1] Not only is Christ central for the identity of the MCM, but Jesus is also central to the motivation and direction in which the MCM moves. Frost adds: "It is Christ in us, the hope of glory, that fills us with energy and vigor for the missional cause."[2]

When considered further, this view reveals that the MCM perceives Jesus' character as evangelistic. In describing the way Jesus is revealed in the gospel of John, Bowen sketches a trajectory that supports this character focus. He writes: "Jesus never took a day off from being God incarnate. His mission was his whole life—all of his deeds and words, lived in obedience to God's will." Continuing, Bowen describes Jesus' obedience in terms of revealing God's glory: "At its simplest, God's glory is God's character, seen in all its beauty and purity, its love and power. And so to glorify God means to show God's character. God is glorified when people see what God is like." He then adds that Jesus reveals God's character in such a way that others are called to respond: "As people are confronted with God in human form, with the view through the window-that-is-Jesus—his holiness, his compassion, his anger at evil, his gentleness with pain—they find they cannot remain neutral. They have a choice to make."[3] In a similar way, Goheen also observes that Jesus' call for the people of Israel to repent and return to God is engaged through a commitment to follow Jesus. "The summons to repent

---

1. Hirsch, *Forgotten Ways*, 94. Emphasis original.
2. Frost, *Road to Missional*, 130.
3. Bowen, *Evangelism for "Normal" People*, 57–58.

and believe demands that one offer one's whole life to Jesus, be willing to abandon one's home and family, and set aside all other responsibilities for the sake of the kingdom."[4] Even more explicitly, Wright asserts: "Jesus is not merely the agent through whom the knowledge of God is communicated (as any messenger might be). He is himself the very content of the communication."[5] From an MCM perspective, Jesus is God's good news. It's not that Jesus does evangelism, but that Jesus—the very character of who he is—is evangelistic.

Therefore, to be formed in Jesus' character is to become a good-newsing people,[6] a people who embody God's good news—that is, embody Jesus— and, therein, become evangelistic in the very character of who they are. In this vein, Boren contends that "the church has nothing to offer the world if it does not embody the message of Good News that it aims to share."[7] Even more emphatically, Hirsch and Hirsch contend that "the Great Commission is not about 'evangelism' as we have come to understand it—that is, simply telling people what Jesus has done for them and leaving it at that. It is not just about the transfer of vital information, a data download, but rather the transfer of the very life of Christ through the medium and message of our own discipleship."[8] To the extent that the people of God embody the character of Jesus Christ, they become evangelistic, even as Jesus is.

Implications for a Missional Approach to Evangelism

Two specific implications for a missional approach to evangelism emerge from this character emphasis. The first is that the praxis-oriented discipleship of God's people also serves as the context through which others are welcomed into the people of God. The second implication is that a missional approach to evangelism is primarily concerned with the faithfulness of God's people in embodying Jesus' character rather than with specific word or deed based activities.

Along these lines, Ashlin-Mayo wonders: "What if evangelism, sharing one's faith, wasn't the result of growing in your relationship with Christ but a key and foundational part of this process?"[9] His question accentuates the integral nature of discipleship and evangelism present within MCM

---

4. Goheen, *Light to the Nations*, 86.
5. Wright, *Mission of God*, 123.
6. Percy, *Good News People*.
7. Boren, *Missional Small Groups*, 35.
8. Hirsch and Hirsch, *Untamed*, 147.
9. Ashlin-Mayo, "You Are NOT a Machine."

conversations. The same practices that occasion growth as disciples also serve to welcome others into the community of God's people. As Jesus' character is formed by the Spirit's transformative presence among God's people through their worship and discipleship, others experience the invitation of Jesus' evangelistic character being embodied among God's people. In this way, Jesus' character, embodied among God's people, extends a welcome to others, inviting them to become participants with God's people in the continued unfolding story of God's mission. In other words, evangelism does not follow discipleship, as if it is a culminating activity only engaged by the spiritually mature. Rather, a praxis-oriented discipleship is from the beginning evangelistic, so that God's people make known the good news of Jesus Christ even as they learn to embody Jesus' character in their life together.

In affirming this combination of discipleship and evangelism, Guder contends that every aspect of the Christian community is connected, "either obediently or disobediently," to this calling.[10] Likewise, Chester points to this capacity when he writes: "Proclamation cannot take place apart from a context. The question is whether that context is congruent with the message of transforming grace in Jesus Christ."[11] In short, the discipleship of God's people is in itself an evangelistic expression of the gospel because it is bent on forming the evangelistic character of Jesus Christ among God's people. Therefore, the integrated approach to worship and discipleship advanced in this project always has in view both the formation of those who are already following Jesus Christ and the evangelization of those who are not yet part of God's people.

Reflecting on how this view changes the goal of evangelism, Fitch contends: "The goal is to immerse the stranger into the salvation of Jesus Christ . . . It reflects a salvation that is from God, embodied in a people's character and a way of life. This vision of success aims toward faithfulness in being the body of Christ before the watching world."[12] In a very real sense then, as the church takes on Christ's character, the body of Christ becomes the proclamation and the invitation of the gospel: that in Jesus Christ, God is reconciling all things. Hammond and Cronshaw exemplify how this praxis-oriented discipleship, evangelistic invitation, and the character of Jesus can come together in a community's life together:

> We get to know each other's spouses and kids. We eat in one another's homes. We are as generous as we can be. We want to do the same with those we serve and love and lead. We want

---

10. Guder, "Worthy Living," 428.
11. Chester, *Justice, Mercy, and Humility*, 3.
12. Fitch, *Great Giveaway*, 43.

everyone we mentor and disciple, everyone we partner with in God's mission, to experience this kind of community, because it is a way to experience the character and nature of God. We want to live this way because Jesus did.[13]

The communal context and practices through which God's people learn to faithfully live as Jesus lived serves as the entry point for others to enter the community and "experience the character and nature of God." In this way, evangelism occurs simultaneously with the integrated worship-discipleship formation of Jesus' character among the people of God.

Additionally, focusing discipleship and evangelism on the character of Jesus in this way repositions the word/deed debate within a MCM understanding of evangelism. Newbigin offers an initial insight into this perspective: "It is clear that to set word and deed, preaching and action, against each other is absurd. The central reality is neither word nor act, but the total life of a community enabled by the Spirit to live in Christ, sharing his passion and the power of his resurrection."[14] Hirsch develops this idea further:

> In a very real and sobering way, we must actually become the gospel to the people around us—an expression of the real Jesus through the quality of our lives. We must live our truths. Or as Paul says it, we ourselves are living letters whose message is constantly being read by others (2 Cor. 3:1–3). In the final analysis, the medium is the message, and the phenomenal movements of God seemed to be able to express the message authentically through the media of both their personal and communal lives together. This is what made it believable and transferable.[15]

Within the MCM, then, the emphasis on the character of Jesus shifts the perception of evangelism away from the either/or prioritizing tensions of proclamation versus social action[16] toward a view of evangelism as an embodied proclamation through which the whole life of God's people makes known the good news of Jesus Christ. Goheen accentuates this perspective:

---

13. Hammond and Cronshaw, *Sentness*, 139–40.

14. Newbigin, *Gospel in a Pluralist Society*, 137.

15. Hirsch, *Forgotten Ways*, 114. Hirsch is drawing on Marshall McLuhan contending that the people of God are the medium and, therefore, the message by which Jesus Christ is made known.

16. See Packer, *Evangelism and the Sovereignty of God*, 45–50; and also Webster, "What Is Evangelism?" 26–40, both of whom distinguish evangelism as distinct from social action, compassion, justice, and other dimensions of Christian witness or mission. See also the Lausanne Covenant, section 4, "The Nature of Evangelism," and section 5, "Christian Social Responsibility" (http://www.lausanne.org/covenant).

> Flowing from its communal life are words and deeds that point to Christ, the source of this new life. The missional church is an evangelizing church that speaks the good news pointing to Christ. It also enacts the good news with deeds of mercy and justice. In all this, the messianic community follows Jesus, who made known the good news of the kingdom in his own words and deeds.[17]

Since the emphasis is on faithful embodiment of the gospel, the question is not whether the people of God should participate in word- or deed-based ministries, but on how both word- and deed-based ministries provide opportunities for the people of God to faithfully embody the character of Jesus Christ.

To this end, the fruit of the Spirit could serve as a helpful barometer for discerning how faithfully a word or deed based ministry assists God's people in cohering with Jesus' character.[18] The fruit of the Spirit provides an accessible list of potential characteristics to guide discernment through questions such as: How will this proclamation assist us in embodying the love of Jesus? Or, what could it look like for us to embody Christ's patience and faithfulness with our neighbors? While not an exhaustive formula, the fruit of the Spirit provides a lens for attending to God's people's faithfulness in embodying Jesus' character. To the extent that God's people "keep in step with the Spirit," their embodiment of Jesus' character through the fruit of the Spirit can also invite questions from their neighbors. While pointing to the absence of New Testament commands to evangelize, Bowen emphasizes other passages that urge God's people to be ready to respond to questions from a watching world who are attracted to (even though they might not understand) the character God's people are embodying.[19]

In this light, a missional approach to evangelism is primarily concerned with God's people conveying the character of Jesus Christ through all that they are, say, and do together. In short, the MCM recognizes that the communal life of Jesus' disciples is inherently evangelistic. As such, the MCM does not see evangelism so much as a particular activity, presentation, conversation, or strategic relationship that needs to be mastered, delivered, or

---

17. Goheen, *Light to the Nations*, 198.

18. While not the only biblical description of God's character—see Psalm 103:8, which describes God as "compassionate and gracious, slow to anger and abounding in love"—the Galatians 5:22–23 text has the advantage of recognizing the Holy Spirit's transformative presence in God's people and their actions.

19. Bowen, *Evangelism for "Normal" People*, 189, in reference to Colossians 4:6 and 1 Peter 3:15.

engaged apart from discipleship.[20] This viewpoint does not exclude typical evangelism methodologies and emphases from supporting roles as potential resources. Rather, the primary understanding of evangelism in the MCM shifts toward a way of communally embodying the character of Jesus Christ *in situ* so that others are invited and welcomed into the community of God's people, among whom they will encounter Jesus Christ and can begin participating in his evangelistic character among God's people.

Two Missional Perspectives on Evangelism

Exploring further what embodying Jesus' character *in situ* can look like, the second conversation engages two missional perspectives on evangelism: why prepositions matter and the relationship of belonging and believing. As a means of exemplifying the impact of these perspectives, this conversation offers a few further thoughts on the practices of hospitality and compassion.

Prepositions Matter

As presented in chapters 1 and 3, the MCM considers the relationship between God's people and their specific local contexts essential for discerning how the church is called to engage within the story of God's mission. Because of this emphasis on location, the prepositions used to describe the relationship between God's people and their neighbours take on a new importance.

Four prepositions are commonly used to describe mission: *to, for, in,* and *with*.[21] Mission has often been understood through the imperative *go*, with the implication that mission involved leaving one's home and going *to* a new place where mission would take place. Mission was elsewhere and assumed to be cross-cultural. The MCM has consistently pushed against this notion of mission, with some contending that God's mission frequently involves staying.[22] Many of the accusations regarding the colonial presuppositions inherent in Christian mission rest on this *to* understanding of mission.

---

20. Fitch, *Great Giveaway*, 48–49.

21. I have encountered these prepositions in a variety of personal conversations related to the MCM during the past six years, but I am not aware of the original source. Though not utilizing the prepositions in the same way I am here, Sparks, Soerens, and Friesen describe mission postures in various historical epochs, arguing that the missional use of *with* is strictly relational and lacks a locational rootedness (*New Parish*, 37–45)—a perspective with which I disagree because of the missional movement's underlying emphasis on place.

22. Hammond and Cronshaw, *Sentness*, 54–55.

Occasionally, mission has been understood as something the people of God do *for* others. This emphasis has been particularly true with regard to missions geared toward alleviating physical suffering. The MCM tends to dismiss this approach quickly, insisting that mission is more than "a project in which those of us inside the church perform some action for those outside the church."[23] The underlying paternalistic assumptions associated with this preposition operate with an economic stereotype of the sending organization having all the resources and the receiving culture having all of the need. Unfortunately, though filled with good intentions, mission *for* others has often resulted in reinforcing the economic and cultural differences that may exist between the church and those they are attempting to serve.

As missiologists and mission practitioners have grown in cultural intelligence[24] and distanced themselves from the perceived colonial practices, a greater emphasis has been placed on doing ministry *in* a specific location. Mission *in* a place involves taking time to understand and respect a culture and developing a long-term commitment to the people of a particular community, so as to value the relationships between people in the sending and receiving communities. While such an emphasis allowed some to focus on mission *in* their own backyards, such attempts to be *in* a specific community still were often expressed through underlying paternalistic expectations connected with mission *for* approaches.

In contrast to these first three approaches, the missional church emphasis has shifted to focus on mission *with* and *within*[25] the neighborhoods in which God's people live. Roxburgh and Boren argue that "[t]he task of the local church in our present situation is to reenter our neighborhoods, to dwell with and to listen to the narratives and stories of the people."[26] Their emphasis on dwelling *with* allows the people of God to be accessible to their neighbors. *With* also recognizes that the Spirit is already at work in the world and among the people in the church's neighborhood. Moreover, *with* seeks to avoid the colonial and paternal assumptions that the church has all the knowledge and resources to recognize and fix the perceived problems for the community. Instead, *with* leads God's people to become part of the community, placing ownership for the community's well-being on the whole community. Taking this posture expects God's people will live as a tangible presence of God in their neighborhoods.

23. Boren, *Missional Small Groups*, 34.

24. See Livermore, *Serving with Eyes Wide Open*.

25. Sparks, Soerens, and Friesen prefer the combined preposition *within*, so as to emphasize the relational aspect of mission *with* neighbours as well as *in* to emphasize the rooted location of God's people (*New Parish*, 46–48).

26. Roxburgh and Boren, *Introducing the Missional Church*, 85.

This emphasis on mission *within* a community reflects the attention above to the worship-discipleship cultivation of an evangelistic character through which others encounter Jesus among the people of God. Huckins contends that not only do the people of God engage their "apprenticeship in the way of Jesus" *within* community, but also through their presence *within* community their neighbors are invited into community with God's people. "The radical invitation is the beginning of redemption, of the restoration God has in mind for all of his people. It is the beginning of a faith that does not remain in the minds of individuals, but is lived in the context of a community of faith."[27] Evangelism as the evangelistic character of God's people *in situ* depends on relational engagement of God's people *with* their neighbors and *within* their neighborhoods.

The Relationship of Belonging and Believing

The second missional perspective on evangelism revolves around the relationship between belonging and believing. This perspective is concerned with whether people profess belief in Jesus before they may belong to the church or if there is room for them to belong before they believe. Noting a shift away from belief preceding belonging, Maddix and Akkerman point to how, "[i]n practical terms, evangelism in many circles has stressed belief before belonging: one must accept the gospel before becoming assimilated into the church. Missional engagement reverses the trend, stressing belonging first (often tempered by Christian practices), trusting that belief will follow."[28] Kreider and Kreider emphasize that this missional posture is congruent with the early church: "The early Christian preachers did not urge their hearers to evangelize their friends; instead they urged them to obey Jesus' teachings and to 'imitate' his way in their lives."[29] Contrasting this approach with the Engel Scale,[30] which divides evangelism and discipleship based on whether a person has made a personal commitment to Christ, Hirsch and Hirsch argue that "discipleship started long before a person became a convert."[31] As such, belonging is not merely an evangelism methodology but, more importantly, an integral part of the praxis-oriented

---

27. Huckins, *Thin Places*, 72–73.
28. Maddix and Akkerman, *Missional Discipleship*, 20.
29. Kreider and Kreider, *Worship and Mission*, 138-39.
30. Engel and Norton, *What's Gone Wrong with the Harvest?*
31. Hirsch and Hirsch, *Untamed*, 150–51. Also Bowen, *Evangelism for "Normal" People*, 76–86.

discipleship of God's people. In this sense, discipleship and evangelism are not readily distinguishable activities within the MCM.

From an MCM perspective, this shift to belonging before believing is necessary because of underlying assumptions connected to a prioritization of belief. Bowen articulates these assumptions well: "One is that individual faith in Christ and life in the Christian community are somehow separate realities. Another is that mental assent to the message of Christ is a separate thing from living by the message of Christ. There is also the assumption that a split-second decision is more significant than a lengthy process." He further contends that, when combined with an emphasis on determining whether someone is a Christian or not, "the purpose of evangelism is then to persuade outsiders to become insiders, to cross the line from darkness into light."[32] These assumptions run the risk of objectifying the person who is being evangelized, reducing their personal worth, and conditioning any potential for future relationship with them on whether or not they agree in the immediate moment with the particular articulation of the gospel being presented to them.

The emphasis on belonging before believing typically relies on a distinction between centered and bounded sets as a means for locating someone in relationship to Jesus Christ.[33] In their seminal work, *The Shaping of Things to Come*, Frost and Hirsch advocate for a centered-set approach within the MCM. From their perspective, a bounded set is concerned with whether people have expressed intellectual assent that Jesus is their Savior and Lord and agreed to adhere to a specific set of behaviors that demonstrate this belief in order to belong to the church. In this set, God's people are responsible to help those outside the boundaries make a personal commitment to Christ so they can gain access to life among God's people. Frost and Hirsch contend that in the bounded set insider Christians have all the spiritual answers and outsider non-Christians all of the need.[34]

On the other hand, they assert that a centered-set approach focuses attention on a person's relational direction and distance from Jesus Christ. Within this approach, everyone belongs among God's people because each and every person has a relationship—even if it is distant, defiant, indifferent, or static—to the center, Jesus Christ. The evangelistic role of God's people is to live in such a way that others can see and experience what life can be like when moving closer toward Jesus Christ. In this model, everyone has the

---

32. Bowen, *Evangelism for "Normal" People*, 45.

33. Discussion on bounded and centered sets is much broader than MCM sources indicate. See Yoder et al., "Understanding Christian Identity in Terms of Bounded and Centered Set Theory," 177–88.

34. Frost and Hirsch, *Shaping of Things to Come*, 47–51.

opportunity to learn from each other and to contribute to others because no one has yet fully arrived at Christ.[35] Belonging in relationship with Jesus and with those who are seeking to follow Jesus precedes belief.

While Frost and Hirsch argue strictly for a centered-set approach, others in the MCM recognize that Jesus' life displayed a mixed approach of bounded and centered sets. Relying on concentric circles, Bowen describes how there appear to be clusters of people at different relational distances from Jesus: the crowds, the women who followed Jesus, the Twelve, and even an inner circle of three. Bowen also observes how the directional movement of their relationship to Jesus gained importance. In affirming Bowen's insight, one could think of Zacchaeus as an outlier, even among the crowds, who was suddenly brought into close relationship with Jesus; of the rich young ruler, who, though affirmed by Jesus, turned and walked away; or of Judas, who belonged to the Twelve but betrayed Jesus with a kiss. Noting how Jesus frequently provided room for the different circles to intermingle with each other, Bowen observes: "there was no distinction between those who were already disciples and those who were, as we would say, checking him out."[36] As such, professed faith in Jesus was not a prerequisite to belonging with and among Jesus' disciples; yet, as one moved toward Jesus their belief in Jesus became more apparent.

From a missional perspective, then, the community of God's people embodying Jesus' evangelistic character becomes the context within which belief is made possible. As a brief aside, this particular viewpoint would be greatly enhanced by dialogue with scholarship surrounding Taylor's social imaginaries and Berger's plausibility structures. Though to directly engage these philosophical and sociological conversations is beyond the scope of this project, the engagement with Smith's *Desiring the Kingdom* in chapter 4 highlights a potential entry point into Taylor's social imagination. Similarly, Sire's *Naming the Elephant*, which explores the formation and place of worldviews, could serve as a helpful means of entering Berger's work. For example, Sire describes a plausibility structure as "the worldview of society, the heart of a society," regardless of the community's size or function (religious, social, academic, political). He continues, adding that "one of the main functions of a plausibility structure is to provide the background of beliefs that make arguments easy or hard to accept." Sire then outlines how the elevation of a particular plausibility structure can silence conversation because conclusions seem obvious and, in the other direction, how the advent of pluralism has undermined a broadly accepted plausibility structure

---

35. Ibid.
36. Bowen, *Evangelism for "Normal" People*, 45–48.

reducing reality to individualized perceptions.[37] Engagement with these broader conversations would strengthen the MCM's understanding of how belonging to a community that embodies the good news cultivates an environment within which believing Jesus becomes possible.

Returning to the conversation at hand, the MCM has emphasized belonging within the community of God's people (and learning to participate in the life of that community) as the experiential context within which belief in Jesus as God's good news makes sense. Thus, with regard to evangelism, the emphasis shifts from a more traditional approach of conveying information about God in order to persuade someone to convert to Christianity, to a slower evangelism where Jesus becomes believable as people are welcomed into the shared life of God's people.

Further Reflections on Hospitality and Compassion

In chapter 5, hospitality and compassion were described as discipleship practices through which the people of God learn to embody the character of Jesus Christ in their relationships with one another and in their engagement with their neighbours. Yet these practices are not simply about discipleship. As Frost remarks, "By living expansive lives of justice, kindness, hospitality, and generosity, we model the life of Jesus to those who would never attend a church service or read the New Testament."[38] In this light, discipleship practices of hospitality and compassion are also evangelistic practices through which others can enter into the shared life of God's people and encounter Jesus Christ.

Several missional authors point to hospitality as a compelling evangelistic practice through which people "far from God" can encounter Jesus Christ. Fitch asserts that "the time-honored practice of hospitality is so exceedingly rare today that just doing it at all speaks volumes about what it means to be a Christian in a world of strangers." He remarks further that "inviting a stranger into one's home alongside another church friends shares and immerses that person in some of the bounty of fellowship and commonality Christians share."[39] Framing hospitality in relationship to a retelling of Jesus going to a dinner party at Matthew's house, Bowen notes how both host and guests are drawn closer to Jesus (centered set) through the diversity of guests "that cut across all social distinctions" (belonging).[40]

37. Sire, *Naming the Elephant*, 109–16.
38. Frost, *Exiles*, 73–74.
39. Fitch, *Great Giveaway*, 60.
40. Bowen, *Evangelism for "Normal" People*, 48–51.

Reflecting on how hospitality can convey God's generosity, Chester and Timmis add an admonishing comment: "the grace of God meant that Jesus hung out with unrespectable people. People complained about his companions. If our congregations are full of respectable people, then it may be that we have not truly grasped the radical grace of God."[41] In these ways, hospitality serves as an evangelistic practice, drawing others into the community of God's people and toward Jesus.

In similar fashion, compassion is also an evangelistic practice. *The New Parish* authors emphasize that compassion is geared toward God's kingdom becoming a lived reality defined by God's economy in their local context rather than by more broadly accepted allegiances.[42] Similarly, Fitch and Holsclaw insist: "Every local practice of justice plants the seeds for justice to flow wider and higher in the entire world."[43] Particularly within cultural contexts of violence and shattered relationships, Fitch contends that "[w]hen the church reaches out to actually minister justice or mercy to a victim of sin and pray for the victimizer, it witnesses to the gospel in ways words can never do."[44] Speaking more directly to acts of compassion, Gorman remarks: "When we act with Christlike compassion by feeding the hungry, giving a cup of clean water to the thirsty, loving the stranger, clothing the naked, and visiting those who are sick or in prison, we make visible the love of God in our world."[45] From a missional perspective, the discipleship practice of compassion, manifested in doing justice and loving mercy, cultivates an evangelistic character among God's people through which the world around them experiences the good news of Jesus Christ.

These practices of hospitality and compassion reveal a missional approach to evangelism that is focused on the people of God embodying the character of Jesus Christ in their relationships with one another and in their engagement with their neighbours. Kreider and Kreider note how this approach resonates with practices in the early church: "The early Christian preachers did not urge their hearers to evangelize their friends; instead they urged them obey Jesus' teachings and to 'imitate' his way in their lives."[46] In this way, discipleship practices like hospitality and compassion create an environment where the church becomes evangelistic and their neighbors can begin to believe that Jesus really is the good news.

---

41. Chester and Timmis, *Total Church*, 84.
42. Sparks, Soerens, and Friesen, *New Parish*, 39.
43. Fitch and Holsclaw, *Prodigal Christianity*, 140.
44. Fitch, *Great Giveaway*, 60.
45. Gorman, "Ripple Effect," 132. Also Bowen, *Evangelism for "Normal" People*, 93.
46. Kreider and Kreider, *Worship and Mission*, 138–39.

Affirmations from Conversations in Post-Christendom Evangelism

In recent history, approaches to Christian evangelism and apologetics have relied on presentations of rational arguments in an attempt to persuade "non-believers" to convert and to defend the veracity of Christian beliefs. Arguments in favour of Christianity have hinged largely upon the capacity of individual apologists to articulate acute defenses of Christianity over against other religious perspectives. In contrast, the MCM locates the persuasiveness of the Christian faith within the communal lifestyle of God's people, not on the capacity of an individual to clearly present a propositional understanding of the gospel. Fitch writes: "For postmodern evangelism, this means that truth is best communicated as it is lived in the life of a body of Christ out of its (his)tory and its stories, not one-on-one combat via evidentiary apologetic." [47] Some, like Kreider and Kreider, connect this approach to the early church, contending that "Christian apologists did not talk about their appealing worship services. Instead they claimed that the Christians behaved differently from other people."[48] This emphasis on the lives of God's people points toward a communally embodied apologetic.

In this regard, the MCM resonates with two conversations related to post-Christendom evangelism. The first conversation centers on Stone's *Evangelism after Christendom*, in which he calls for a communally embodied approach to Christian witness. The second conversation emerges from dialogue around the need for an embodied apologetics,[49] for which Stackhouse's *Humble Apologetics* serves as a primary example. Both of these works are highlighted briefly here as a means of affirming the MCM emphasis on the formation of a communally embodied apologetic for the gospel.

Stone's Evangelism after Christendom

In *Evangelism after Christendom*, Stone offers a substantive reflection on the theology and practice of evangelism within a post-Christendom context, contending that "the most evangelistic thing the church can do today is to

---

47. Fitch, *Great Giveaway*, 57

48. Kreider and Kreider, *Worship and Mission*, 138–39.

49. Sire points to this need when describing apologetics as presenting "the watching world such a winsome embodiment of the Christian faith that for any and all who are willing to observe there will be an intellectually and emotionally credible witness to its fundamental truth" (*Little Primer on Humble Apologetics*, 26).

be the church."[50] Part 1 explains the nature of a practice,[51] exploring the essential role of narrative, tradition, and virtues in discerning core practices.[52] With this framework, he asserts that there is both an evangelistic characteristic to the whole of Christian life and a specific practice of evangelism that together establish evangelism as a constitutive practice of Christianity.[53]

In part 2, Stone reflects on the biblical narrative's social imagination, in which Israel's election to embody God's concern for all of creation[54] serves as the context for Jesus' embodied proclamation of God's reign, tangibly extended as both gift and summons into the narrative of God's kingdom.[55] The narrative trajectory of God's mission continues with the formation of the *ecclesia*, founded in Jesus' resurrection as the community of the Spirit,[56] who then embody Jesus' reign in their life together as they continue to be "narrated by the story of Jesus" even while "narrating it to others" in expectation of Jesus' return.[57]

In part 3, Stone attends to two opposing narratives: Constantinianism and modernity. Relying heavily on Yoder's critique of Constantinianism[58] and engaging modernity through MacIntyre's *After Virtue*,[59] Stone critiques strategies focused on seeker-friendly worship, on meeting felt needs,[60] and on positioning Christianity as a modest "option among a plurality of options."[61] Instead, Stone calls the church to become a countercultural, communal embodiment of God's reign within a postmodern context.[62]

Drawing on Yoder's ecclesiology, Stone argues in part 4 that the church offers "a radical alternative" to the surrounding culture, while also serving as a "credible witness to the world" and *for* the world.[63] Such credibility, Stone contends, comes through the church's sacramental politics (baptism)[64] and

50. Stone, *Evangelism after Christendom*, 15.
51. Ibid., 30–37.
52. Ibid., 37–45.
53. Ibid., 45–53.
54. Ibid., 65.
55. Ibid., 80–84.
56. Ibid., ch. 4.
57. Ibid., 106.
58. Ibid., 120–29.
59. Ibid., 131–35.
60. Ibid., 143–46.
61. Ibid., 153–54.
62. Ibid., 170.
63. Ibid., 176–77.
64. Ibid., 180–88. Stone contends that "salvation is, in the first place, a distinct form of social existence."

economics (Eucharist),[65] which mark the *ecclesia* as the alternative public of the Holy Spirit,[66] who makes Christ known through the *ecclesia*'s embodied life. [67] In this light, conversion is "the acquisition of a way of life," remaking the whole person "through the stories, practices, and traditions of the church,"[68] and faithful witness is the *ecclesia*'s adherence to the "distinctively upside-down set of priorities embodied in the life and ministry of Jesus."[69]

In part 5, Stone reflects on the character of evangelism as "a life patterned after the story of Christ through a lived participation in the ecclesial fellowship."[70] He highlights four virtues of evangelistic practice: *presence* through which faith is tangibly embodied; *patience* as "an active confidence that we live in God's time"; *courage* to embody God's reign in the presence of opposing narratives; and *humility* to "become dispossessed of every pretense to gaining a foothold in the world for themselves or their cause."[71] These virtues require the additional virtue of the community's practical wisdom, in which "the traditions, stories, memories, exemplars, and patterns of the church provide a deep *habitus* . . . through which the Holy Spirit guides the church."[72]

Stone then concludes his consideration of evangelism as a practice, appealing to the church to be distinctive so as to give the world "something to see—and to touch and to try."[73] He states that "the practice of evangelism is a complex and multilayered process—a context of multiple activities that invite, herald, welcome, and provoke and that has as its end the peaceable reign of God and the social holiness by which persons are oriented toward that reign."[74] In the end, for Stone, the practice of evangelism is embodied in the people of God, weak and imperfect as they may be, so that "the visibility of the people of God may be understood as a sign and foretaste of what has already arrived and a promise of what is to come."[75]

Overall, Stone's extensive treatment of evangelism as a communal practice in *Evangelism after Christendom* is congruent with much of the

---

65. Ibid., 202.
66. Ibid., 224–30.
67. Ibid., 231–42.
68. Ibid., 262–63.
69. Ibid., 275.
70. Ibid., 277.
71. Ibid., 285–306.
72. Ibid., 310–11.
73. Ibid., 315.
74. Ibid., 316.
75. Ibid., 318.

MCM emphasis on the embodied evangelistic character of God's people. While Stone's explicit reference to Yoder leaves his analysis open to critiques of Yoder's ecclesiology, of whether Stone has faithfully represented Yoder, and some additional concerns,[76] his attempt to engage conversations regarding social imaginaries and practices could serve as profitable models for further dialogue within the MCM. Moreover, Stone's thesis, "that the most evangelistic thing the church can do today is be the church,"[77] resonates with the missional emphasis of the church's sent identity.

In working out his thesis, Stone offers at least four other contributions that affirm the direction of this project. The first contribution is his argument that evangelism is "an intrinsic characteristic of every Christian practice and of the comprehensive practice of Christian faith itself," so that "the fellowship, disciplines, practices, and social patterns by which we are made witnesses are themselves the very signs of God's mercy and judgment and a living invitation to a 'watching world.'"[78] Secondly, Stone recognizes that evangelism, as a practice, is defined by the internal goal of faithful witness rather than any external goals of conversion, church growth, or cultural influence.[79] Thirdly, Stone portrays evangelism as communal, asserting that the church is "constituted, vivified, and renewed by the Holy Spirit"[80] as "the social embodiment of God's new creation in Christ, the very news that is to be heralded as good."[81] Finally, Stone understands evangelism as intimately involved with the church's character. Stone argues that evangelism "is a matter of being present in the world in a distinctive way such that the alluring and 'useless' beauty of holiness can be touched, tasted, and tried."[82] As such, evangelism is concerned with "the way Christians eat together, keep time, celebrate, forgive debts, express thanks, show hospitality, demonstrate compassion, live simply, and share their materials resources with one another" as "an actual participation in the life of the triune God."[83] Thus,

---

76. See Willimon who affirms Stone's work and offers a critique regarding the limited attention to Christology ("Evangelism after Christendom," 35–37). Also Krabill, "Evangelism after Christendom," 93–94. One also wonders why Stone does not provide as robust of a critique of postmodernity as he does Constantinianism and modernity.

77. Stone, *Evangelism after Christendom*, 15.

78. Ibid., 27.

79. Ibid., 34.

80. Ibid., 25.

81. Ibid., 48.

82. Ibid., 21.

83. Ibid., 202.

conversion is "the acquisition of a way of life that is embodied and passed along in community."[84]

Embodied Apologetics

A similar emphasis has emerged among the discipline of Christian apologetics, calling for an apologetic that is embodied in the life of a community of God's people rather than simply in the intellectual argument of one person attempting to persuade others of the gospel's truth. Stackhouse's *Humble Apologetics* illustrates this perspective.

Offered as both a reflective memoir and a vision for an expanded view of apologetics, *Humble Apologetics* affords Stackhouse an opportunity to argue for a holistic apologetic. Pointing to how "the very thing to be discussed in apologetics is more than a matter of mere intellection," Stackhouse asserts that "apologetics itself must extend beyond the merely intellectual."[85] In broadening the general understanding of apologetics, Stackhouse contends: "*anything* that helps people take Christianity more seriously than they did before, *anything* that helps defend and commend it, properly counts as apologetics."[86] His argument unfolds in three parts.

In part 1, Stackhouse considers four challenges to Christianity present in the North American context: pluralism, postmodernism, plausibility, and consumerism. After reflecting on the pluralistic culture in which Christianity contends, Stackhouse argues that there are actually multiple postmodernisms at work, contributing to the current implausibility of Christianity within postmodernity.[87] Alongside these challenges, Stackhouse notes how consumerism leads people to see themselves as the primary judge of good and the belief that "everything that matters can somehow be obtained by commercial means."[88] In this context, religion is commodified, faith is privatized, and "genuine religion" in the public sphere is perceived as a "threat to the values and order of consumerism."[89]

Through part 2, Stackhouse explores the idea of conversion, arguing that the goal of Christian mission is not to convert people to Christianity but to help others journey toward conversion, which scripture and theology

---

84. Ibid., 259–60.
85. Stackhouse, *Humble Apologetics*,115.
86. Ibid., 115. Emphasis original.
87. Ibid., 40.
88. Ibid., 54–59.
89. Ibid., 60–63.

speak of as repentance, regeneration, sanctification, and glorification[90]—a holistic portrayal that stands in stark contrast to the single-moment, change-in-mind conversion often emphasized among evangelicals.[91] Moreover, in light of the finite and fallen nature of humanity, Stackhouse contends that all knowledge is faith-based and is, therefore, best expressed in terms of "graduated assent" rather than as coherence to absolute truth, making religious certainty humanly impossible.[92] Arguing further that the "fundamental human problem is not ignorance or deprivation, but sin,"[93] he contends that religious certainty is not the *telos* of apologetics. Rather, the question of apologetics and religion is about "what or whom we love." Stackhouse asserts that since rational "argument cannot produce affection" for God, conversion needs to be seen as a matter of the Holy Spirit, not of apologetics.[94] Therefore, apologetics is more appropriately focused on the virtuousness, or character, of Christianity rather than on winning intellectual arguments.[95]

In part 3, Stackhouse's primary concern is with establishing guidelines for apologetic conversations. In framing these guidelines, Stackhouse insists that apologetics concerned entirely with words and truths "will literally fail to communicate Christianity, but instead necessarily distort it by shrinking it to what words and truths can portray,"[96] while also cautioning that the particular content of God's love in Jesus Christ "cannot possibly be inferred from mere good Christian behavior."[97] "Therefore," Stackhouse argues, "we are to offer, as God Incarnate did, both word and flesh, both message and life, to our neighbors in apologetics."[98] Offering twelve guidelines for humble apologetics, Stackhouse emphasizes sympathetic listening to neighbors and maintaining a clear focus on Jesus,[99] while cautioning against a reduced mission in pursuit of an immediate decision for Christianity.[100] Reflecting on other modes of apologetics, Stackhouse points to the apologetic witness

---

90. Ibid., 71–77.
91. Ibid., 76–85.
92. Ibid., 85–110.
93. Ibid., 112.
94. Ibid., 113.
95. Ibid., 114–20.
96. Ibid., 131.
97. Ibid., 132–34.
98. Ibid., 135.
99. Ibid., 161–205.
100. Ibid., 203.

of Christian character communicated in how Christians carry themselves,[101] particularly as evident in Christian communities, which Stackhouse calls *plausibility places*. These communities express "God's care for the earth, for the financially and socially needy, for beauty and joy, and for the intellectual life," not in pursuit of "saving souls" but in order to cooperate with God, "who is at work to redeem the whole world."[102]

Stackhouse concludes with an appeal for a *humble apologetic* that reflects the limits of human knowledge,[103] communicates respect for others' intelligence and spiritual journeys,[104] and consistently recognizes the apologist's own dependence on God.[105] Ultimately, this humility maintains a posture of expectation that God is at work "bringing people into his Kingdom" and calling Christians to participate in God's mission.[106]

While there is much to commend in this book—the clear, concise explanation of postmodernity and postmodernisms[107] and the positioning of faith as the basis for knowledge,[108] for example—and certainly some room for critique,[109] including the question of how Stackhouse's apologetics relates to those of other apologists,[110] two key aspects of Stackhouse's presentation affirm the direction of this project.

Throughout *Humble Apologetics*, Stackhouse asserts that "apologetics itself must extend beyond the merely intellectual."[111] He returns consistently to this conviction, contending for a holistic apologetic because "serious decisions are resolved by the whole person, not merely by the intellectual,

---

101. Ibid., 213–23.
102. Ibid., 224–26.
103. Ibid., 228.
104. Ibid., 229.
105. Ibid., 230.
106. Ibid., 231
107. Beghuis, "Humble Apologetics," 381–82.
108. Ryan provides a balanced review of Stackhouse's book, observing that Stackhouse does not adopt postmodernism but sees that in this culture "we must argue from a position of plausibility, asking those in front of us to consider: 'Might not this be true?'" ("Humble Apologetics," 127–28).
109. A chapter on the narrative shape of scripture and faith could have bolstered his argument that conversion to the Christian faith is more than a change of mind. Also, more attention to biblical patterns of apologetics at the end of chapter 7 would have been beneficial.
110. For example, Strange who critiques Stackhouse from a presuppositionalist posture ("Humble Apologetics," 231–38).
111. Stackhouse, *Humble Apologetics*, 115.

moral, spiritual, physical, sociological, and psychological."[112] Rooting this broadened apologetic in his understanding of the gospel, Stackhouse writes:

> Since the Christian message fundamentally is an invitation extended to human beings (not just human brains) to encounter and embrace the person of Jesus Christ (rather than merely to adopt a doctrinal system or ideology) it is then obvious that establishing the plausibility and credibility of that message will depend upon more than intellectual argument. It will depend instead on the Holy Spirit of God shining through all the lamps of good works we can raise to the glory of our Father in heaven.[113]

As such, apologetics cannot be limited to intellectual persuasion, but must extend to include the whole person, and include the whole Christian community. However, it would be misleading to suggest that Stackhouse is somehow discarding or even minimizing reason and intellectual engagement in apologetics. He comments:

> Indeed, it would seem odd that in a religion whose God tells us to love him with our minds as well as with the rest of our being, and who gives his people a highly complex set of sacred writings in the Bible, intellectual explanation and defense would not play at least some part in helping at least some audiences come to faith and then grow up in it.[114]

Yet Stackhouse wisely notes that broadening apologetics is also accompanied by recognition that Christian apologetics is rooted in the question of "whether one loves God, and no one does that without conversion—the exclusive activity of the Holy Spirit."[115] Therefore, "conversion is a gift."[116] This perspective affirms the emphasis within MCM conversations that evangelism is more about the faithfulness of God's people than about winning converts. Recognizing that the real human problem is not disordered thinking but the "pathology of our deranged hearts," Stackhouse writes: "Apologetics that merely speaks, then, to the mind as if people merely lack correct information will never speak to the central problem that the gospel says we face."[117] The aim of apologetics, then, is not simply to provide con-

---

112. Ibid., 160.
113. Ibid., 226.
114. Ibid., 126.
115. Ibid., 113.
116. Ibid., 228.
117. Ibid., 186.

vincing arguments but to "love our neighbors as best we can each moment according to the need and opportunity."[118]

The second affirmation that *Humble Apologetics* makes to this project is how apologetics is concerned with the character of the Christian community. Stackhouse sees that the character displayed in conveying the message of the gospel is essential for a holistic apologetic, recognizing the challenge "to complement our proclamation of the gospel with public demonstrations of God's care for the earth, for the financially and socially needy, for beauty and joy, for the intellectual life."[119] In similar fashion, an experience of poor Christian character lies at the heart of some of the most significant objections to Christianity. Stackhouse notes:

> Over and over again, talk-radio shows that featured religion were besieged by callers who wanted to report on personal disappointments with people who had called themselves Christians. An abusive father here, a repressive mother there; a flirtatious pastor or a licentious youth leader; a thieving church treasurer or a dishonest employee who loudly proclaimed his faith—over and over again, people of all walks of life reported encounters with repellent Christians. This particular person symbolized Christianity to their victims, and the pain they caused sticks to the religion they professed.[120]

What becomes clear through both types of testimony is that the character of Christians and of Christian communities significantly shapes people's experiences of Christianity.

In this light, Stackhouse sees the Christian community as a *plausibility place*, wherein people are able to "listen to Jesus, and watch Jesus, and hang around Jesus by listening to, and watching, and hanging around Christians—each Christian as an individual, yes, but especially Christians in our life together as congregations."[121] Encountering a community "of otherwise ordinary people in which the Christian faith is taken for granted as true and life-giving powerfully helps it to make sense to newcomers. In such communities, Christianity becomes plausible because it is lived with integrity."[122] Stackhouse asserts that churches that "truly live out the Christian ideals of faith, truth, hope, and especially love, are also among the very

---

118. Ibid., 203.
119. Ibid., 225.
120. Ibid., 45.
121. Ibid., 192–93.
122. Ibid., 194.

best arguments in favor of Christianity's claims."[123] Throughout *Humble Apologetics*, Stackhouse identifies the Christian community, and particularly its character, as a living, embodied apologetic for the gospel in ways that support the argument being advanced in this project.

Communally Embodied Expressions of the Gospel of Jesus Christ

This project has argued that the MCM can more fully cultivate Jesus' character among God's people by integrating a missional approach to worship with a praxis-oriented discipleship. Building on that foundation, this chapter has considered Jesus' character—and, therefore, the communally embodied character of God's people—as evangelistic, which, in turn, led to exploring a missional approach to evangelism. Rather than securing conversions, a missional approach to evangelism focuses on God's people being with their neighbors, particularly through practices of hospitality and compassion, in which belief in Jesus becomes possible. Having seen parallel conversations within post-Christendom evangelism on the character of God's people as a communally embodied apologetic, this project now turns to the final thought of the thesis: expressions of the gospel of Jesus Christ.

In short form, a communally embodied apologetic expresses the gospel of Jesus Christ by forming locally contextualized gatherings of God's people. While the word *church* and the practice of church planting certainly fit inside this understanding, they frequently carry with them reductionistic images of a building with a Sunday morning worship service, paid clergy and ministry staff, and budgeted resources.[124] However, the emphasis here on locally contextualized gatherings seeks to expand the possibilities of what can be considered *church* given the particularities and peculiarities of any given setting. Such a goal relies on Hunsberger's insight that "[e]very church everywhere will embody a local, particular expression of the gospel."[125]

Those particular expressions will gather in a wide range of settings and structures. Boren's small groups, the house church approach advocated by Chester and Timmis, and the missional communities evident in Huckins's and Roxburgh's writings can all serve as locally contextualized gatherings of God's people. Likewise, the more formally structured gatherings of a congregation with robust worship, highly structured discipleship efforts, access, and influence that can be seen in Fitch's and Goheen's descriptions also

---

123. Ibid., 193.
124. Harder, "New Shoots from Old Roots," 49–62.
125. Hunsberger and Van Gelder, *Church between Gospel and Culture*, xvi.

participate as expressions of the gospel. Hammond and Cronshaw contend that "whether a church is missional or not has very little to do with the size of the congregation or how they worship. Multisite or monastic, chapel or cathedral, alternative or automobile drive-through—take whatever helps you and others connect with God."[126] Whether a gathering is just being planted or a gathering has been together for multiple generations, the emphasis is not on the particular ways in which they are currently structured, but on how they faithfully embody the good news of Jesus Christ together. Instead of the typical numeric and structural emphases, the focus is on the purposes for which God's people form a local gathering. As Hendrik contends, gatherings of God's people "become a sign pointing beyond themselves to God's reign" with a goal of modelling "now the truth and the final purpose of God, even if imperfectly."[127]

In many ways, these purposes go back to the initial description of the MCM provided in chapter 1, allowing for and encouraging broad diversity in how and where the people of God are gathered as a communally embodied expression of the gospel of Jesus Christ. Communally embodied expressions will seek to imitate the Trinity, thereby participating in the *missio trinitatis*. Bowen remarks that "[i]t seems that God invented this imitation idea. Human beings, after all, were made in the image of God, to live out God's character in the world. Just as children imitate their parents, we were made to imitate God."[128]

A gathering of God's people will also understand itself as being sent into its particular context, even as the Father sent the Son and the Spirit. To this end, *The New Parish* authors insist that "[j]ust as Christ 'became flesh and blood, and moved into the neighborhood,' so also the people that comprise the local church in the parish are meant to be a tangible expression of God's love in the everyday reality of life."[129]

Moreover, these particular, local expressions of the gospel of Jesus Christ will see themselves as a community of servants. Fitch conveys this servant vision well: "I hope our churches become known for servanthood in their neighborhoods and warm hospitality that invites strangers into our homes. I pray that the home of every evangelical person becomes an incubator for evangelism, inviting strangers to the gospel out of their lostness and into the love and grace of life in our Lord Jesus Christ."[130]

126. Hammond and Cronshaw, *Sentness*, 58.
127. Hendrick, "Congregations with Missions vs. Missional Congregations," 306.
128. Bowen, *Evangelism for "Normal" People*, 65.
129. Sparks, Soerens, and Friesen, *New Parish*, 27.
130. Fitch, *Great Giveaway*, 229.

Finally, a gathering of God's people lives into the narrative of God's mission in which the people of God participate in God's reconciliation and restoration of all things in Jesus Christ. Fitch and Holsclaw envision a future when "[w]herever such communities come into being, sin is overcome, evil is defeated, and death no longer holds power. The kingdom is breaking in."[131] In these ways, the gospel of Jesus Christ is expressed in and through the shared life of God's people as they embody the evangelistic character of Jesus Christ.

Perhaps, then, Newbigin expressed the vision of these local expressions quite well when he wrote:

> How is it possible that the gospel should be credible, that people should come to believe that the power which has the last word in human affairs is represented by a man hanging on a cross? I am suggesting that the only answer, the only hermeneutic of the gospel is a congregation of men and women who believe it and live by it. I am, of course, not denying the importance of the many activities, campaigns, distribution of Bibles and Christian literature, conferences, and even books such as this one. But I am saying that these are all secondary, and that they have power to accomplish their purpose only as they are rooted in and lead back to a believing community.[132]

From an MCM perspective, then, God's people, as they express the gospel in their life together within their respective and particular contexts, communally embody Jesus' character so that others might hear, see, and believe that Jesus is the Christ, the Son of God, sent to reconcile and restore the world.

Implications and Potential Contours for Further Conversations

This project concludes with a few brief comments regarding implications and potential contours for further conversations related to both the content and the methodology engaged in this project. Relating to both the academy and to practitioners, these implications and suggestions for further dialogue are offered in recognition that there is still much to be discerned and discovered with regard to the relationship of worship, discipleship, and evangelism within the MCM.

---

131. Holsclaw, *Prodigal Christianity*, 113.
132. Newbigin, *Gospel in a Pluralist Society*, 227.

In relationship to the academy, there are four implications that emerge through this project. First, the scope of this project contends for a generalist approach within academic studies. In a context where academic contributions bend toward specialization, this project has sought to develop the theological interconnectedness of three broad areas within the life of God's people: worship, discipleship, and evangelism. While not novel, such an approach is deliberately engaged here with the hope of demonstrating the value of expanding and strengthening the breadth of theological research and not only the depth of particularized investigation.

Secondly, this project operated with the premise that the MCM has developed enough history and enough breadth of internal conversation that the movement can serve as a legitimate subject area for research in the area of practical theology. While certainly engaged within Doctorate of Ministry degrees, the MCM has received significantly less attention from Doctorates of Theology or Philosophy in areas of practical theology, like ethics, pastoral care, and preaching. Hopefully, in a small way, this project can encourage further research around the MCM within practical theology.

The third implication emerges from the methodology of this project, by offering an initial attempt at integrating aspects from three different conversational fields within practical theology—liturgical theology, Christian ethics, and post-Christendom evangelism—that have not often found occasion to dialogue with each other. While this project barely skimmed the surface of these other conversations, the benefit of further collaboration between practical theology conversations became more evident throughout this project, as they provided developed means of addressing gaps within the MCM conversation.

Finally, this project sought to develop a theological understanding of evangelism that is not entangled in the colonial and paternalistic practices for which Christian mission has been significantly and justifiably critiqued. As referenced in this chapter, conversations in post-Christendom evangelism, along with the MCM, have begun to pursue an approach to evangelism that is more concerned with nurturing a faithful character among God's people than with perfecting particular techniques of presenting a propositional understanding of the gospel. A guarded concern that God's people not lose their ability to articulate the gospel with winsome clarity and intellectual integrity is still needed. Yet, shifting from persuasion for in-the-moment conversions toward communally embodying Jesus' character is a healthy transition away from the pitfalls of Western and intellectual centric approaches to evangelism.

With regard to practitioners, this project sought to develop a robust place for worship, discipleship, and mission within the life of the church.

Rather than isolating these aspects from each other, the project pursued a trajectory that sought to strengthen each area by its connection with the other areas. Worship, discipleship, and outreach need not compete with each other, but can legitimately find their fullest expression through integration as together their practices cultivate Jesus' character among God's people.

Additionally, an implication of this project is that practitioners can encourage evangelism as a way of life in community together rather than as the exclusive responsibility of a few well-trained and particularly gifted people. This approach does not negate the benefit of training around rational apologetics or developing clear and culturally relevant means of communicating the gospel. Rather, the emphasis shifts from evangelism toward encouraging God's people to embody the love of God in Christ Jesus—to love their neighbors—in the daily rhythms of their lives.

Beyond these implications, this project exposes numerous opportunities for further conversations regarding worship, discipleship, and evangelism within the MCM. Without attempting to identify all these potential conversations, two areas stand out with regard to practitioners and four areas related to the academy.

With practitioners, there would be great value in developing worship- and discipleship-related resources that assist with making the integration of worship and discipleship explicit. For instance, what might a greeting in worship look like that values the particular stories emerging from practices of hospitality within a local neighborhood? Or, what creative ways can a congregation's artists assist the people in moving from celebration of the Eucharist into a discipleship opportunity to care for creation, to enter the upheaval experienced by recent refugees, or to depict the grand narrative of scripture as public art within the local community? Testimony could be revived in this sense not merely as spoken words, but also as visual art drawing people into the life of God's people.

Additionally, how might practitioners give attention to practices of hospitality and compassion with a similar conviction as to more individual disciplines of reading scripture and prayer? More dialogue with and among practitioners is needed to identify barriers and opportunities for elevating and engaging these practices as essential to the communal formation of God's people.

In regard to the academy, there are at least four potential areas for furthering this conversation. One such conversation is to encourage dialogue with sources that are more fluent in disciplines of phenomenology and ritual studies and with philosophers like Taylor and Berger. Such disciplines have the potential to deepen understandings of how the character of Jesus Christ is formed in God's people through the rhythms of remembering and anticipating and how the communal character of God's people creates social imaginaries and plausibility structures conducive to faith formation.

Secondly, another conversation focused on the inclusion of educational theory, particularly recent discussions surrounding project-based learning, would enrich the conversation around a praxis-oriented discipleship. These contributions could deepen the idea that discipleship is not merely the transmission of information but more profoundly is the formation of personal character within a community.

Thirdly, this project recognizes that the MCM is closely related to at least five other recent renewal movements: fresh expressions, emergent church, integral mission, Christian community development, and new monasticism. A comparative study of worship and discipleship practices, the formation of character, and evangelism approaches within these various movements could be quite fruitful.

Finally, an examination and evaluation of how MCM advocates assess Christendom, postmodernism, and post-Christendom would be of great value in discerning cultural and historical biases present within the MCM. Such an endeavor also would move MCM conversations into dialogue with scholars in historical theology, a discipline with which the MCM has had little direct engagement.

Bibliography

Abraham, William. *The Logic of Evangelism*. Grand Rapids: Eerdmans, 1989.
Adeney, Frances. *Graceful Evangelism: Christian Witness in a Complex World*. Grand Rapids: Baker Academic, 2010.
Ashlin-Mayo, Bryce. "You Are NOT a Machine: Post-Industrial Discipleship." Blog post, July 2012. http://bryceashlinmayo.com/2012/07/you-are-not-a-machine-post-industrial-discipleship/.
Aune, Michael. "Ritual Practice: In the World, Into Each Human Heart." In *Inside Out: Worship in an Age of Mission*, edited by Thomas Schattauer, 151–80. Minneapolis: Fortress, 1999.
Ballor, Jordan. *Ecumenical Babel: Confusing Economic Ideology and the Church's Social Witness*. Grand Rapids: Christian's Library, 2010.
Bangert, Mark. "Holy Communion: Taste and See." In *Inside Out: Worship in an Age of Mission*, edited by Thomas Schattauer, 59–86. Minneapolis: Fortress, 1999.
Bartholomew, Craig, and Michael Goheen. *The Drama of Scripture: Finding Our Place in the Biblical Story*. Grand Rapids: Baker Academic, 2004.
Bavinck, Herman. *Reformed Dogmatics*, vol. 4. Edited by John Bolt and translated by John Vriend. Grand Rapids: Baker Academic, 2008.
Bavinck, Johan H. *An Introduction to the Science of Missions*. Translated by David H. Freeman. Phillipsburg, NJ: Presbyterian and Reformed, 1960.
Bauckham, Richard. BIBLE AND MISSION: CHRISTIAN WITNESS IN A POSTMODERN WORLD. Grand Rapids: Baker Academic, 2003.
Bechtel, Carolyn. "Can We Talk? An Invitation to the Reformed and Missional Dialogue." *Perspectives* 23/8 (August 2008) 4–5.
Beghuis, Kent D. "Humble Apologetics: Defending the Faith Today." *Bibliotheca Sacra* 161/643 (2004) 381–82.
Bensen, Bruce Ellis. *Liturgy as a Way of Life: Embodying the Arts in Christian Worship*. Grand Rapids: Baker Academic, 2013.
Berger, Peter. *The Sacred Canopy: Elements of a Sociological Theory of Religion*. New York: Doubleday, 1967.
Berger, Peter, and Thomas Luckman. *The Social Construction of Reality: A Treatise in the Sociology of Knowledge*. New York: Doubleday, 1966.
Berghoef, Bryan. *Pub Theology: Beer, Conversation, and God*. Eugene, OR: Cascade, 2012.
Berkhof, Louis. *Systematic Theology*. Grand Rapids: Eerdmans, 1996.

Bessenecker, Scott. *The New Friars: The Emerging Movement Serving the World's Poor.* Downers Grove, IL: InterVarsity, 2006.

Bevans, Stephan, and Roger Schroeder. *Constants in Context: A Theology of Mission for Today.* Maryknoll, NY: Orbis, 2008.

Bickers, Dennis. *Intentional Ministry in a Not-So-Mega Church: Becoming a Missional Community.* Kansas City: Beacon Hill, 2009.

Billings, Todd. "Being Missional in the Reformed Tradition." *Perspectives* 24/5 (May 2009) 3–5.

Bolt, John. "Does the Church Today Need a New 'Mission Paradigm'?" *Calvin Theological Journal* 31/1 (April 1996) 196–208.

Boren, M. Scott. *Missional Small Groups: Becoming a Community that Makes a Difference in the World.* Grand Rapids: Baker, 2010.

Borger, Joyce, Martin Tel, and John D. Witvliet, eds. *Lift Up Your Hearts: Psalms, Hymns, and Spiritual Songs.* Grand Rapids: Faith Alive Christian Resources, 2013.

Bosch, David J. *Transforming Mission: Paradigm Shifts in Theology of Mission.* Maryknoll, NY: Orbis, 1991.

Bouma-Prediger, Steven, and Brian Walsh. *Beyond Homelessness: Christian Faith in a Culture of Displacement.* Grand Rapids: Eerdmans. 2008.

Bowen, John. *Evangelism for "Normal" People: Good News for Those Looking for a Fresh Approach.* Minneapolis: Augsburg Fortress, 2002.

———, ed. *Green Shoots Out of Dry Ground: Growing a New Future for the Church in Canada.* Eugene, OR: Wipf & Stock, 2013.

———. "Liturgical and Missional: Do I Have to Chose?" *Good Idea!*, Institute of Evangelism, March 11, 2011. http://institute.wycliffecollege.ca/2011/03/liturgical-and-missional-do-i-have-to-choose/.

———. "Towards Scholarly Evangelists and Evangelistic Scholars: The Teaching of Evangelism in Theological Seminaries." *McMaster Journal of Theology and Ministry* 6 (2003) 113–25.

Braaten, Carl, and Robert Jensen, eds. *Marks of the Body of Christ.* Grand Rapids: Eerdmans, 1999.

Brachlow, Stephen. "John Robinson and the Lure of Separatism in Pre-Revolutionary England." *Church History* 50/3 (September 1981) 288–301.

Bradbury, Steve. "The Micah Declaration on Integral Mission." In *Justice, Mercy and Humility: Integral Mission and the Poor,* edited by Timothy Chester, 13–16. Waynesboro, GA: Paternoster, 2002.

Breen, Mike. "Why the Missional Movement Will Fail, Part 2." Blog post, September 20, 2011. http://mikebreen.wordpress.com/2011/09/20/why-the-missional-movement-will-fail-part-2/.

Breen, Mike, and Steve Cockram. *Building a Discipling Culture: How to Release a Missional Movement by Discipling People Like Jesus Did.* 2nd ed. Pawleys Island, SC: 3Dimension Movements, 2011.

Brownson, James. "Speaking the Truth in Love: Elements of a Missional Hermeneutic." *International Review of Mission* 83/330 (July 1, 1994) 479–504.

Brownson, James, Inagrace Dietterich, Barry Harvey, and Charles West. *StormFront: The Good News of God.* Grand Rapids: Eerdmans, 2003.

Brunner, Emil. "One Holy Catholic Church." Translated by Bruce Metzger. *Theology Today* 4/3 (October 1947) 318–31.

———. *The Word and the World.* New York: Scribner, 1931.

Brueggemann, Walter. *Cadences of Home: Preaching among Exiles*. Louisville: Westminster John Knox, 1997.

———. *The Word that Redescribes the World: The Bible and Discipleship*. Edited by Patrick Miller. Minneapolis: Fortress, 2006.

Bryant, Scott. "The Optimistic Ecclesiology of Walter Rauschenbusch." *American Baptist Quarterly* 27/2 (2008 2008) 117–35.

Bucer, Martin. *Instruction in Christian Love*. Translated by Paul Fuhrmann. Richmond, VA: John Knox, 1952.

Cahill, Mark. *One Thing You Can't Do in Heaven*. Bartlesville, OK: Genesis, 2004.

Calvin, John. *Institutes of the Christian Religion*. Edited by John T. McNeill, translated by Ford Lewis Battles. Library of Christian Classics 20–21. Philadelphia: Westminster, 1960.

Canty, Kyle. "A Black Missional Critique of the Missional Movement." *The Rooftop*, July 16, 2013. http://thecityrooftop.com.

Cavanaugh, William. *Being Consumed: Economics and Christian Desire*. Grand Rapids: Eerdmans, 2008.

———. *Theopolitical Imagination: Christian Practices of Space and Time*. New York: T & T Clark, 2002.

Chan, Francis, and Mark Beuving. *Multiply: Disciples Making Disciples*. Colorado Springs, CO: David Cook, 2012.

Chan, Simon. *Liturgical Theology: The Church as Worshiping Community*. Downers Grove: InterVarsity Academic, 2006.

Chester, Timothy. *Everyday Church: Gospel Communities on Mission*. Wheaton, IL: Crossway, 2012.

———, ed. *Justice, Mercy and Humility: Integral Mission and the Poor*. Waynesboro, GA: Paternoster, 2002.

Chester, Tim, and Steve Timmis. *Total Church: A Radical Reshaping around Gospel and Community*. Wheaton, IL: Crossway, 2008.

Christian Reformed Church in North America. *Our World Belongs to God*. Rev. ed. Grand Rapids: CRC, 2008.

———. *What It Means to Be Reformed*. Grand Rapids: CRCNA, 2016. https://www.crcna.org/sites/default/files/what_it_means_to_be_reformed.pdf.

Chilcote, Paul. "The Integral Nature of Worship and Evangelism." In *The Study of Evangelism: Exploring a Missional Practice of the Church*, edited by Paul Chilcote and Lacy Warner, 246–263. Grand Rapids: Eerdmans, 2008.

Chilcote, Paul, and Lacy Warner, eds. *The Study of Evangelism: Exploring a Missional Practice of the Church*. Grand Rapids: Eerdmans, 2008.

Church of England Mission and Public Affairs Council. *Mission-Shaped Church: Church Planting and Fresh Expressions of Church in a Changing Context*. 2nd ed. London: Church House, 2009.

Claiborne, Shane. "Marks of New Monasticism." In *New Monasticism as Fresh Expression of Church*, edited by Graham Cray, Ian Mobsby, and Aaron Kennedy, 19–36. Nowich, UK: Canterbury, 2010.

Condor, Tim. "The Existing Church/Emerging Church Matrix: Collision, Credibility, Missional Collaboration, and Generative Friendship." In *An Emergent Manifesto of Hope*, edited by Doug Pagitt and Tony Jones, 97–107. Grand Rapids: Baker, 2007.

Cosper, Mike. *Rhythms of Grace: How the Church's Worship Tells the Story of the Gospel*. Wheaton, IL: Crossway, 2013.

Conner, Benjamin. *Practicing Witness: A Missional Vision of Christian Practice.* Grand Rapids: Eerdmans, 2011.

Costello, Tim. "Integral Mission with the Poor." In *Justice, Mercy and Humility: Integral Mission and the Poor*, edited by Timothy Chester, 102–11. Waynesboro, GA: Paternoster, 2002.

Cray, Graham. "On Not Knowing the End at the Beginning." *Journal of Missional Practice* 2 (Autumn 2013). http://journalofmissionalpractice.com/on-not-knowing-the-end-at-the-beginning/.

———. "Why Is New Monasticism Important?" In *New Monasticism as Fresh Expression of Church*, edited by Graham Cray, Ian Mobsby, and Aaron Kennedy, 1–11. Nowich, UK: Canterbury, 2010.

Davies, J. G. *Worship and Mission.* London: SCM, 1966.

Dawn, Marva. "Reaching Out without Dumbing Down: A Theology of Worship for the Church in Postmodern Times." In *Confident Witness, Changing World: Rediscovering the Gospel in North America*, edited by Craig Van Gelder, 270–82. Grand Rapids: Eerdmans, 1996.

———. *Reaching Out without Dumbing Down: A Theology of Worship for this Urgent Time.* Grand Rapids: Eerdmans, 1995.

———. *A Royal Waste of Time: The Splendor of Worshiping God and Being Church for the World.* Grand Rapids: Eerdmans, 1999.

———. "Worship to Form a Missional Community." *Direction* 28/2 (September 1999) 139–52.

DeRoo, Neal, and Brian Lightbody, eds. *The Logic of the Incarnation: James K. A. Smith's Critique of Postmodern Religion.* Eugene, OR: Pickwick. 2009.

DeYoung, Kevin, and Greg Gilbert. *What Is the Mission of the Church?: Making Sense of Shalom, Social Justice, and the Great Commission.* Wheaton, IL: Crossway, 2011.

Donovan, Vincent. *Christianity Rediscovered.* 25th anniversary ed. Maryknoll, NY: Orbis, 2003.

DuBose, Francis. *God Who Sends: A Fresh Quest for Biblical Mission.* Nashville: Broadman, 1983.

Engel, James, and Wilbert Norton. *What's Gone Wrong with the Harvest?: A Communication Strategy for the Church and World Evangelization.* Grand Rapids: Zondervan, 1975.

Everts, Don, and Doug Schaupp. *I Once Was Lost: What Postmodern Skeptics Taught Us about Their Path to Jesus.* Downers Grove, IL: InterVarsity, 2008.

Fennell, Robert. "Canada's Ever-Changing Contexts: Mission in a Radically Pluralistic Society." In *Green Shoots out of Dry Ground: Growing a New Future for the Church in Canada*, edited by John Bowen, 21–34. Eugene, OR: Wipf & Stock, 2013.

Fitch, David. *The Great Giveaway: Reclaiming the Mission of the Church from Big Business, Parachurch Organizations, Psychotherapy, Consumer Capitalism, and Other Modern Maladies.* Grand Rapids: Baker, 2005.

———. "'Knitting While Detroit Burns?': The Reformed 'Both/And' vs. the Anabaptist 'First/Then.'" *Reclaiming the Mission* (blog), August 27, 2013. http://www.missioalliance.org/knitting-while-detroit-burns-the-reformed-"bothand"-versus-the-anabaptist-"first-then"/.

———. "The Production of Experience." In *The Great Giveaway: Reclaiming the Mission of the Church from Big Business, Parachurch Organizations, Psychotherapy, Consumer Capitalism, and Other Modern Maladies*, 95–125. Grand Rapids: Baker, 2005.

Fitch, David, and Geoff Holsclaw. *Prodigal Christianity: 10 Signposts into the Missional Frontier*. San Francisco: Jossey-Bass, 2013.

Flett, John. "Missio Dei: A Trinitarian Envisioning of a Non-Trinitarian Theme." *Missiology* 37/1 (January 1, 2009) 5–18.

Foust, Thomas, George Hunsberger, Andrew Kirk, and Werner Ustorf, eds. *A Scandalous Prophet: The Way of Mission after Newbigin*. Grand Rapids: Eerdmans, 2002.

Francis, Pope. *Evangelii Gaudium* ("The Joy of the Gospel"). Apostolic exhortation, November 24, 2013. http://w2.vatican.va/content/francesco/en/apost_exhortations/documents/papa-francesco_esortazione-ap_20131124_evangelii-gaudium.html.

Frost, Michael. *Exiles: Living Missionally in a Post-Christian Culture*. Peabody, MA: Hendrickson, 2006.

———. "Exiles at the Altar." In *Exiles: Living Missionally in a Post-Christian Culture*, 275-300. Peabody, MA: Hendrickson, 2006.

———. *The Road to Missional: Journey to the Center of the Church*. Grand Rapids: Baker, 2011.

Frost, Michael, and Alan Hirsch. *The Shaping of Things to Come: Innovation and Mission for the 21st-Century Church*. Peabody, MA: Hendrickson, 2003.

Fullenweider, Jann. "Proclamation: Mercy for the World." In *Inside Out: Worship in an Age of Mission*, edited by Thomas Schattauer, 23–38. Minneapolis: Fortress, 1999.

Galbreath, Paul. "Desiring the Kingdom: Worship, Worldview, and Cultural Formation," *Interpretation* 65/4 (October 2011) 432.

Geweke, Deborah. "Ampersand Faith: Re-Integrating Liturgy & Life through a Reappropriation of Mystical Theology and Praxis." *Currents in Theology and Mission* 38/4 (August 2011) 256–71.

Gilbert, Pierre. "The Missional Relevance of Genesis 1-3." *Direction* 43/1 (2014) 49–64.

Goheen, Michael. "'As the Father Has Sent Me, I Am Sending You': J. E. Lesslie Newbigin's Missionary Ecclesiology." PhD diss., University of Utrecht, 2001. http://dspace.library.uu.nl/handle/1874/597.

———. *A Light to the Nations: The Missional Church and the Biblical Story*. Grand Rapids: Baker Academic, 2011.

———. "The Missional Church: Ecclesiological Discussion in the Gospel and Our Culture Network in North America." *Missiology* 30/4 (October 2002) 479–90.

———. "Nourishing Our Missional Idenitity." In *In Praise of Worship: An Exploration of Text and Practice*, edited by David Cohen and Michael Parsons, 32–55. Eugene, OR: Wipf & Stock, 2010.

Gorman, Joe. "The Ripple Effect: How the Local Church Can Change the World through Missional Partnerships." In *Missional Discipleship: Partners in God's Redemptive Mission*, edited by Mark Maddix and Jay Akkerman, 131–46. Kansas City: Beacon Hill, 2013

Gornik, Mark. *To Live in Peace: Biblical Faith and the Changing Inner City*. Grand Rapids: Eerdmans, 2002.

Gray-Reeves, Mary, and Michael Perham. *The Hospitality of God: Emerging Worship for a Missional Church*. New York: Seabury, 2011.

Green, Garret. *Imagining God: Theology and the Religious Imagination*. Grand Rapids: Eerdmans. 1999.

Grenz, Stanley. "Ecclesiology." In *The Cambridge Companion to Postmodern Theology*, edited by Kevin Vanhoozer: 252–68. Cambridge: Cambridge University Press, 2003.

Guardini, Romano "The Playfulness of the Liturgy." In *Primary Sources of Liturgical Theology: A Reader*, edited by Dwight Vogel, 38–45. Collegeville, MN: Liturgical, 2000.

Guder, Darrell. *The Continuing Conversion of the Church*. Grand Rapids: Eerdmans, 2000.

———. "Evangelism and Justice: From False Dichotomies to Gospel Faithfulness." *Church and Society* 92/2 (November 2001) 14–20.

———. "Missio Dei: Integrating Theological Formation for Apostolic Vocation." *Missiology* 37/1 (January 2009) 63–74.

———, ed. *Missional Church: A Vision for the Sending of the Church in North America*. Grand Rapids: Eerdmans, 1998.

———. "Theological Significance of the Lord's Day for the Formation of the Missional Church." In *Sunday, Sabbath, and the Weekend: Managing Time in a Global Culture*, edited by Edward O'Flaherty, Rodney Peterson, and Timothy Norton, 105–17. Grand Rapids: Eerdmans, 2010.

———. "Worthy Living: Work and Witness from the Perspective of Missional Church Theology." *Word and World* 25/4 (September 2005) 424–32.

Hageman, Howard. "Liturgy and Mission." *Theology Today* 19/2 (July 1, 1962) 169–70.

Hammond, Kim, and Darren Cronshaw. *Sentness: Six Postures of Missional Christians*. Downers Grove, IL: InterVarsity, 2014.

Harder, Cam. "New Shoots from Old Roots: The Challenge and Potential for Mission in Rural Canada." In *Green Shoots out of Dry Ground: Growing a New Future for the Church in Canada*, edited by John Bowen, 49–62. Eugene, OR: Wipf & Stock, 2013.

Hardy, Douglas, and William L. Selvidge. "Review Essay of Some Recent Work on Spirituality and Mission." *Journal of Spiritual Formation and Soul Care* 6/1 (March 1, 2013) 109–21.

Hauerwas, Stanley. *A Community of Character: Toward a Constructive Christian Social Ethic*. Notre Dame: University of Notre Dame Press, 1981.

———. *The Hauerwas Reader*. Edited by John Berkman and Michael Cartwright. Durham, NC: Duke University Press, 2001.

———. "A Story-Formed Community: Reflections on Watership Down." In *The Hauerwas Reader*, edited by John Berkman and Michael Cartwright, 171–98. Durham, NC: Duke University Press, 2001.

———. *With the Grain of the Universe: The Church's Witness and Natural Theology*. Grand Rapids: Brazos, 2001.

———. "Worship, Evangelism, Ethics: On Eliminating the And." In *The Study of Evangelism: Exploring a Missional Practice of the Church*, edited by Paul Chilcote and Lacy Warner, 205–18. Grand Rapids: Eerdmans, 2008

Hauerwas, Stanley, and Samuel Wells, eds. *The Blackwell Companion to Christian Ethics*. 2nd ed. Malden, MA: Blackwell, 2011.

Haugen, Gary. "Integral Mission and Advocacy." In *Justice, Mercy and Humility: Integral Mission and the Poor*, edited by Timothy Chester, 187–200. Waynesboro, GA: Paternoster, 2002.

Helland, Roger, and Leonard Hjalmarson. *Missional Spirituality: Embodying God's Love from the Inside Out*. Downers Grove, IL: InterVarsity, 2011.

Hendrick, John. "Congregations with Missions vs. Missionary Congregations." In *Church between Gospel and Culture*, edited by George Hunsberger and Craig Van Gelder, 298–307. Grand Rapids: Eerdmans, 1996.

Heuertz, Christopher, and Christine Pohl. *Friendship at the Margins: Discovering Mutuality in Service and Mission*. Downers Grove, IL: InterVarsity, 2010.

Hirsch, Alan. "Defining Missional." *Leadership Journal*, Fall 2008. http://www.christianitytoday.com/le/2008/fall/17.20.html.

———. *The Forgotten Ways: Reactivating the Missional Church*. Grand Rapids: Brazos, 2006.

———. "What Is Missional Discipleship?" Verge Network, August 12, 2013. http://www.vergenetwork.org/2013/08/12/what-is-missional-discipleship-alan-hirsch/.

Hirsch, Alan, and Debra Hirsch. *Untamed: Reactivating a Missional Form of Discipleship*. Grand Rapids: Baker, 2010.

Hirsch, Alan, and Tim Catchim. *The Permanent Revolution: Apostolic Imagination and Practice for the 21st Century Church*. San Francisco: Jossey-Bass, 2012.

Holsclaw, Geoff. "More than Splitting the Difference: Intro." *Into the Far Country* (blog), August 8, 2013. http://geoffreyholsclaw.net/more-than-splitting-the-difference-intro/.

Huckins, Jon, with Rob Yackley. *Thin Places: 6 Postures for Creating and Practicing Missional Community*. Kansas City, MO: House Studio, 2012.

Hunsberger, George. *Bearing the Witness of the Spirit: Lesslie Newbigin's Theology of Cultural Plurality*. Grand Rapids: Eerdmans, 1998.

———. "Birthing Missional Faithfulness: Accents in a North American Movement." *International Review of Mission* 92/365 (April 2003) 145–52.

———. "Features of the Missional Church: Some Directions and Pathways." *Reformed Review* 52/1 (October 1998) 5–13.

———. "Proposals for a Missional Hermeneutic: Mapping a Conversation." *Missiology* 39/3 (July 2011) 309–21.

Hunsberger, George, and Craig Van Gelder, eds. *The Church between Gospel and Culture: The Emerging Mission in North America*. Grand Rapids: Eerdmans, 1996.

Hollinghurst, Steve. *Mission Shaped Evangelism: The Gospel in Contemporary Culture*. Norwich, UK: Canterbury, 2010.

Hybels, Bill. *Just Walk Across the Room: Simple Steps Pointing People to Faith*. Grand Rapids: Zondervan, 2006.

Irwin, Kevin. "Lex Orandi, Lex Credendi—Origins and Meaning: State of the Question." *Liturgical Ministry* 11 (March 2002) 57–69.

Jethani, Skye. WITH: RECLAIMING THE WAY YOU RELATE TO GOD. Nashville, : Thomas Nelson, 2011.

Johnson, Ben Campbell. *Rethinking Evangelism: A Theological Approach*. Philadelphia: Westminster John Knox, 1987.

Jones, Paul. "We Are How We Worship: Corporate Worship as a Matrix for Christian Identity Formation." *Worship* 69/4 (July 1995) 346–60.

Kallenberg, Brad. *Live to Tell: Evangelism in a Postmodern Age*. Grand Rapids: Brazos, 2011.

Keifert, Patrick. *Welcoming the Stranger: A Public Theology of Worship and Evangelism*. Minneapolis: Fortress, 1992.

Keller, Timothy. "Being Salt & Light in Culture." Interview by D. J. Chuang at the 2006 Desiring God National Conference. http://www.youtube.com/watch?v=i1Q6Zun2v-8.

———. *Center Church: Doing Balanced, Gospel-Centered Ministry in Your City*. Kindle ed. Grand Rapids: Zondervan, 2012.

———. *Generous Justice: How God's Grace Makes Us Just*. New York: Dutton, 2010.

Kenneson, Philip. "Gathering: Worship, Imagination, and Formation." In *The Blackwell Companion to Christian Ethics*, edited by Stanley Hauerwas and Samuel Wells. 2nd edition. Malden, MA: Blackwell, 2011.

Kerr, David. "Christian Understandings of Proselytism." *International Bulletin of Missionary Research* 23/1, (1999) 8–12

Kilmartin, Edward. "Theology as Theology of the Liturgy." In *Primary Sources of Liturgical Theology: A Reader*, edited by Dwight Vogel, 103–9. Collegeville, MN: Liturgical, 2000.

Kim, Nami. "A Mission to the 'Graveyard of Empires'?: Neocolonialism and the Contemporary Evangelical Missions of the Global South." *Mission Studies* 27/1 (January 2010) 3–23.

Kimball, Dan. *Emerging Worship: Creating Worship Gatherings for New Generations*. Grand Rapids: Zondervan, 2004.

Kinnaman, David, and Gabe Lyons. *UnChristian: What a New Generation Really Thinks about Christianity and Why It Matters*. Grand Rapids: Baker, 2012.

Kirk, Andrew. "Following Modernity and Postmodernity: A Missiological Investigation," *Mission Studies* 16/12 (2000) 217–39.

———. *What Is Mission?: Theological Explorations*. Minneapolis: Fortress, 2000.

Klug, Eugene. "Luther's Understanding of 'Church' in His Treatise On the Councils and the Church of 1539." *Concordia Theological Quarterly* 44/1 (January 1980) 27–38.

Knight, Steve. "What Does Missional Mean?" *Mission Shift* (blog), Patheos, May 17, 2012. http://www.patheos.com/blogs/missionalshift/2012/05/what-does-missional-mean/.

Koester, Anne, ed. *Liturgy and Justice: To Worship God in Spirit and Truth*. Collegeville, MN: Liturgical, 2002.

Kostamo, Leah, and Markku Kostamo, "Creation Care as Christian Mission." In *Green Shoots Out of Dry Ground: Growing a New Future for the Church in Canada*, edited by John Bowen, 167–79. Eugene, OR: Wipf & Stock, 2013.

Krabill, James R. "Evangelism after Christendom: The Theology and Practice of Christian Witness." *Conrad Grebel Review* 26/3, (2008) 93–94.

Kreider, Alan, and Eleanor Kreider. *Worship and Mission after Christendom*. Harrisonburg, VA: Herald, 2011.

Laing, Mark. "Missio Dei: Some Implications for the Church." *Missiology* 37 (January 2009) 89–99.

Lange, Dirk. "Communal Prayer and the Missional Church." *Svensk Missionstidskrift* 100/1 (January 2012) 9–21.

Lathrop, Gordon, and Timothy Wengert. *Christian Assembly: Marks of the Church in a Pluralistic Age*. Minneapolis: Fortress, 2004.

Leiderbach, Mark, and Alvin Reid. *The Convergent Church: Missional Worshipers in an Emerging Culture*. Grand Rapids: Kregel, 2009.

Leithart, Peter. *Defending Constantine: The Twilight of an Empire the Dawn of Christendom*. Downers Grove, IL: InterVarsity Academic, 2010.

Lieburg, Frederik Angenietus van. "Interpreting the Dutch Great Awakening (1749-1755)." *Church History* 77/2 (June 2008) 318–36.

Livermore, David. *Serving with Eyes Wide Open: Doing Short-Term Missions with Cultural Intelligence*. Grand Rapids: Baker, 2006.

Luther, Martin. "On the Councils and the Churches." In *Works of Martin Luther*, vol. 5. Philadelphia ed. Grand Rapids: Baker, 1982.

MacIlvaine, Rodman, III. "What Is the Missional Church Movement?" *Bibliotheca Sacra* 167/665 (January 2010) 89–106.

Maddix, Mark. "Missional Communities." In *Missional Discipleship: Partners in God's Redemptive Mission*, edited by Mark Maddix and Jay Akkerman, 15–26. Kansas City: Beacon Hill, 2013.

Maddix, Mark, and Jay Akkerman, eds. *Missional Discipleship: Partners in God's Redemptive Mission*. Kansas City: Beacon Hill, 2013.

Marsden, George. "Fundamentalism as an American Phenomenon: A Comparison with English Evangelicalism." *Church History* 46/2 (June 1977) 215–32.

Marshall, Glen. "A Missional Ecclesiology for the 21st Century." *Journal of European Baptist Studies* 13/2 (January 2013) 5–21.

McKenna, John H. "Eucharist and Memorial." *Worship* 79/6 (November 2005) 504–22.

———. "Liturgy: Toward Liberation or Oppression?" *Worship* 56/4 (July 1982) 291–308.

McKnight, John, and Peter Block. *The Abundant Community: Awakening the Power of Families and Neighborhoods*. San Francisco: Berrett Koehler, 2012.

McKnight, Scot. *The Jesus Creed: Loving God, Loving Others*. Brewster, MA: Paraclete, 2004.

Meyers, Ruth. "Missional Church, Missional Liturgy." *Theology Today* 67/1 (April 2010) 36–50.

Mikaelsson, Lisbeth. "Missional Religion – with Special Emphasis on Buddhism, Christianity and Islam." *Svensk Missionstidskrift* 92/4 (January 1, 2004) 523–38.

Minitrea, Milfred. *Shaped by God's Heart: The Passion and Practices of Missional Churches*. San Francisco: Jossey-Bass, 2004.

Mobsby, Ian, and Mark Berry. *A New Monastic Handbook: From Vision to Practice*. London: Canterbury, 2014.

Moltmann, Jurgen. *The Church in the Power of the Spirit: A Contribution to Messianic Ecclesiology*. London: SCM, 1977.

Moore-Keish, Martha. *Do This in Remembrance of Me: A Ritual Approach to Reformed Eucharistic Theology*. Grand Rapids: Eerdmans, 2008.

Morgenthaler, Sally. *Worship Evangelism: Inviting Unbelievers into the Presence of God*. Grand Rapids: Zondervan, 1995.

Murray, Michael J. "Reason for Hope (in the Postmodern World)." In *Reason for the Hope Within*, edited by Michael J. Murray, 1–19. Grand Rapids: Eerdmans, 1999.

Myers, Bryant. *Walking with the Poor: Principles and Practices of Transformational Development*. Maryknoll, NY: Orbis Books, 1999.

Nelson, Gary. *Borderland Churches: A Congregational Introduction to Missional Living*. St. Louis: Chalice, 2008.

Nessan, Craig. *Beyond Maintenance to Mission: A Theology of the Congregation*. 2nd ed. Minneapolis: Fortress, 2010.

———. "Christian Imagination and Congregational Evangelism." *Currents in Theology and Mission* 28/1 (February 2001) 38–46.

Neufeld, Tim. "Can Mennonite Brethren Be Missional?" *Direction* 39/1 (March 2010) 41–55.

Newbigin, Lesslie. *The Gospel in a Pluralist Society*. Grand Rapids: Eerdmans, 1989.

———. "What Is a Local Church Truly United." *Ecumenical Review* 29/2 (April 1977) 115–28.

Oldenburg, Mark. "Liturgical Year: Within the World, Within Its Time." In *Inside Out: Worship in an Age of Mission*, edited by Thomas Schattauer, 87–106. Minneapolis: Fortress, 1999.

Olson-Smith, Clark. "Becoming Contemplative Worshippers: Attending to Our Communal Heart." *Currents in Theology and Mission* 38/4. (August 2011) 272–83.

Oppenhiemer, Mark. "Evangelicals Find Themselves in the Midst of a Calvinist Revival." *New York Times*, January 3, 2014. http://www.nytimes.com/2014/01/04/us/a-calvinist-revival-for-evangelicals.html.

Pachuau, Lalsangkima. "Missiology in a Pluralistic World: The Place of Mission Study in Theological Education." *International Review of Mission* 59 (October 2000) 539-55.

———. "Missio Dei." In *Dictionary of Mission Theology: Evangelical Foundations*, edited by John Corrie, Samuel Escobar, and Wilbert Shenk, 234. Downers Grove, IL: InterVarsity, 2007.

Packer, J. I. *Evangelism and the Sovereignty of God*. American ed. Downers Grove, IL: InterVarsity. 2008.

Padilla, Rene. "Integral Mission and its Historical Development." In *Justice, Mercy and Humility: Integral Mission and the Poor*, edited by Timothy Chester, 42–58. Waynesboro, GA: Paternoster, 2002.

———. "Integral Mission Today." In *Justice, Mercy and Humility: Integral Mission and the Poor*, edited by Timothy Chester, 59–64. Waynesboro, GA: Paternoster, 2002.

———. *Mission between the Times: Essays on the Kingdom*. Rev. ed. Carlisle, UK: Langham Monographs, 2010.

Pagitt, Doug, and Tony Jones, eds. *An Emergent Manifesto of Hope*. Grand Rapids: Baker, 2007.

Parker, Garry. "Missional Evangelism: Verbal Proclamation and the Struggle for Justice." In *Mission of the Church in Methodist Perspective*, edited by Alan G. Padgett, 121–35. Lewiston, NY: Edwin Mellen, 1992.

Plantinga, Cornelius, Jr. *Engaging God's World: A Christian Vision of Faith, Learning, and Living*. Grand Rapids: Eerdmans, 2002.

Penner, James, Rachel Harder, Erika Anderson, Bruno Desorcy, and Rick Hiemstra. *Hemorrhaging Faith: Why and When Canadian Young Adults are Leaving, Staying, and Returning to the Church*. Toronto: Evangelical Fellowship of Canada, 2011. http://www.hemorrhagingfaith.com.

Pennings, Ray. "Can We Hope for a Neocalvinist-Neopuritan Dialogue?" *Comment*, December 1, 2008. http://www.cardus.ca/comment/article/1559/can-we-hope-for-a-neocalvinist-neopuritan-dialogue/.

Percy, Harold. *Good News People: An Introduction to Evangelism for Tongue-Tied Christians*. Toronto: Anglican Book Centre, 1996.

Perkins, John. *Beyond Charity: The Call to Christian Community Development*. Grand Rapids: Baker, 1993.

———. *With Justice for All: A Strategy for Community Development*. Rev. ed. Venture, CA: Regal, 2008.

Pohl, Christine. *Living into Community: Cultivating Practices that Sustain Us*. Grand Rapids: Eerdmans, 2012.

———. *Making Room: Recovering Hospitality as a Christian Tradition*. Grand Rapids: Eerdmans, 1999.

Powers, Mark. *Going Full Circle: Worship that Moves Us to Discipleship and Missions*. Eugene, OR: Wipf & Stock, 2013.

Putman, Jim. *Real-Life Discipleship: Building Churches the Make Disciples*. Colorado Springs, CO: NavPress, 2010.

Raj, A. R. Victor. "Missional or Missionary." *Missio Apostolica* 16/2 (November 2008) 101–03.

Rankin, Stephen. "A Perfect Church: Toward a Wesleyan Missional Ecclesiology." *Wesleyan Theological Journal* 38/1 (March 2003) 83–104.

Resner, Andre, Jr. "To Worship or To Evangelize? Ecclesiology's Phantom Fork in the Road." *Restoration Quarterly* 36/2 (January 1994) 65–80.

Richardson, Rick. "Emerging Missional Movements: An Overview and Assessment of Some Implications for Mission(s)." *International Bulletin of Missionary Research* 37/3 (July 2013) 131–36.

Richebacher, Wilhelm. "Missio Dei: The Basis of Mission Theology or a Wrong Path?" International Review of Mission 92/367 (October 2003) 588–605.

Roberts, Paul. "Rethinking Worship as an Emerging Christian Practice." In *The Gospel after Christendom: New Voices, New Cultures, New Expressions*, edited by Ryan Bolger, 179–94. Grand Rapids: Baker Academic, 2012.

Robinson, Bob. "So What's Wrong with Neo-Calvinism?" Re-Integrate, May 27, 2014. http://www.re-integrate.org/2014/05/27/whats-wrong-neocalvinism.

Roessingh, Hetty, and Wendy Chambers. "Project-Based Learning and Pedagogy in Teacher Preparation: Staking Out the Theoretical Middle Ground." *International Journal of Teaching and Learning in Higher Education* 23/1 (2011) 60–71. http://files.eric.ed.gov/fulltext/EJ938579.pdf.

Rollins, Peter. *Insurrection: To Believe Is Human; to Doubt, Divine*. New York: Howard, 2011.

Roxburgh, Alan. *Missional: Joining God in the Neighborhood*. Grand Rapids: Baker, 2011.

———. "Practices of a Missional People." *Journal of Missional Practice*, Fall 2013. http://journalofmissionalpractice.com/practices-of-a-missional-people/.

Roxburgh, Alan, and M. Scott Boren. *Introducing the Missional Church: What It Is, Why It Matters, How to Become One*. Grand Rapids: Baker, 2009.

Ryan, Mark P. "Humble Apologetics: Defending the Faith Today." *Presbyterion* 30/2, (2004) 127–28.

Saliers, Don. "Liturgy and Ethics: Some New Beginnings." *Journal of Religious Ethics* 7/2 (September 1979) 173–89.

———. *Worship as Theology: Foretaste of Glory Divine*. Nashville: Abingdon, 1994.

Samartha, S. J. "Mission in a Religiously Plural World: Looking Beyond Tambaram 1938." *International Review of Mission* 77/307 (July 1988) 320–21.

Sanneh, Lamin. *Translating the Message: The Missionary Impact on Culture*. 2nd rev. ed. Maryknoll, NY: Orbis, 2009.

Scandrette, Mark. "Growing Pains: The Messy and Fertile Process of Becoming." In *An Emergent Manifesto of Hope*, edited by Doug Pagitt and Tony Jones, 21–32. Grand Rapids: Baker, 2007.

Schattauer, Thomas, ed. *Inside Out: Worship in an Age of Mission*. Minneapolis: Fortress, 1999.

———. "Liturgical Assembly as Locus of Mission." In *Inside Out: Worship in an Age of Mission*, edited by Thomas Schattauer, 2–14. Minneapolis: Fortress, 1999.

Schell, Donald. "Discerning Open Table in Community and Mission." *Anglican Theological Review* 94/2 (March 2012) 245–55.

Schmemann, Alexander. *For the Life of the World: Sacraments and Orthodoxy.* Crestwood, NY: St. Vladimir's Seminary Press. 1973.

Schmit, Clayton. *Sent and Gathered: A Worship Manual for the Missional Church.* Grand Rapids: Baker Academic, 2009.

Schoon, Chris. "Confessions of a Former Skeptic: Questions for Institutional Vocation in the Garden." *Comment*, January 9, 2014. http://www.cardus.ca/comment/article/4128/confessions-of-a-former-skeptic-questions-for-institutional-vocation-in-the-garden/.

———. "Lamenting and Celebrating in the Still Unfolding Story." Presentation give at the Edifide Educators Convention, Redeemer University College, October 24, 2014. https://vimeo.com/113787641.

———. "Missional Worship for Missional Living." CRCNA webinar, May 7, 2014. http://network.crcna.org/worship/missional-worship-missional-living.

———. "Ruminating around a Backyard Fire." *Perspectives* 26/4 (April 2011) 7–10.

———. "Unveiling God's Face." ThM thesis,. Calvin Theological Seminary, 2007.

Scott, Elenora. "A Theological Critique of the Emerging, Postmodern, Missional Church/Movement." *Evangelical Review of Theology* 34/4 (October 2010) 335–46.

Seibel, Cory. "The Heart of God in the Heart of the City: Missional Vocation and the Urban Congregation." *Direction* 39/1 (2010) 56–70.

Sine, Tom. *The New Conspirators.* Downers Grove, IL: InterVarsity, 2008.

Sire, James. *A Little Primer on Humble Apologetics.* Downers Grove, IL: InterVarsity, 2006.

———. *Naming the Elephant: Worldview as a Concept.* Downers Grove, IL: InterVarsity, 2004.

Small, Joseph. "Who's In, Who's Out?" *Theology Today* 58/1 (April 2001) 58–71.

Smith, Efrem. "Expanding the Missional Church Conversation." Blog post, November 21, 2011. http://www.efremsmith.com/category/blog/2011/11/expanding-the-missional-church-conversation.

Smith, James K. A. *Desiring the Kingdom: Worship, Worldview, and Cultural Formation.* Grand Rapids: Baker Academic, 2009.

———. "Knitting While Detroit Burns?" *Cardus Daily* (blog), August 21, 2013. http://www.cardus.ca/blog/2013/08/knitting-while-detroit-burns.

———. *Letters to a Young Calvinist: An Invitation to the Reformed Tradition.* Grand Rapids: Brazos. 2010.

Sparks, Paul, Tim Soerens, and Dwight Friesen. *The New Parish: How Neighborhood Churches are Transforming Mission, Discipleship, and Community.* Downers Grove, IL: InterVarsity, 2014.

Stackhouse, John, Jr. *Humble Apologetics: Defending the Faith Today.* New York: Oxford University Press. 2002.

Stiller, Karen, and William Metzger. *Going Missional: Conversations with 13 Canadian Churches who Have Embraced Missional Life.* Winnipeg, MB: World Alive, 2010.

Stone, Bryan. *Evangelism after Christendom: The Theology and Practice of Christian Witness.* Grand Rapids: Brazos. 2007.

Strange, Alan D. "Humble Apologetics: Defending the Faith Today." *Mid-America Journal of Theology* 14 (2003) 231–38.

Taylor, Charles. *Modern Social Imaginaries.* Durham, NC: Duke University Press, 2004.

Teig, Mons. "Holy Baptism: Promise Big Enough for the World." In *Inside Out: Worship in an Age of Mission*, edited by Thomas Schattauer, 39–58. Minneapolis: Fortress, 1999.

Thiessen, Elmer. *The Ethics of Evangelism: A Philosophical Defense of Proselytizing and Persuasion*. Downers Grove, IL: InterVarsity Academic, 2011.

Tiefel, James. "Liturgical Worship for Evangelism and Outreach." *Logia* 21/3 (January 2012) 73–88.

Tineou, Tite. "Dare to Make New Mistakes: Doing Christian Mission without Historical Guilt." *Touchstone* 28/3 (September 2010) 19–29.

Tizon, Al. *Missional Preaching: Engage, Embrace, Transform*. Valley Forge, PA: Judson, 2012.

Tshimanga, Hippolyto. "Communion as a Missional Ordinance." *Conrad Grebel Review* 24/3 (October 2010) 78–94.

Turley, Richard. "Practicing the Kingdom: A Critical Appraisal of James K. A. Smith's Desiring the Kingdom." *Calvin Theological Journal* 48/1 (April 2013) 131–42.

Van Dyk, Leanne. "The Church in Evangelical Theology and Practice." In *The Cambridge Companion to Evangelical Theology*, edited by Timothy Larson and Daniel Treier, 125–41. Cambridge: Cambridge University Press, 2007.

Van Engen, Charles. *God's Missionary People: Rethinking the Purpose of the Local Church*. Grand Rapids: Baker, 1991.

———. Mission on the Way: Issues in Mission Theology. Grand Rapids: Baker, 1996.

Van Gelder, Craig. "The Church Needs to Understand Its Missionary Nature: A Response to John Bolt and Richard Muller." *Calvin Theological Journal* 31/2 (November 1996) 504–19.

———. *Confident Witness, Changing World: Rediscovering the Gospel in North America*. Grand Rapids: Eerdmans, 1999.

———. *The Essence of the Church: A Community Created by the Spirit*. Grand Rapids: Baker, 2000.

———. "From Corporate Church to Missional Church: The Challenge Facing Congregations Today." *Review and Expositor* 101/3 (June 1, 2004) 425–50.

———. "The Future of the Discipline of Missiology: Framing Current Realities and Future Possibilities." *Missiology* 42/1 (January 2014) 39–46

———. *The Ministry of the Missional Church: A Community Led by the Spirit*. Grand Rapids: Baker, 2007.

———, ed. *The Missional Church and Leadership Formation: Helping Congregations Develop Leadership Capacity*. Grand Rapids: Eerdmans, 2009.

———, ed. *The Missional Church in Context: Helping Congregations Develop Contextual Ministry*. Grand Rapids: Eerdmans, 2007.

———. "Some 'Further' Reflections on Church and World, Worship and Evangelism." *Calvin Theological Journal* 27/2 (1992) 372–76.

Van Rheenan, Gailyn. "Contrasting Missional and Church Growth Perspectives." *Restoration Quarterly* 48/1 (March 2006) 25–32.

Viola, Frank. "Rethinking the Five-Fold Ministry." *Beyond Evangelical* (blog), October 27, 2010. http://frankviola.org/2010/10/27/rethinking-the-five-fold-ministry.

Vogel, Dwight, ed. *Primary Sources of Liturgical Theology: A Reader*. Collegeville, MN: Liturgical, 2000.

Volf, Miroslav. "Worship as Adoration and Action: Reflections of a Christian Way of Being-in-the-World." In *Worship: Adoration and Action*, edited by D. A. Carson, 203–211. Grand Rapids: Baker Academic, 1993.

Walsh, Brian, and Richard Middleton. *The Transforming Vision: Shaping a Christian Worldview*. Downers Grove, IL: InterVarsity Academic, 1994.

Webber, Robert E. *Ancient-Future Evangelism: Making Your Church a Faith-Forming Community*. Grand Rapids: Baker, 2003.

———. *Ancient-Future Worship: Proclaiming and Enacting God's Narrative*. Grand Rapids: Baker, 2008.

———. "Liturgical Evangelism." *Covenant Quarterly* 64/1–3 (February 2006) 144–53.

Webster, Douglas. "What Is Evangelism?" *Journal of Theology for Southern Africa* (June 1973) 26–40.

Wells, Samuel. *God's Companions: Reimagining Christian Ethics*. Malden, MA: Blackwell, 2006.

Williamson, Joseph. "The Marks of the Church: A Recurring Protestant Dilemma." *Andover Newton Quarterly* 6/2 (November 1965) 24–34.

Willimon, William H. "Evangelism after Christendom: The Theology and Practice of Christian Witness." *Christian Century* 124/13 (2007) 35–37.

Wilson, Paul Scott. *The Four Pages of the Sermon: A Guide to Biblical Preaching*. Nashville: Abingdon, 1999.

Wilson-Hartgrove, Jonathan. *New Monasticism: What It Has to Say to Today's Church*. Grand Rapids: Brazos, 2008.

Wittmer, Michael. "Don't Stop Believing: A Theological Critique of the Emergent Church." *Reformed Review* 61/3 (Fall 2008) 119–32.

Wolters, Al. *Creation Regained: Biblical Basics for a Reformational Worldview*. Grand Rapids: Eerdmans, 1985.

Wolterstorff, Nicholas. *Hearing the Call: Liturgy, Justice, Church, and World*. Edited by Mark Gornik and Gregory Thompson. Grand Rapids: Eerdmans, 2011.

Woodbridge, Noel. "Living Theologically – Towards a Theology of Christian Practice in Terms of the Theological Triad of Orthodoxy, Orthopraxy and Orthopathy as Portrayed in Isaiah 6:1–8: A Narrative Approach." *HTS Teologiese Studies/Theological Studies* 66/2 (2010) art. 807. DOI: 10.4102/hts.v66i2.807.

Woodward, J. R. *Creating a Missional Culture: Equipping the Church for the Sake of the World*. Downers Grove, IL: InterVarsity, 2012.

Wright, Christopher. *The Mission of God: Unlocking the Bible's Grand Narrative*. Downers Grove, IL: InterVarsity, 2006.

———. *The Mission of God's People: A Biblical Theology of the Church's Mission*. Grand Rapids: Zondervan, 2010.

Wright, N. T. *The New Testament and the People of God*. Christian Origins and the Question of God 1. London: SPCK, 1992.

Yoder, Michael, Michael Lee, Jonathan Ro, and Robert Priest. "Understanding Christian Identity in Terms of Bounded and Centered Set Theory in the Writings of Paul G. Hiebert." *Trinity Journal* 30/2 (September 2009) 177–88.

Zscheile, Dwight, ed. *Cultivating Sent Communities: Missional Spiritual Formation*. Grand Rapids: Eerdmans, 2012.

Subject Index

Ashlin-Mayo, Bryce, 143, 170
Athanasian Creed, 113
Augsburg Confession, 92
Aune, Michael, 67–68, 119

baptism, 11, 67, 79, 91, 95, 132, 139–40, 182
Bauckham, Richard, 8n32, 8n35, 34, 60n108, 159
Belgic Confession, 11n51, 91–92
Bosch, David, 2n4, 10n46, 20–21, 33n150, 89n64,
Bowen, John, 6n22, 7n28, 10n46, 31, 94n42, 103n86, 106–7, 109, 147, 159–60, 169, 173, 176n31, 177–80, 192
Breen, Mike, 3n6, 20n93, 30–31, 34, 48n33, 50–52, 110, 115n15, 160
Boren, M. Scott, 20n88, 28n132, 37, 46n23, 49n44, 146n13, 164n76, 166, 170, 175, 190
Brownson, James, 4n14, 8n32, 8n35, 34
Brunner, Emil, 22n103, 95
Bucer, Martin, 115

Calvin, John, 11n51, 91, 92n37, 94n45, 115, 117–18
Chan, Simon, 119n42, 134n105
Chester, Tim, 37n166, 52–54, 57n93, 59n106, 154, 171, 180, 190
Chilcote, Paul, 15, 66, 77–78, 150–51
Christendom, 3, 20, 23, 27, 33, 36–37, 40, 51n56, 58, 63, 68, 70, 79–86, 90, 96, 115, 125, 129n95, 142, 195

Christian community development, 19n83, 30, 35–36, 38n176, 43n5, 195
Claiborne, Shane, 38, 167n98
colonialism, 5–6, 84, 129n95, 174–75, 194
Communion (see Eucharist)
compassion, 41, 69, 72, 103, 143, 164, 166–69, 172n16, 174, 179–80, 184, 190, 194
Cosper, Mike, 133n104, 144
Cray, Graham, 35
Cronshaw, Darren, 24, 58, 81, 100–102, 127, 133n104, 144, 171–72, 174, 191

Dawn, Marva, 15, 65, 74–76, 112n2, 114, 116, 123n71, 129, 157
discipleship, 1, 3–4, 6, 11, 16–17, 30–34, 36, 38–41, 44, 46, 48–52, 54–56, 70, 72, 76, 78–79, 81, 89, 104, 11, 113, 122, 140–44, 146–48, 149–61, 164, 166–68, 170, 172, 174, 176–77, 179–80, 190, 192–95
Donovan, Vincent, 8, 10n46

ecclesiology, 4, 6n21, 14–15, 18, 22–23, 33, 38–40, 62, 66, 79, 81, 83–110, 115, 168–69, 182, 184
emergent church movement, 19n83, 35, 37–38, 43, 87, 195
ethics, 1, 4–5, 10, 12, 16, 30–31, 43, 62, 80, 104, 116, 143, 144n4, 148–49, 153–54, 167, 193

SUBJECT INDEX

Eucharist, 11, 61–62, 66–69, 73, 78–79, 91, 95, 96n51, 121, 124, 131–32, 136, 138, 149–52, 183, 194
evangelism, 1, 4–6, 11–12, 15–17, 20n92, 29, 31–32, 40–41, 55, 74–78, 89, 124, 156, 168, 170–74, 176–77, 179–84, 188, 190–95
evangelistic character, 1–4, 6, 12–14, 16, 27, 31–32, 36, 39–44, 46–47, 49, 52–54, 56–57, 62, 65, 67, 70, 75–80, 82, 97, 110, 113, 119–20, 122, 141, 167–71, 173–74, 176–84, 190, 192

Fitch, David, 7n31, 15, 54, 60, 65, 72–74, 81, 92n37, 96, 100–103, 106, 112, 115, 122n66, 123–24, 128, 146n14, 157, 164n76, 167n95–96, 171, 174n20, 179–81, 190–92
fresh expressions, 19n83, 35, 195
Frost, Michael, 3n11–12, 4n14, 15, 18, 20n89–90, 25–29, 33, 44n9, 47n23, 48n33, 57, 61, 63–65, 81, 90, 102–3, 105–8, 114–16, 123n71, 125n79, 126, 129n95, 153n36, 156n50, 159, 165n82, 167n92, 169, 177–79

Goheen, Michael, 7–9, 15, 18, 25–27, 33n151, 34, 45–46, 65, 66n142, 76–77, 80, 82–83, 86, 95n48, 97–100, 105, 108–10, 123, 125, 127, 130, 146, 152n31, 153n35, 154, 157, 169–70, 172–73, 190–91
Gospel and Our Culture Network, 19, 33, 39, 89
Guder, Darrell, 3, 4n14, 5n16, 15, 18, 19n86–87, 23n105, 26n119, 33, 66, 78–80, 93, 95n47, 96n49, 98, 100–101, 103–6, 109–10, 127–29, 142–43, 147, 157, 171

Hammond, Kim, 24, 58, 81, 100–102, 127, 133n104, 144, 171–72, 174, 190
Hauerwas, Stanley, 5n17, 6n26, 7–9, 41, 44n7, 141n113, 143, 147–55
Helland, Roger, 2n5, 52–53, 85n1, 96n51, 106–7, 113, 144n4, 157, 164n76

Hirsch, Alan, 3n6, 4n14, 17, 20n89, 23n106, 25–27, 30n141, 33, 140n182, 44n9, 47n23, 48n33, 48n36, 49n39, 49n44, 50–53, 58, 60, 86, 89–90, 93n40, 99–100, 102–8, 112, 113n10, 115n15, 123n71, 126, 153, 156n50, 169–70, 172, 176–78
Hjalmarson, Leonard, 2n5, 52–53, 85n1, 96n51, 106–7, 113, 144n4, 157, 164n76
Holsclaw, Geoff, 15n68, 54, 60, 100–103, 180, 192
Holy Spirit, 11, 22, 29, 33, 41, 50–51, 58, 81, 101, 102n79, 111–19, 121–22, 128, 134–35, 137–42, 145, 147, 152, 160–62, 173n18, 183–84, 186, 188
hospitality, 28, 41, 60, 69, 143, 164–68, 174, 179–80, 184, 190–91, 194
Huckins, Jon, 3n6, 31, 54–56, 58–59, 102n79, 106, 112–13, 115n15, 122n66, 123n71, 128–29, 144n7, 156n49, 160, 162n71, 176, 190
Hunsberger, George, 4n14, 15n68, 19, 27n128, 29, 33, 44n8, 102n80, 104n90, 156, 190

integral mission, 19n83, 35–37, 38n176, 43n5, 195

Jesus, 1, 6–11, 20, 23, 25–26, 28–32, 36, 40–42, 46n18, 48n36, 49–55, 61–63, 68, 73–73, 76–79, 82, 85–86, 88–90, 99–113, 124–25, 128, 133–40, 142–43, 145–47, 149–52, 154, 157–74, 176–80, 182–86, 188–94

Keller, Timothy, 7n30, 20n90–92, 166n86, 167n91
Kenneson, Philip, 148, 152–53, 155–56
Kirk, Andrew, 20n93, 22
Krieder, Alan and Eleanor, 14–15, 30n141, 65, 68–70, 83, 93n39, 96, 99, 102–3, 112, 115n15, 122n67, 124n77, 125, 139n111, 144–45, 159, 176, 180–81

liturgical theology, 1, 4–5, 16, 43, 193
liturgy, 12–13, 17, 30, 52, 57, 62–63, 67–69, 71–73, 77, 87n14, 93–97, 119, 121–22, 131, 144, 146, 148–52, 157
Lord's Supper (see eucharist)

Maddix, Mark, 3n6, 49–50, 52, 60, 142n1, 165, 167n99, 176
marks of the church, 15, 40, 85–86, 90, 93–97, 104
missio dei, 2–3, 14n64, 17–22, 31–34, 68, 129, 145, 147
missio trinitatis, 17, 19–20, 22, 34, 38, 40, 42, 65, 67–68, 70–72, 81, 85–86, 89–90, 93, 97, 100, 103–5, 110, 114, 123–24, 127, 134, 139, 142, 145, 153, 161, 162n71, 191
Moore-Keish, Martha, 11n51, 12n56, 151

Newbigin, Lesslie, 1–2, 4, 8n32, 15n68, 18–19, 28n132, 29, 33, 35–36, 42, 82, 87, 99–100, 104n90, 145, 155n44, 172, 192
new monasticism, 19n83, 30, 35, 38–39, 43n5, 195
Nicene Creed, 91, 113, 134
notae ecclesia, 15, 40, 86, 89–97

ordo, 62–63, 74, 96, 97, 98n58, 130, 148
order of worship, 40, 73, 130–40
Our World Belongs to God, 11n51, 23–24

Padilla, Rene, 36–37
parish, 56–57, 115, 162, 191
Pohl, Christine, 28, 163–65, 167
post-Christendom, 4–5, 16, 33, 41–42, 63, 68–69, 100, 168, 181, 190, 193, 195
postmodernism, 83, 185–86, 195
proselytism, 5–6

Roxburgh, Alan, 4n15, 20n88, 24–25, 26n123, 28n132, 33–34, 37,
46n23, 86n5, 107, 123n71, 140, 166, 175, 190

Saliers, Don, 5n19, 119n42
Schattauer, Thomas, 3n12, 14–15, 65–68, 76, 79, 81, 112n2, 113–15, 116n21, 128n92, 133n103
Schmit, Clayton, 6, 14, 57, 61–63, 72, 81
Smith, James K. A., 7n31, 9, 10n50, 40, 44n7, 73n183, 111, 112n1, 118–22, 124n74, 134n105, 155n45, 158, 178
Stackhouse, John Jr., 181, 185–90
Sire, James, 124n74, 178–79, 181n49
Stone, Bryan, 6n21, 41, 168, 181–85

Timmis, Steve, 52–54, 57n93, 59n106, 154, 180, 190
Tizon, Al, 3n10, 15, 18–19, 21n97, 65, 71–72, 100
Trinitarian, 14n64, 19–23, 32–33, 90, 102n75, 123

Van Gelder, Craig, 3n9, 6n22, 16n69, 19, 26, 30n141, 33–34, 45n15, 47, 58–59, 80–81, 86n2, 88–89, 101, 110, 112, 114, 123, 141, 156n48, 190n125

Webber, Robert, 6, 14, 57, 61–63, 64n137, 81, 123n69, 124–26, 150
Wells, Samuel, 5n17, 41, 44n7, 143, 147–55
Westminster Confession, 64, 92
Willingen (1952), 22, 33
Woodward, J. R., 2n5, 33n153, 47–49, 108n108, 110, 129, 155
worship, 1–6, 11–17, 30, 37–44, 46, 53, 57–86, 89, 92–97, 106, 108–58, 163–65, 167–69, 171–72, 176, 181–82, 190–95
Wright, Christopher, 8–9, 19n86, 23n108, 34, 45, 59–60, 68, 89, 105n94, 107, 110, 112, 123, 127–28, 135n107, 156n49, 170

www.ingramcontent.com/pod-product-compliance
Lightning Source LLC
Chambersburg PA
CBHW070253230426
43664CB00014B/2520